CLASSIC
ELECTRICS
A VISUAL HISTORY OF
GREAT GUITARS

WALTER CARTER

Jawbone

An imprint of Outline Press Ltd

2A Union Court, 20–22 Union Road,

London SW4 6JP, England

www.jawbonepress.com

ISBN: 978-1-906002-19-0

TEXT: Walter Carter
EDITOR: Peter Chrisp
DESIGN: Paul Cooper Design

Origination and print by Colorprint (Hong Kong)

1 2 3 4 5 12 11 10 09 08

CONTENTS

classic electrics CONTENTS

CONTENTS

classic electrics

HOLLOWBODY GUITARS 186

CONTENTS

CONTENTS

classic electrics

SOLIDBODY GUITARS

ELECTRIC SOLIDBODY

Electric solidbody guitars have hardly been around long enough to be called classics – at least not in the sense that a Shakespeare play, a Renaissance cathedral, a Stradivari violin, or even a 19th-century "classical" guitar is a classic design. The "test of time" that traditionally defines a classic hasn't even started yet for the solidbody guitar, since many of the first generation of solidbody players are still alive today. But in a world where technological advances have accelerated the passing of one era into another, the "real time" of a single generation can correspond to centuries in earlier times. In that context, these solidbody designs have more than passed the "classic" standard, by their influence as well as their endurance.

It took the guitar world almost 20 years to accept the fact that an electric guitar did not have to look like a traditional guitar. While the solidbody seemed to do away with much of the traditional art and craft of making a fine guitar, it established new standards of quality based more on aesthetics and electronics. Still, the solid guitar might be a curiosity except for one property – the reduced tendency to "feed back" through an amplification system – that distinguished its performance from all other hollow electric and acoustic styles and made it the best design for an amplified world. That, even more than the aesthetic freedom it offered to guitar makers, propelled the electric solidbody guitar – and, of course, the music and musicians associated with it – into one of the strongest, most influential forces that popular music has ever experienced. These classic instruments are the tools with which those musicians changed our culture.

Alembic guitars are less frequently sighted than Alembic basses but, like the basses, they are easily identifiable by the "hippie sandwich" – the multi-piece neck-thru-body construction – along with the rich, handcrafted look of exotic wood and brass "fittings."

Alembic started as a consulting company with the task of making the Grateful Dead sound better. Founded in 1969 by Ron and Susan Wickersham, who were joined a year later by Rick Turner, Alembic put active pickups in the guitars of the Dead's Bob Weir and Jerry Garcia. It was Alembic's basses, however, that put them on the map as instrument makers. With brass bridges and nuts, neck-thru design and highly figured walnut, maple, and purple heart wood, Alembic basses led the way for many high-end bass makers.

Numerous influential bassists, ranging from Jack Casady (who had #001) to Stanley Clarke, have played Alembics. While the company's guitars were never as pervasive, an elite group of guitarists, most notably blues legend Johnny Winter and David Bowie bandmembers Carlos Alomar and Adrien Belew, have played Alembics.

11

MODEL
Alembic Series I

YEAR
1978

PRODUCTION
1970s

AMPEG

The "see-through" Ampeg guitars of 1969–71 represented three legendary names in electric guitar history. Ampeg pioneered electric basses with an amplification device in the end peg – hence the name Ampeg. In 1968 the Linden, New Jersey-based company tapped New York luthier and session musician Dan Armstrong to develop a guitar made of transparent acrylic glass, known by such trade names as Lucite and Plexiglas. Armstrong in turn tapped Bill Lawrence, a German-born musician, to help design not just one but six easily interchangeable pickups, giving guitarists a bass or treble option for rock, country and jazz (Rock Treble, Country Bass, etc.).

Its unique look and tonal versatility, plus onstage use by Rolling Stone Keith Richards, should have put the "see-throughs" over the top, but they lasted only three years. Ampeg continued to make basses and bass amps, Armstrong developed a line of effects boxes, and Lawrence went on to design pickups for Fender, Gibson and Peavey. Thanks in part to Dave Grohl's (Foo Fighters) use of a Dan Armstrong, Ampeg launched a reissue in 1998.

12

MODEL
Ampeg Dan Armstrong

YEAR
1969

PRODUCTION
1968 to 1971

This Diamond-brand 12-string from 1968 marked the end of an era for the Japanese-based Aria company, which was founded as an import company in 1956 by classical player Shiro Aria. In the 1960s, Aria gained a foothold in the U.S. market with cheap instruments that looked expensive.

The ADSG 12T took Fender's Jazzmaster body and gave it a sleeker look with more pointed horns and a more elongated shape. The pickups, pickguard, knobs and three-tone sunburst finish also had a Fenderish look, while the "tiger stripe" wood grain of the top evoked memories of Gibson's sunburst Les Paul Standards of 1958–60 – a look that Gibson abandoned in the 1960s – and the pearl dot fingerboard inlays were no doubt inspired by Gretsch's edge-hugging "thumbprint" inlays.

Through 1968, Arias competed directly with American budget brands such as Harmony and Kay, playing a major role in driving those two giants out of business. A year later, following Gibson's reintroduction of the Les Paul, Aria changed directions and took aim for the major makers with their first copy of Gibson's Les Paul.

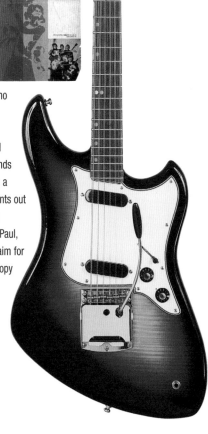

MODEL
Aria ADSG 12T

YEAR
Circa 1968

PRODUCTION
1960s

13

ARIA

Cheaper production cost was not the only advantage Aria enjoyed over the long-established guitarmakers in the 1970s and '80s. As this Aria Urchin Deluxe illustrates, the Japanese company was unencumbered by any identification with traditional designs, while the Gibsons and Fenders of the world had great difficulty establishing new models that strayed too far from Les Pauls, Stratocasters and other designs that dated back to the 1950s.

By the early 1980s, the angular bodies and sharply pointed horns of Bernie Rico's guitars, marketed under his B.C. Rich brand, were capturing the attention of guitar buyers, and Aria jumped on the bandwagon from with a series of Urchin guitars, produced from 1982–84, that clearly drew their inspiration from B.C. Rich.

Ironically – or appropriately, many of Aria's "victims" from the 1960s and '70s might say – Aria's success was eventually undermined by cheap imports, and by the end of the 1980s Aria had moved most of its production to Korea.

MODEL
Aria Urchin Deluxe

YEAR
Circa 1983

PRODUCTION
1982 to 1984

14

The pickguard says Baldwin but the three-piece pickguard design is the signature of Jim Burns of London. Although the Double Six model name might suggest a double-necked six-string, it does accurately describe the standard configuration of a 12-string guitar with six pairs of strings. Not only does the Double Six look like a 12-string version of the Burns Hank Marvin model, it was part of Marvin's arsenal of instruments. And in the hands of Mike Pender it played a prominent role in the sound of The Searchers.

Baldwin was founded as a piano retailer in Cincinnati, Ohio, in 1857 and became one of America's leading piano makers by the turn of the 20th century. In the 1960s Baldwin branched out into guitars, but after making little headway into the market with its own designs, the company bought Burns of London in 1965 and then Gretsch in 1967. As the Double Six illustrates, the Burns connection provided some of the more memorable, if least successful, instruments from the two acquisitions, and Baldwin stopped making Burns guitars in 1970.

MODEL
Baldwin Double Six

YEAR
Circa 1967

PRODUCTION
1965 to 1970

15

BIGSBY

Paul Bigsby's most successful invention was his vibrola tailpiece, but the Downey, California, inventor's most important contribution to the world of musical instruments may well be this soldibody electric guitar that he made for singer-songwriter Merle Travis in 1948.

Though not the very first solidbody electric, it predated Leo Fender's Broadcaster by two years. It featured neck-thru-body construction, a style that would distinguish some of the early Rickenbacker solidbodies and would be appear in the 1960s on Gibson's Firebirds. Its most obvious influence on future guitars was its headstock, which Travis reportedly drew up on a napkin for Bigsby. The six-on-a-side tuner configuration not only became a standard feature on Bigsby's instruments, it appeared in a very similar form on the Fender Stratocaster in 1954.

Bigsby continued to make electric guitars in the 1960s, including a doubleneck for Nashville legend Grady Martin and the pedal steel guitar that Bud Isaacs played on the 1954 hit "Slowly," ushering in the modern era of pedal steel, but he never expanded production custom orders for individuals.

MODEL
Bigsby Custom guitar for Merle Travis

YEAR
1948

PRODUCTION
1948

Sharply pointed horns highlighted the new fashion looks of 1961 in the solidbody guitar world. In America, Gibson overhauled its Les Pauls with the new body style, while in England, Burns of London put pointed horns on its new Bison model. The Bison trumped Gibson's top model, the three-pickup Custom, with four low-impedance pickups, a better vibrato system, a flashier pickguard, and a sleek tuner-post cover. Even the name Bison – aka the American buffalo – was better than Gibson's, which soon became the unimaginative SG (for Solid Guitar).

After the first 50 Bisons, Burns backed it down to three pickups, a bolt-on neck, and a simpler vibrato. While it was never the company's best seller, it provided the most memorable image of Jim Burns's innovative ideas. It survived the acquisition of Burns by Baldwin in 1965, but disappeared with the entire Burns line in 1970. A new Burns London, founded in 1992, revived it as the Bison 64, and it can be sighted today in the hands of band members of Dead Poets Society.

17

MODEL
Burns Bison (four pickups)

YEAR
1961

PRODUCTION
1961

BURNS

As lead guitarist with the Shadows, who had dual fame as an instrumental group and as pop star Cliff Richard's band, Hank Marvin was England's most influential rock guitarist in the late 1950s and early '60s. In 1964, the leading player teamed up with the leading British guitarmaker, Jim Burns, to create the Burns Hank Marvin model.

Prior to his association with Burns, Marvin was "joined at the hip" with his 1959 Fender Stratocaster with Fiesta Red finish – believed to have been the first Stratocaster in England – and it became the starting point for Marvin's signature model. The double-cutaway body and three single-coil pickups are basic Strat features, but the double-bar handrest, the three-piece pickguard, and the peghead scroll are distinctive Burns touches.

Only a year after Burns London introduced the Hank Marvin model, Burns sold his company to the Baldwin Piano & Organ Co. As Marvin was still virtually unknown in the U.S., Baldwin did not continue the model. A new Burns London company brought the Marvin model back in limited production in 2004.

MODEL
Burns Hank Marvin

YEAR
1964

PRODUCTION
1964 to 1965

The Stratocaster-inspired body of this 1989 Contemporary Spectrum reflects the origin of the Charvel company as a parts house specialising in such items as Stratocaster-style bodies, while the pointed headstock angling off to the bass side – the opposite direction from a conventional Fender – and the "dive-bomb" vibrato exemplify the innovative ideas that gave rise to new guitar companies in the 1970s, as Gibson and Fender began to show their age.

Ironically, the Charvel designs did not come from Wayne Charvel, who founded the business in 1974 in Los Angeles and went on to design guitars for several major guitar makers. They came from Grover Jackson, a Charvel employee who bought the company in 1977 and began marketing guitars under his own name as well as Charvel.

By the late 1980s, Charvels were among the most respected of high-end Japanese-made guitars, and production was expanded to Korea (Charvette by Charvel) and back to the U.S. in the 1990s. The run ended for Charvel when Aria bought the company in 1997.

MODEL
Charvel
Contemporary Spectrum

YEAR
1989

PRODUCTION
1989 to 1991

classic electrics DANELECTRO

The Danelectro U2 offered 1950s guitarists an electric guitar in its simplest, most basic form and, when it found its way into the Sears Roebuck catalog, it became the starter guitar for a generation of budding American rock'n'rollers.

Nat Daniel started his career building amplifiers for Epiphone, and he founded the Danelectro company in New York in 1946 to supply amps to catalog companies. His guitars, which debuted in 1956, were case studies in frugality. The top and back were of a hardboard construction material called Masonite, and the pickups were not just nicknamed "lipstick tube," they used real lipstick tubes. The "adjustable" bridge saddle was a single piece of rosewood that swiveled on a screw.

The U1 (single pickup) and U2 (double pickup) were successful enough, but when Daniel installed a small amplifier in a guitar case and Sears offered the guitar and case as a set, they proved to be an irresistibly cheap way for parents to get their kids started on the rock'n'roll dream.

MODEL

Danelectro U2
(Silvertone G01301L)

YEAR

Circa 1958

PRODUCTION

1956 to 1958
(Danelectro),
1958 to 1959
(Silvertone)

The typical Egmond electric guitar of the 1950s and '60s was, like this Model 3, inexpensive, unoriginal, and unremarkable. The Rosetti 3 (Rosetti was the importer), had eye-catching pearloid and an unusual textured finish but took most of its inspiration from a Fender Jazzmaster, including the "offset waist" body shape, the vibrola (or "tremolo" in Fender terminology) design, and the peghead shape with "six-in-line" tuners.

Made in the Netherlands, Egmonds would be largely forgotten today if not for their place in early Beatles history. Paul McCartney bought an Egmond-made Rosetti Solid 7 model in 1960, just as The Silver Beetles were becoming The Silver Beatles. The Egmond was McCartney's main stage axe through The Beatles' first trip to Hamburg, until he switched to bass when Stu Sutcliffe left the group.

Acoustic Egmond models also played a role in the Beatles story. George Harrrison's very first guitar was an Egmond flat-top. And Eric Griffiths played an Egmond in John Lennon's pre-Beatles group, The Quarry Men.

21

MODEL
Egmond Model 3

YEAR
1965

PRODUCTION
Mid 1960s

EKO

Italian guitar designs have never achieved quite the same level of respect and influence as Italian cars and shoes, but the Eko guitars of the 1960s, exemplified by this 1964 model 700/4V, turned heads nevertheless with their unconventional body shapes and abundance of knobs and switches.

Ekos came from Oliviero Pigini & Co. of Recanati, Italy, which was founded in the 1950s as an accordion company. The Eko line of electric guitars debuted in 1960, initially imported from Yugoslavia but produced in Recanati beginning in 1964. An American distribution agreement with LoDuco of Milwaukee, Wisconsin, in 1961 brought the line to the U.S.

The 700/4V was a catalog cover model, showing off a pearloid-covered body with scooped-out lower bout and outwardly curving horns. A vibrola, four pickups, and a plethora of pushbuttons and other electronic controls offered every tonal possibility imaginable to a guitarist of 1964. Eko went out of business in 1970 but was revived in 1980 and today offers retro versions of its 1960s classics.

MODEL
Eko 700 4V

YEAR
1964

PRODUCTION
1962 to 1965

The Epiphone Crestwood of 1958 was the first solidbody offered under the venerable Epiphone name and, moreover, it served notice that the Epiphone was alive and well under its new owners – the Gibson company. Epiphone had been one of Gibson's most formidable competitors in the tenor banjo market of the 1920s and the archtop guitar market of the 1930s, but when Epiphone faltered after World War II, Chicago Musical Instrument Co. (Gibson's parent company) bought its former foe.

Although Gibson introduced such innovative designs as the solid Flying V and Explorer, and the semi-solid ES-335 in 1958, the new Epiphone Crestwood featured a more derivative, proven body shape, which was essentially a Fender Telecaster with a mirror-image double-cutaway.

Epiphones were made in Gibson's Kalamazoo, Michigan, factory but were priced slightly below comparable Gibsons and consequently were quite successful. The Crestwood received a body makeover and an upgrade in name to Crestwood Custom in 1963 and continued to lead the Epiphone solid line until Gibson moved Epi production overseas in 1970.

23

MODEL
**Epiphone Crestwood
(first version)**

YEAR
1959

PRODUCTION
1958 to 1962

FENDER

Except for the name on the peghead, the Fender Broadcaster is familiar throughout the guitar world as the Telecaster – the instrument that revolutioned the music world as the first commercially successful solidbody electric.

The Broadcaster debuted in October 1950 as a two-pickup version of Fender's first model, the Esquire. The Gretsch company, a prominent guitar maker and instrument distributor since the turn of the 20th century, had marketed a Broadkaster drum model, and Gretsch asked Leo Fender to find another name. Fender complied immediately by clipping the "Broadcaster" part off the logo decal (examples of which are known today as "No-casters"). Early in 1951 the model was rechristened Telecaster.

The Broadcaster/Telecaster established the solidbody electric guitar – as well as the Fender company – as a force to be reckoned with. It was overshadowed by the three-pickup, contoured-body Stratocaster in 1954, but the Telecaster was the guitar of choice for such influential players as Buck Owens, James Burton, Albert Lee and Danny Gatton and it continues to play a vital role in Fender's success today.

MODEL
Fender Broadcaster

YEAR
1950

PRODUCTION
1950 to early 1951

I n June 1950, a small California-based maker of electric Hawaiian guitars and amplifiers debuted a solidbody "electric Spanish" guitar called the Esquire. And thus began a revolution in the guitar world.

Like Leo Fender's Hawaiian models, the Esquire had a simple, almost crude design compared to the elegant carved-top hollowbody models of Gibson, Gretsch and Epiphone. The Esquire's "slab" body could have been fashioned by anyone with access to a band saw. The neck did not have a separate fingerboard and was simply bolted on to the body. And it only had a single pickup at a time when other makers were offering two and even three pickups.

The Esquire offered one advantage that hollow guitars did not have: reduced feedback, which meant it could be played at higher volume than conventional electrics. That, coupled with the restless, rebellious attitude of post-World World War II America, made the plebeian Esquire an attractive alternative to traditional guitars. The double-pickup Broadcaster (soon to be renamed Telecaster), introduced three months later, would put Fender over the top.

MODEL
**Fender Esquire
(black pickguard)**

YEAR
1952

PRODUCTION
1950 to 1954

FENDER

The black pickguard identifies the first version of the Telecaster, which began in 1950 as the Broadcaster, then became the "No-caster" in 1951 (with no model name on the peghead) before Fender finally came up with the Telecaster name. The classic "black guard Tele" look features the wide, grayish wood grain of an ash body showing through the slightly translucent "blonde" finish, which often ages to a butterscotch hue.

Among the first prominent Telecaster players were musicians from Fender's home area in southern California. Bill Carson, playing a black-guard Tele in Hank Thompson's Brazos Valley Boys, demonstrated the solidbody guitar's capability of being turned up loud enough to be heard in a Western swing band without feeding back. The Tele's bright tone and clean attack enhanced the lightning-fast licks of Jimmy Bryant, famed for his duet work with steel guitarist Speedy West, as he became the archetype for the hot-picking country guitarist.

The black guard Tele established not just Fender, but the electric solidbody guitar, as a viable new force in the guitar world.

MODEL
**Fender Telecaster
(black pickguard)**

YEAR
1953

PRODUCTION
1952 to 1954

26

A white pickguard appeared on the Fender Telecaster in 1955, presumably because it would not show wear like the earlier Bakelite black guard, but the model was otherwise unchanged. With the white guard, the "butterscotch" look of the early Teles changed to a more opaque finish that aged to a rich ivory color.

Although Fender introduced a "new and improved" solidbody, the Stratocaster, in 1954, it would be several years before the Strat overtook the Tele in sales. In the meantime, the Telecaster continued to gain a foothold in Los Angeles recording studios.

James Burton's string-bending work on Ricky Nelson's hits, beginning in 1958, helped establish the "twangy" sound that would forever associate the Telecaster with the rockabilly element of country music. Buck Owens, prior to his emergence as a country superstar, brought his Telecaster to numerous L.A. sessions in the late 1950s. California's top studio guitarists, including Barney Kessel, Tommy Tedesco and Howard Roberts even bought Telecasters along to sessions to keep up with the new sounds in popular music.

MODEL

Fender Telecaster (white pickguard)

YEAR

1957

PRODUCTION

1955 to 1981

FENDER

The familiar, distinguishing look of Fender's one-piece maple neck changed in the late 1950s when the company adopted a more durable rosewood fingerboard. At the same time, Fender standardized a palette of custom finish colors that offered guitarists a range of individual expression from bright Fiesta Red to shining Gold metallic to basic Black.

The most famous custom color Tele from that era is the red guitar played by blues legend Muddy Waters. Not surprisingly, a red Tele also appeared in the hands of one of Muddy's disciples in England, Eric Clapton of The Yardbirds.

Although Fender's more expensive models, the Stratocaster and Jazzmaster, had become more popular with California surf bands, the Tele thrived in blues-based music of the early 1960s. Chicago guitarist Mike Bloomfield used a blonde-finish rosewood-fingerboard Tele as he began laying the groundwork for the guitar styles that would dominate rock music in the late 1960s, and Memphis session man Steve Cropper used a Tele for the memorable, minimalist licks that provided musical hooks on the instrumental hits of Booker T. and the MGs.

MODEL
Telecaster
(Fiesta Red finish)

YEAR
1960

PRODUCTION
1958 to 1969

Although the Stratocaster had overtaken the Telecaster in popularity as the 1950s came to a close, Fender maintained faith in the company's original model, as shown by a series of upscale Tele variations that began with the Telecaster Custom in 1959.

The "slab" body style of the Telecaster offered one aesthetic opportunity that the rounded edges of the more expensive Stratocaster, Jazzmaster and Jaguar could not accommodate, and that was body binding. Fender introduced this enhanced Telecaster (and Esquire) in mid 1959 as the Telecaster Custom. Along with the body binding, the Telecaster Custom was further delineated from the regular Telecaster by its sunburst finish.

Fender literature promoted the Telecaster Custom as a "startling new look," although vintage guitar aficionados would consider it more beautiful than startling. The startling look came in 1965, when Fender offered the Custom in a traditional "Tele blonde" finish that was enhanced by contrasting black body binding. The Telecaster Custom would never rival the standard Tele in popularity, but it remains a favorite of collectors today.

29

MODEL
Telecaster Custom

YEAR
1963

PRODUCTION
1959 to 1972

FENDER

Clarence White injected a hot country/bluegrass guitar style into rock'n'roll music when he began playing sessions with members of The Byrds in the mid 1960s, but when he wanted to play pedal-steel style licks on his Telecaster, he found himself in need of a third hand to bend the strings. He enlisted drummer Gene Parsons, who had grown up in his father's machine shop, to bring the pedal steel to the Telecaster.

Parsons engineered a system of springs and levers that raised the B string by a full step when White pushed down on the neck. White used the pedal-steel effect through his tenure with The Byrds from 1968 until his death (killed by a drunk driver) in 1973.

Bernie Leadon of The Eagles used a Parsons-White B-bender to create the string-bending lead guitar solo on "Peaceful Easy Feeling," and country star Marty Stuart not only uses a B-bender, he uses the actual guitar that formerly belonged to Clarence White. Fender today offers the Nashville B-Bender Telecaster as a standard model.

MODEL
Fender Telecaster (Sonic Blue, custom B-bender)

YEAR
1964

PRODUCTION
1964

Although Fender's golden era ended when Leo Fender sold the company to the CBS broadcasting conglomerate in 1965, the new management did come up with some attractive variations on Fender's proven models, starting with the Telecaster Thin Line of 1968.

The Thin Line was not actually thinner, just lighter in weight than the regular Tele, thanks to a hollowed out bass side. The f-hole was a nice aesthetic touch, as were the modernized lines of the pearloid pickguard and the natural or sunburst finish on the ash body (or on the rarely seen mahogany body).

The Thin Line sported standard Tele electronics with two single-coil pickups until late 1971, when it became the first Fender model with two humbucking pickups. Humbuckers were almost foreign to the accepted Fender sound and were more closely associated with Gibson – the company that invented the double-coil hum-canceling pickup. Consequently the Thin Line was never a stellar seller, but it lasted through the 1970s and was reissued in both single-coil and humbucking versions in 1997.

31

MODEL
Fender Telecaster Thin Line

YEAR
1968

PRODUCTION
1968 to 1979

FENDER

Brazilian rosewood has been the preferred wood for acoustic guitar bodies since the mid 1800s, appreciated for its bold grain patterns as well as its rich tonal qualities. Curiously, it was late in 1968 before Fender became the first company to exploit the aesthetic appeal of rosewood on a solidbody guitar.

Fender gave the prototype of the Rosewood Telecaster to The Beatles' George Harrison, who used it on the album *Let It Be* and in the accompanying movie. Fender couldn't have asked for a better endorsement for a new model, but the company's timing proved to be horrible. Brazil put an embargo on the export of uncut rosewood logs in 1969, thereby forcing most guitarmakers to switch to the less dramatically figured Indian rosewood.

Fender made the Rosewood Telecaster through 1972, but the importation problems with Brazilian rosewood, coupled with the heavy weight of a solid rosewood guitar, doomed it to very limited production. A Japanese-made reissue revived interest in the model but it, too, was only made in limited numbers, from 1989 to the mid 1990s.

MODEL
**Fender Rosewood
Telecaster**

YEAR
1968

PRODUCTION
1968 to 1972

Around 1970, Fender set its sights on a share of the guitar market represented by those players who preferred the thicker sound of Gibson's double-coil humbucking pickups to Fender's single-coils. Fender had the means to implement a formidable humbucking pickup in the person of Seth Lover, who had invented the humbucker for Gibson and by this time worked for Fender.

The Telecaster Thinline and Telecaster Deluxe had a pair of humbuckers, but that was not what players wanted. The "model" they wanted was already in use by such influential guitarists as Mike Bloomfield, Albert Lee, and Keith Richards, all of whom were playing Telecasters that had been customized with a humbucking pickup in the neck position.

In 1972, Fender offered that single-coil and humbucker configuration but gave it the confusing name of Custom Telecaster. It did not have the bound body of the earlier Telecaster Custom, and Fender further confused the two models by referring to the new model in literature as the Telecaster Custom. Although it seemed to be the perfect combination of Fender and Gibson sounds, it never caught on with players and was discontinued in 1980.

33

MODEL
Fender Custom Telecaster

YEAR
1977

PRODUCTION
1972 to 1979

FENDER

The Telecaster was pushed down near the bottom of Fender's model line in the 1960s by such flashy new models as the Jazzmaster and Jaguar, but by the early 1980s, the stars of the '60s had fallen and disappeared from the line, and the Telecaster and Stratocaster reemerged as the company's most popular models. Not only had they maintained a loyal following among guitarists, they were now beginning to attain iconic status.

Bill Schultz, who became Fender president in 1981 and would lead the employee group that bought Fender in 1985, recognized the Telecaster's fan base and began offering fancier versions of the basic model, exemplified by the Gold Elite Telecaster of 1983.

The Elite's upgrades included active electronics with a pair of white-covered poleless pickups, a bound top and a tremolo bridge with six individual saddles and drop-in string loading. For the elite of the Elite, Fender added gold-plated hardware and pearloid tuner buttons to create the Gold Elite. A Walnut Elite with black walnut body and neck completed the Elite family.

MODEL

**Fender Telecaster
Gold Elite**

YEAR

1983

PRODUCTION

1983 to 1985

It was officially called the Marble Telecaster, but the swirling, multi-color finish that appeared on Fenders in 1984 quickly earned them the nickname Bowling Ball Telecaster.

Designer Darren Johansen developed the finish technique and brought it to Fender in 1984. Fender committed to 300 instruments, 50 of which were Telecasters and 250 of which were Stratocasters. Most have a red-black-white or blue-black-yellow color scheme while a few (45 total) have a gold-silver-yellow finish. The base model was the short-lived (1982–84) and ironically named Standard Telecaster, which featured a non-standard six-saddle bridge, with strings anchored at the bridge rather than through the body.

By 1985, when the Marble Teles and Marble Strats were shipped to dealers, the attention of Fender's owners had been distracted from model design and refocused on selling the struggling company to a group of employees (the sale was finalized in March 1985), and a followup order for marble-finish guitars was never placed. Johansen applied his technique to clothing and went on to greater success as a clothing designer.

35

MODEL
Fender Marble Telecaster

YEAR
1984

PRODUCTION
1984

FENDER

With the Telecaster Contemporary of 1985, Fender seemed to show a fundamental misunderstanding of the Telecaster's appeal. It had always been a basic, no-frills guitar, and there was a limit to the degree of modification or enhancement that the Tele crowd would endure.

The Contemporary looked good in theory. It brought a popular Stratocaster mod to the Tele in the form of a humbucker and two single-coil pickups, better known as the "Fat Strat" configuration. An optional pickup configuration offered two humbuckers. Coil-tap capability was provided as a sort of afterthought, as if Fender had suddenly realized that the signature sound of the Telecaster had always come from its single-coil bridge-position pickup. The tremolo unit, too, was not really proper on a Telecaster; in the minds of guitarists, it belonged on a Strat. The black chrome hardware only added to the incongruity.

Like many Fenders of 1985, the Telecaster Contemporary was made in Japan, which did not endear it to U.S. buyers, and it lasted only two years.

MODEL
Fender Contemporary Telecaster

YEAR
1987

PRODUCTION
1985 to 1987

The American Standard Telecaster appeared in 1988, after a three-year hiatus in regular Telecaster production. Fender had been successful with a reissue of the 1952 Tele, introduced in 1981, but not everyone wanted the features of the original model, particularly the three-piece saddles and the maple neck/fingerboard.

The American Standard introduced a new Telecaster that could be updated with new features as they became available, while the reissue could maintain vintage specifications for traditinalists. To that end, the new version came with a modern six-saddle bridge, optional rosewood fingerboard, smaller fingerboard radius (9.5 inches compared to 12 inches on the reissue), and finish colors ranging from vintage white to lipstick red, from traditional sunburst to Caribbean Mist.

Many Fenders had been made overseas in 1985 while a new ownership developed new production facilities in Corona, California, and the model name of the American Standard Telecaster (like the American Standard Stratocaster that preceded it by two years) clearly stated that the Telecaster had come home to the U.S.A.

37

MODEL
Fender American Standard Telecaster

YEAR
1991

PRODUCTION
1988 to current

FENDER

One of the "battlefronts" in the long-running war between Fender and Gibson has been the neck joint. Fenders have a bolt-on neck, designed by Leo Fender himself so that a player could perform a do-it-yourself neck replacement if his fingerboard wore out. Gibsons have a "set" neck that is glued into the body. Neither side was been able to venture into the other's territory with much success until the 1990s.

Fender's Set Neck Telecaster of 1990 spearheaded the attack. The model name only began to describe its Gibson-esque design. It had a mahogany body (routed to reduce the weight) with a curly maple top cap, just like Gibson's Les Paul Standard but without the top carving. The neck, too, was mahogany, like a standard Gibson neck. It came with various optional pickup and tremolo configurations: two humbuckers, two humbuckers and Strat-style tremolo, two humbuckers and single-coil, plus a Custom Shop version with a coil-tapped neck-position humbucker.

Fender pushed Set Neck Telecasters (and Stratocasters) through the 1990s but ultimately retreated to the safety of its bolt-neck design in 2000.

MODEL

**Fender Telecaster
Set Neck**

YEAR

1992

PRODUCTION

1990 to 1999

38

Fender introduced the American Deluxe series in 1998 to offer just what the name suggests: upscale, American-made versions of its standard Teles and Strats – in essence, custom guitars without the Custom Shop price – or exclusivity.

The regular Telecaster in the American Deluxe series featured a bound alder body, six-saddle bridge, pearloid pickguard, abalone fingerboard dots and "Noiseless" pickups. Otherwise the American Deluxe retained the same basic look – pickguard shape, control plate, pickup configuration etc. – as a traditional Telecaster.

Not so with the QMT and FMT that Fender introduced in 2004. To show off the Quilted Maple Top and Flamed Maple Top, Fender did away with the pickguard and mounted the controls directly into the top. Although most of the models in the series featured new Samarium Cobalt Noiseless pickups, designed by Bill Lawrence (the man responsible for many of Gibson's 1970s pickup designs), the Telecaster QMT and FMT opted for the extra power of a pair of "Enforcer" humbucking pickups. Transparent stained finishes, in amber, sunburst cherry or blue, enhanced the figuration of the maple top.

MODEL

Fender American Deluxe Telecaster QMT

YEAR

2004

PRODUCTION

2004 to current

FENDER

As successful as Fender's Telecaster was, it soon became apparent that the design left plenty of room for improvement. With input from musician Bill Carson and several Fender employees, Leo Fender went back to the drawing board.

Fender abandoned the Telecaster's "slab" body design for a sleek, double-cutaway shape with contours to fit the player's body. He added a third pickup. He upgraded the Tele's three-piece adjustable saddle system to six pieces – one for each string. He introduced a new vibrato – which Fender erroneously called "tremolo" – that offered players a truer return to pitch than the Bigsby design that had been the industry standard. And he upgraded the blonde, whitewashed finish of the Tele with a two-tone sunburst finish. Don Randall, Leo Fender's partner in Fender's sales and marketing division, named the new model Stratocaster.

Starting with Buddy Holly's first hits in 1957, the Strat became a vital element of rock'n'roll, and it gained iconic status in the hands of such artists as Jimi Hendrix and Eric Clapton. It remains today the foundation of Fender's continuing success.

MODEL
**Stratocaster
(two-tone sunburst
finish)**

YEAR
1957

PRODUCTION
1954 to 1959

The Stratocaster of the early 1960s had the same basic design as the original, but several details changed in the late 1950s. The most obvious new feature was the fingerboard, which switched from the integrated maple neck/fingerboard to a separate rosewood board (although the maple neck remained an option). The pickguard, originally single-ply, gained several laminate layers along with beveled edges to simulate multi-ply binding.

Fender had introduced a handful of custom color options in 1958 and 1959. An expanded selection of colors in 1963 included Candy Apple Red, which became the most popular of the custom finishes in the 1960s.

In the early 1960s, the Jazzmaster held the top place in the Fender line, but the Strat remained the most popular model. Today, Stratocasters made prior to CBS's acquisition of Fender in 1965 are among the most prized guitars in the vintage guitar market, with custom-color models bringing a premium over standard sunburst-finish examples.

MODEL

Stratocaster (Sonic Blue finish with rosewood fingerboard, small headstock)

YEAR
1964

PRODUCTION
1958 to 1965

FENDER

By the mid 1960s, Leo Fender was tiring of the electric guitar business, and in January 1965, he sold Fender to the CBS broadcasting conglomerate for $13 million. At that point, Fender quality – design quality as well as production quality – began to decline.

The first design change on the Strat initiated by the CBS ownership group was a simple, seemingly innocent one: They made the headstock of the Stratocaster larger. Today, the large headstock, which appeared near the end of 1965, is considered by the vintage guitar world as the mark of the true end of Leo Fender's guitars and the beginning of the CBS era.

Despite the damage that CBS would do to the Stratocaster in its 20 years of Fender ownership, the Strat began to reemerge in the late 1960s. George Harrison gave his 1966 Strat important exposure in 1967 on The Beatles' *Magical Mystery Tour* performances. That same year, Jimi Henrix's album *Are You Experienced* took rock guitar to a new plane as Hendrix brought the Strat back into the spotlight, making it once again Fender's premier model.

MODEL
Stratocaster (Lake Placid Blue finish, large headstock)

YEAR
1966

PRODUCTION
1965 to 1985

Fender began referring to its basic Stratocaster as the Standard Stratocaster in the 1980s to distinguish it from such offshoot models as the Anniversary and the '57 Reissue, but in 1983, shortly after the introduction of the first reissue Stratocaster, the standard-production version received a makeover that seemed to gut the Strat's identity and tradition.

The new version had only two knobs – the input jack took over the third knob position – and the traditional tremolo bridge, which required the strings to load from the back of the guitar, was simplified into a top-loading design.

Among the first moves from the new ownership group, which purchased Fender from CBS in 1985, was to fix the Strat, to right the "wrongs" that had been committed with the 1983 Standard. In late 1986, the Standard was overhauled with a new tremolo system, a new truss-rod design, and a selection of new colors. To reassure guitarists that this new Strat was made in the U.S.A., Fender named it the American Standard. It remains, as its name suggests, the standard, basic, production-model Stratocaster in Fender's line today.

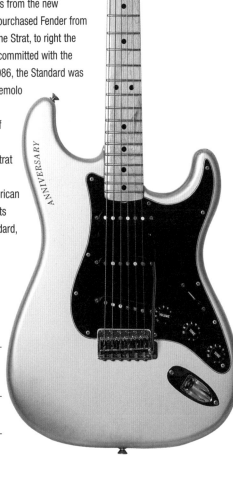

MODEL
Fender Stratocaster 25th Annivesary

YEAR
1979

PRODUCTION
1979

FENDER

As Fender struggled in the shaky U.S. guitar market in the early 1980s, demand for Fenders in Japan grew to the point that in 1982 Fender organized the Fender Japan company with Japanese partners.

Despite great improvement in the quality of Japanese-made instruments, the "Made in Japan" label would have been viewed in the U.S. as a sign that yet another once-proud American company had succumbed to overseas competition. Consequently, the first guitars from Fender Japan were offered only to the Japanese market. Within a few years, however, Fender could not ignore the commercial potential of Asian-made guitars, and the Squier name was appropriated (from a string-making company Fender owned) to distinguish the imports from the U.S.-made models.

In 1985, Squier production moved to Korea, and Squiers have since been sourced from various factories in Mexico, China, and Indonesia. Unlike Gibson's Epiphone import line, which maintained a model line separate from Gibson's in the 1980s, Fender's Squiers capitalized on the Stratocaster and other established Fender models and were quickly accepted as inexpensive but well-made alternatives to the real thing.

MODEL
Fender Squier Stratocaster

YEAR
1982

PRODUCTION
1982 to current

44

Fender marked the 25th anniversary of the Stratocaster in 1979 with a special model touting "Anniversary" on the bass horn, but curiously, nowhere does it indicate the number of the anniversary.

With its large headstock, 1970s logo and tuners, two string trees, and black-and-silver color scheme (the earliest had a pearl white finish), it was clearly a commemorative model rather than a reissue of the 1954 original. Although the Anniversary Strat was intended to be a limited-edition model, Fender made around 10,000 of them.

The Anniversary's success may well have been the result of the small walnut plug in the headstock, just above the nut. Since 1971, there had been a metal "bullet" in that spot, an indicator of the "Tilt Neck" adjustment and three bolts (screws, actually) securing the neck to the body. The Anniversary's headstock, however, indicated an old-style four-bolt neck, with the truss-rod adjustment at the body end. It was a welcome sign of changes to come; within two years, Fender had ditched the Tilt Neck and returned to the player-preferred four-bolt neck (but with new truss-rod design).

45

MODEL
Fender American Standard Stratocaster

YEAR
1991

PRODUCTION
1983 to current

FENDER

By the early 1980s, the Stratocaster had emerged as the only model that could carry Fender into the future. While the struggling company was starting to produce some models overseas, a dressed-up, high-end, made-in-U.S.A. Stratocaster helped divert attention from growing financial problems.

Fender had offered cosmetic upgrades in the form of the Walnut Strat and Gold Strat (with black walnut body and gold-plated hardware, respectively) in 1981, but the Elite Stratocaster of 1983 introduced upgraded performance as well. The poleless, white-covered pickups were part of an active electronics system, and the traditional pickup selector switch was replaced by three on-off pushbuttons. The tremolo bridge unit offered drop-in string loading (rather than through-the-back) along with a snap-on whammy bar. And the jack was moved out of the way of the player's right hand, to the rim of the guitar.

In the end, even Walnut Elite and Gold Elite options could not save the Elite Stratocaster, and when the employee group led by Bill Schultz bought Fender from CBS in early 1985, the Elite disappeared.

MODEL
Fender Elite Stratocaster

YEAR
1983

PRODUCTION
1983 to 1984

Prior to 1987, Fender's single-coil pickups were based on Leo Fender's designs, while the company's humbuckers were designed in-house by former Gibson employee Seth Lover. With the Strat Plus of 1987, Fender went outside of the company for the first time and made the new Lace Sensor pickup standard equipment on this model.

Lace Sensors were designed by Don Lace, who had consulted with Fender on speaker designs and pickups as early as 1967 and founded his own electronics company, Actodyne General, Inc., in 1979. In the 1980s, to help Fender alleviate a high rejection rate during the production of its pickups, Lace began developing a single-coil pickup with higher fidelity and more resistance to interference.

The Strat Plus introduced Fender-Lace pickups, along with such "plusses" as locking tuners, a roller bridge, and a pearloid pickguard. Higher-grade models, such as the Deluxe Plus and Ultra Deluxe Plus piled on the extras, including an ash veneer or figured maple veneer. Lace Sensor pickups became established on the Eric Clapton models, but the Plus did not last past 1997.

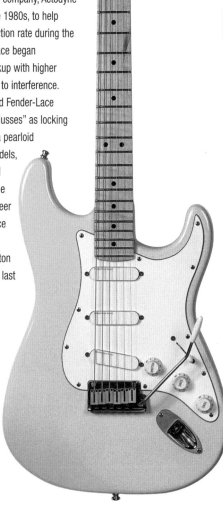

47

MODEL
Fender Strat Plus

YEAR
1990

PRODUCTION
1987 to 1997

FENDER

Although Eric Clapton gained his fame in the 1960s playing Gibson guitars as a member of Cream, he had started out on a Fender – a Telecaster – with the Yardbirds. In 1970, on a visit to Nashville to perform on the Johnny Cash TV show, he purchased a handful of used Stratocasters from Gruhn Guitars (then called GTR) and Sho-Bud Music.

When Clapton's new band, Derek and the Dominos, debuted later in 1970, their hit "Layla" featured Clapton with one of those Strats, nicknamed "Brownie." Another Strat that he pieced together from his Nashville purchases, nicknamed "Blackie," became his most famous instrument.

Fender's Eric Clapton signature model, introduced in 1988, was essentially a 1957 reissue with a blocked tremolo like Blackie's, but it was no Blackie replica (that would come later). The 1988 Clapton sported the new Fender-Lace Sensor pickups, which not only looked different, with their pole-less design, but also produced a "quieter" (not to be confused with softer) signal. The Clapton Strat also came in a lot more colors than the basic black, including Olympic White, Candy Green and Torino Red.

48

MODEL
Fender Eric Clapton Stratocaster

YEAR
1990

PRODUCTION
1988 to current

Jeff Beck never attained the commercial success of the guitarists who preceded him and followed him in the Yardbirds – Eric Clapton and Jimmy Page, respectively – but among rock'n'roll guitarists, Beck is as revered and influential as his fellow Yardbirds alumni.

Fender had wooed Beck in the late 1980s, but Beck demurred, and the model originally developed for him was introduced in 1987 as the Strat Plus. It featured the quiet Lace Sensor pickups, as did the Clapton model that followed it a year later, and as did the Jeff Beck Stratocaster when it finally debuted in 1991.

Like Clapton, Beck had started out with Fenders but developed his signature sound on a humbucker-equipped Gibson. Appropriately, his Fender model featured two adjacent single-coil pickups – in essence a humbucker – in the bridge position. This "fat Strat" configuration was perfect for the thick, distorted tone that Beck was known for, and by the end of the decade, the HSS (humbucker-single-single) had become an established option in the Strat lineup.

MODEL
Fender Jeff Beck Stratocaster

YEAR
1991

PRODUCTION
1991 to current

FENDER

In 1990s, Fender's Custom Shop began banging up new guitars for The Rolling Stones' Keith Richards and other rock stars who wanted the vintage look onstage but did not want to sacrifice their vintage instruments to the rigors of touring.

At a time when collectors had driven the price of original Strats from the 1950s and early '60s well beyond the reach of the average player, the well-worn look of a vintage Strat carried a strong appeal to the average guitar buyer as well. Master Builder J.W. Black recognized this phenomenon and suggested making these guitars available for everyone, and the result was the Relic '50s Stratocaster (with maple neck) and Relic '60s Stratocaster (like this one, with a rosewood fingerboard) first produced in 1996.

By 2000, Fender had refined and developed their "aged" offerings into the Time Machine series: NOS (new old stock) models looked new, out of the box; Closet Classics appeared to have been played for a bit, then stored in a closet; and Relics had the dings and playing wear of a lifelong favorite guitar.

MODEL

Fender Relic '60s Stratocaster

YEAR

1998

PRODUCTION

1996 to current

Most signature models sport special equipment preferred by the artist, but Fender's Rory Gallagher model replicated the well-traveled condition as well as the modifications that the influential Irish blues-rocker made to his 1961 Stratocaster.

The physical condition of Gallagher's guitar was much like his personal condition after years of performing, with the band Taste from 1966–70 and then as leader of his own group until his death from a failed liver transplant (made necessary by alcohol abuse) in 1995. By that time, he had worn most of the finish off his guitar. He had replaced the original Kluson tuners with Sperzels and then replaced one of those with a Gotoh. He replaced the original "clay dot" fingerboard marker at the 12th fret with a white plastic dot. And he used custom-wound pickups.

Fender's Custom Shop reproduced the finish – or what was left of it – the tuners (even the Gotoh), the white dot, and the custom-wound pickups on every Rory Gallagher model, although they stopped short of replicating the corrosion and additional abuses that Gallagher's original guitar suffered.

51

MODEL
Fender Rory Gallagher Stratocaster

YEAR
2007

PRODUCTION
2004 to current

FENDER

I n 1956, only two years after Fender introduced the model that is still considered a pinnacle of electric solidbody guitar design – the Stratocaster – Fender swung its focus in the opposite direction.

The Duo Sonic offered guitarists – especially beginning players or players on a budget – a genuine, two-pickup Fender at an affordable price. Its body was sleeker and thinner than the Stratocaster, though not quite as aesthetically developed, and it had a double-cutaway design, which seemed to make it more attractive than the Telecaster.

The main drawback to the Duo Sonic was its shorter, 22.5-inch scale, which limited its appeal to younger players. That feature was "corrected" in 1964 with an optional 24-inch scale (still shorter than Fender's standard of 25.5 inches). At the same time, the Duo Sonic's body was upgraded to the more contemporary shape of the Mustang. As the Stratocaster began to emerge as the dominant Fender model in the 1969, the Duo Sonic fell by the wayside in 1969.

MODEL
Fender Duo Sonic

YEAR
1959

PRODUCTION
1956 to 1968,
1994 to 1997

From the very beginning, going back to the K&F lap steel guitars made by Leo Fender and Doc Kauffman in 1945, Fender instruments had been designed simply, for efficient production and low cost to the end user. The Esquire of 1950 would seem to have been the most basic, elemental, electric solidbody guitar possible but, in 1956, inspired perhaps by the success Gibson was enjoying with its Les Paul Junior (a simplified, single-pickup version of its Les Paul Model), Fender introduced the Musicmaster.

Although the Musicmaster's double-cutaway body shape was more modern than the Esquire's, it was thinner and lighter in weight so that it did not feel as substantive to a player. Its single pickup did not have the separate polepieces of the Esquire's pickup. And its short scale length of 22.5 inches limited its appeal to beginning players.

Despite its place at the low end of the Fender line, early Musicmasters were outfitted with the gold-colored metal pickguard (made of anodized aluminum) that would appear on Fender's high-end Jazzmaster in 1958.

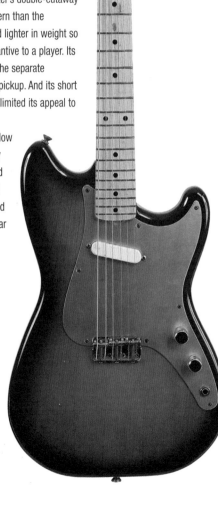

MODEL
Fender Musicmaster

YEAR
1957

PRODUCTION
1956 to 1980

53

FENDER

Although Fender's Stratocaster of 1954 remains, in the opinion of generations of players, the pinnacle of the electric solidbody, Leo Fender continued to refine his designs. They came together in what Fender described as "America's finest electric guitar" in 1958 – the Jazzmaster.

The Jazzmaster took the Strat's modern, curvy body to the next level, with offset "waists" to make it more comfortable for a player who was sitting down. A more refined control system added roller knobs for neck pickup control, plus on/off switches for each pickup. The saddles featured ridges to keep strings from moving, and the tremolo was a new design. In the larger picture of Fender history, the most important feature was the rosewood fingerboard, which would soon be implemented across the line.

The Jazzmaster's pickups gave it a warmer sound than the Strat, a sound that was aimed at jazz players, who never embraced it. Ironically, just as the model was being discontinued in 1980, it found a home in anti-elite music, starting with angry-young-man Elvis Costello and extending into grunge rock bands of the 1980s.

MODEL
Fender Jazzmaster

YEAR
1959

PRODUCTION
1958 to 1979

Its 30-inch scale made it a bass (albeit a short-scale bass), but the tremolo on Fender's Bass VI, along with its guitar-style string spacing, revealed its true identity as a low-tuned guitar.

The Bass VI's body and tremolo came from the Jazzmaster, and the three pickups were Stratocaster-style. Its simple, sensible electronics system consisted of individual on/off switches for each pickup, controlled by a master tone and volume. It was tuned an octave below the guitar, so that it reached the same low range as an electric bass, but its high strings extended well into the mid-range of a guitar.

Fender introduced this hybrid in 1961, inspired possibly by the moderate success of Danelectro's inexpensive six-string bass, but without a clear market demand for such a model. Although it had a unique sound – either a thin, high bass or a low, thick guitar sound, depending on the perspective – that appeared occasionally in a variety of musical settings (Jack Bruce played one on *Fresh Cream*), few bands used the Bass VI on a regular basis, and Fender last made it in 1975.

55

MODEL
Fender Bass VI

YEAR
1962

PRODUCTION
1961 to 1974

Four years after the Jazzmaster, Fender introduced another model aimed at jazz players, and the result would be much the same: The Jaguar of 1962 sold moderately well to everyone *but* jazz guitarists.

The new model had the basic look of the Jazzmaster, including the same body and tremolo. Upgrades included pickup shielding – which look like teeth protecting the sides of the pickups – and even more switches than the Jazzmaster. The main difference was the Jaguar's shorter scale length, prompted, perhaps, by Gibson's Byrdland model (with 23.5 inch scale) and intended to accommodate greater finger stretches for modern jazz chord voicings. Fender settled on a 24-inch scale, an inch-and-a-half shorter than standard.

Fender's best intentions were thwarted when Carl Wilson of The Beach Boys began playing a white Jaguar, and the model was forevermore associated with surf music. Like the Jazzmaster, the Jaguar later found a home in grunge music, thanks in part to a customized Mustang/Jaguar used by Kurt Cobain of Nirvana. Also like the Jazzmaster, the Jaguar has been revived successfully in recent years.

56

MODEL
Fender Jaguar

YEAR
1964

PRODUCTION
1962 to 1975

Despite Fender's expectations, the company's elite, expensive models – the Jazzmaster and Jaguar – failed to inspire jazz players, but they did appeal to younger rock'n'roll guitarists. To capitalize on that demand, Fender crossed the Jaguar with the low-end Duo Sonic model in 1964 and, in keeping with the animal theme, named it the Mustang.

The Mustang featured the Jaguar's offset waists and 24-inch scale (the shorter 22.5-inch scale of the Duo Sonic and Musicmaster was available as an option), but it had the poleless pickups of the lower models.

Fortuitously, the Ford Motor Company introduced its Mustang car that same year, and it immediately captured the youth market before going on to become a collectible classic in the automotive world. Fender's Mustang did not fare quite so well, but with an upgrade in 1969 that featured an automotive racing stripe and an auto-related name – Competition Mustang – it lasted until 1982. Like the Jazzmaster and Jaguar, it then became a favorite of cult bands.

MODEL
Fender Mustang

YEAR
1971

PRODUCTION
1964 to 1982

57

FENDER

Fender's timing for the introduction of the Electric XII could not have been better. It appeared in mid 1965, just after The Byrds brought folk and rock music together with the hit single "Mr. Tambourine Man," which featured a memorable opening guitar lick on an electric 12-string. Unfortunately, the guitar on The Byrds' records was a Rickenbacker 12-string, and Fender was unable to ride on the coattails of Rickenbacker's success.

Shortly after the Electric XII appeared, Fender upgraded it along the same lines as its other top models of the period, the Jazzmaster and the Jazz Bass, changing the fingerboard inlays from dots to blocks and adding binding to the fingerboard.

Although 12-string guitars did find a place in rock music in the late 1960s, it was the same place the acoustic 12-strings had held in folk music, providing tonal enhancement or a change of sonic scenery, but never as an instrument that was a vital element of the genre. Fender last made the Electric XII in 1969.

MODEL
Fender Electric XII

YEAR
1966

PRODUCTION
1965 to 1969

The Fender Bronco, as the name suggests, was a member of the same family as the Mustang. Introduced in 1967, it offered players a less-expensive, single-pickup version of the Mustang. Or, from the opposite perspective, it was an upgraded version of Fender's simplest guitar, the Musicmaster.

The Bronco had a more Fenderlike sound than the Musicmaster, thanks to its pickup placement near the bridge (the Musicmaster's was in the neck position). A pearloid pickguard gave it a classier look than the Musicmaster. And its tremolo was all its own, found on no other Fender.

The Bronco's shorter, 24-inch scale, and its single pickup limited its appeal to beginners or players with small hands. Fender offered it into 1980, but it was never a popular model. It made sporadic appearances in videos as "window dressing" in the hands of such guitarists as Mick Taylor of The Rolling Stones and Billy Corgan of Smashing Pumpkins, but unlike its fellow short-scale models, the Mustang and Jaguar, it was never revived.

MODEL
Fender Bronco

YEAR
circa 1972

PRODUCTION
1967 to 1980

FENDER

Kurt Cobain, left-handed guitar-playing leader of the Seattle band Nirvana, brought "grunge" rock to the forefront of popular culture with a custom Fender that combined his modified Mustang with favorite Jaguar neck. He called it a Jag-stang, and so did Fender when they offered it as a regular production model.

The Jag-Stang's neck copied Cobain's, with the shorter, 24-inch scale that the Jaguar and Mustang shared, and the Jag-Stang had a Mustang tremolo, but the body was different, and the pickups were from neither of the vintage models. Cobain used a humbucker in the bridge position and a vintage-style Stratocaster pickup in the lead position.

As influential as Cobain was, he became even more famous after he committed suicide in April 1994, and it was late 1995 – a year-and-a-half after his death – before Fender put the Jag-Stang into production. As Cobain's notoriety faded, so did the Jag-Stang. It lasted in the line for five years and made a short comeback from 2003–05.

MODEL
Fender Jag-stang

YEAR
1997

PRODUCTION
1995 to 2000,
2003 to 2005

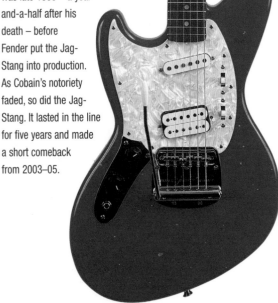

From the wave of publicity that surrounded the 1994 suicide of Nirvana leader Kurt Cobain, Cobain's wife Courtney Love emerged as a star in her own right, as an actress (starring in *The People versus Larry Flynt*) as well as the leader of the band Hole.

In 1997, shortly after Fender introduced the Jag-Stang as a Cobain signature model, the Venus Vista debuted under the Squier brand (in six-string and 12-string versions) as Love's signature model. Its design seemed to show good intentions – a double-cutaway body, a humbucker in the bridge position and single-coil pickup in the neck position, strings anchoring through the body, and a bound fingerboard. But the body shape looked like a squat Stratocaster, the pickguard had the shape of a blob, and the angles of the pickups, bridge and string holes appeared to be at odds with the body and pickguard. The controls were oversimplified, with a three-way switch, one tone, and one volume.

Fender only offered the Squier Venus for two years, but it coincided with the high point of Love's career.

MODEL
Fender Squier Venus

YEAR
Circa 1997

PRODUCTION
1997 to 1998

61

FRAMUS

Twelve-string electric guitars have been a part of blues and folk music since the beginning of those genres, and they migrated to rock music in the mid 1960s, thanks to The Beatles' "A Hard Day's Night" and The Byrds' "Mr. Tambourine Man." However, the inspiration for Framus' nine-string Melodie model of 1965 is unknown.

The nine-string guitar would appear to be simply halfway between a six- and 12-string, but it has its own distinct personality. The three treble strings, which handle most of the melodic work, are doubled for extra strength, while the three bass strings are singles. The result is a more powerful guitar but without the heavy octave-doubling of a 12-string.

The only player to be closely identified with a nine-string was Big Joe Williams (the Delta blues player, not the big band singer) who added three strings to his acoustic. British blues great John Mayall also had a homemade nine-string acoustic. Framus made only an estimated 50 nine-string electrics in the mid 1960s, and they still await their calling.

MODEL
**Framus Melodie
9 string**

YEAR
Mid 1960s

PRODUCTION
Mid 1960s

Framus used the Strato name on numerous models, and the Strato Deluxe (model 5/168) did have three single-coil pickups like a Fender Stratocaster, but most of the Strato Deluxe's features came from a different Fender model: the Jazzmaster. The body is almost an exact copy, and with circuitry overload from five knobs and six switches, plus a mute, a vibrato, and six-on-a-side tuner configuration, the Jazzmaster influence is unmistakable.

This Strato Deluxe from 1965 goes a step beyond the Jazzmaster, and all other guitars of the major manufacturers in the mid 1960s, with its onboard Organtone effect. The player could hook his pinkie finger into the curved switch handle and engage a spring-loaded volume control to create an effect similar to that of the rotating horn of a Leslie organ amplifier.

The Organtone was available on various Framus models, but guitarists quickly showed their reluctance to sound like an organ, and the Strato Deluxe did not make it into the 1970s, much less into the revived Framus line of 1995.

63

MODEL
Framus Strato Deluxe

YEAR
1965

PRODUCTION
1960s

FUTURAMA

The Futurama's three rocker switches provided on/off options for each pickup, providing pickup combinations that the three-pickup Fender Stratocaster could not match. According to British distributor Selmer, that qualified it as "The World's Most Advanced Electric Guitar."

While the inexpensive Czech-made model hardly live up to that billing, the Futurama name did turn out to be significant, as many of the guitar heroes of the future played a Futurama in their early years, including George Harrison of The Beatles, Alvin Lee of Ten Years After, Jimmy Page of Led Zeppelin, and Gerry Marsden of Gerry and the Pacemakers.

When Selmer first brought the model into Britain in 1957, the brand was Resonet and the model was Grazioso. The Futurama name quickly replaced Resonet, and production moved to several other makers, including the Swedish Hagstrom company. The Futurama was continually "advanced" to the point that the Hagstrom-made Futurama Coronado had more than a dozen controls, but Selmer dropped the Futurama entirely after 1965.

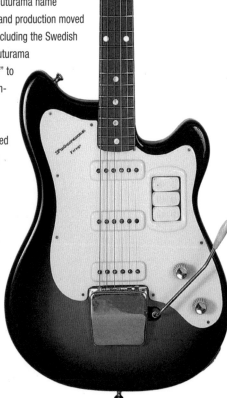

MODEL
Futurama 3

YEAR
Circa 1960

PRODUCTION
1957 to 1965

At G&L, founded by *G*eorge Fullerton and *L*eo Fender in 1979, Fender continued to refine and develop the designs that had defined the Fender company in the 1950s. The Comanche V is a case in point, representing what the Fender Stratocaster might have evolved to in 1989 if Leo had remained at Fender.

The Comanche's body is Stat-based but with more tapered horns. Like the Strat, it sports three pickups, but the Comanche's have the split-coil design that Leo created for the Fender Precision bass, and they have ceramic magnets rather than Fender's traditional Alnicos. The adjustable bridge saddles look as if they would be right at home on Leo's '54 Strat, but the vibrato unit is an improved, dual-fulcrum design developed by Leo at G&L. The selector switch is a five-way (or six-way on the Comanche VI), rather than the three-way on the original Strats.

Production of the Comanche stopped with Fender's death in 1991, but the new owners of G&L revived it in 1998, and it continues to carry on Leo Fender's legacy in today's G&L line.

MODEL
G&L Comanche

YEAR
1989

PRODUCTION
1989 to 1991,
1988 to current

65

In to the future...
from out of the past.

G&L

Leo Fender, worrying about his health and his ability to continue running a guitar company, sold Fender to CBS in 1965 and then proceeded to advance and refine electric solidbody guitar designs for another 26 years – longer than his tenure as head of the Fender company. After nine years of designing and producing instruments for the Music Man company, he partnered with former Fender employee George Fullerton to organize G&L in 1979.

G&L's best-known model appeared in 1985, and it looked a lot like Fender's legendary Telecaster (nee Broadcaster), with its single-cutaway, slab-style body, angled bridge pickup, oblong control plate and six-on-a-side tuner configuration. Leo even tried to name it Broadcaster, but the Fender company objected. Fender historian Richard Smith suggested ASAT, which was military jargon for an anti-satellite missile (it was not short-hand for After Strat, After Tele).

Leo Fender died in 1991, but the new owners, BBE Sound of Huntington Beach, California, continued the ASAT, and it is offered today in over a dozen variations.

MODEL
G&L ASAT

YEAR
1989

PRODUCTION
1985 to current

Gibson employees initially derided Leo Fender's Broadcaster/Telecaster as a crude design that resembled a toilet seat, but by 1952 Gibson could ignore the solidbody electric no longer. Gibson began working on a more elegant design with a carved top that not only identified it with Gibson's tradition as the company that invented the carved-top guitar but also would be difficult for Fender to copy without considerable new tooling.

To ensure maximum publicity and support for the new model, Gibson enlisted the most popular guitarist of the era, Les Paul, who had been an ardent proponent of the solidbody electric guitar for over a decade. Paul contributed his own patented bridge/tailpiece design and suggested a metallic gold top finish to further distinguish the Gibson from a Fender.

The Les Paul Model debuted in 1952, on the heels of Les Paul and Mary Ford's #1 hit "How High The Moon." With Les and Mary both playing Gibson "goldtops," Gibson was instantly established in the solidbody market.

67

MODEL
Gibson Les Paul Model (trapeze tailpiece, left-handed)

YEAR
1952

PRODUCTION
1952 to 1953

Gibson's Les Paul Model, as the "goldtop" was officially called, had one shortcoming, and that was its bridge. Due to a shallow neck-set angle, the combination bridge/tailpiece was too high, requiring the strings to wrap underneath the crossbar. It felt awkward to guitarists, and Gibson fixed the problem in late 1953 by increasing the neck angle and introducing a new bridge/tailpiece.

The "wraparound" bridge, as it has come to be known, took the strings over the top of the bar, and it was anchored more securely than the Les Paul-designed trapeze, by means of two "studs" screwed into the top of the guitar.

In the meantime Les Paul and Mary Ford dominated the radio with hit after hit – including a run of five Top 10 records between August 1952 and March 1953. Despite the Les Paul Model's bridge problem, sales rose in 1953, establishing a strong foundation in the new solidbody market from which Gibson would quickly expand the Les Paul line in both directions.

MODEL
Gibson Les Paul Model
(wraparound bridge)

YEAR
1954

PRODUCTION
1953 to 1954

In 1954, two years after the introduction of the goldtop Les Paul Model, Gibson offered a fancier version called the Les Paul Custom. Personal design input from Les Paul included the black finish – the color of a tuxedo – and low frets to facilitate the speedy runs that Paul was known for. Both features inspired nicknames for the new model: Black Beauty and Fretless Wonder.

The Custom also introduced two Gibson innovations. The neck-position pickup featured height-adjustable Alnico V magnets rather than screws for polepieces, although it was still essentially the same single-coil design as Gibson's standard P-90 pickup. The bridge, however, was a significant improvement over the goldtop's wraparound. Designed by Gibson president Ted McCarty, the "tune-o-matic" offered individually adjustable saddles and overall height adjustment.

Though not quite as versatile as the saddles on Fender's Stratocaster, which was also introduced in 1954, Gibson's tune-o-matic proved more than adequate, and it continues today as the standard Gibson bridge for almost all electric models.

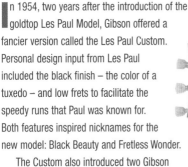

69

MODEL
Gibson Les Paul Custom (Alnico V pickups)

YEAR
1954

PRODUCTION
1954 to 1957

classic electrics

GIBSON

Midway through 1957, Gibson gave the Les Paul Custom a major upgrade, adding a third pickup and, more important, replacing the single-coil pickups with the new double-coil "humbuckers." The gold-plated metal pickup covers added a new dimension of elegance to the Custom's look, and the powerful pickups opened up a new world of sound for guitarists.

It was not the perfect guitar, however. For most players, three pickups was overkill, and the Custom's switching system limited the choices of pickup combinations to neck pickup alone, middle and bridge pickups together, or bridge pickup alone, making it actually less versatile than a two-pickup Gibson. Consequently, the Custom wasn't as popular as the Standard, but it still held a considerable level of status as Gibson's top solidbody.

Despite its shortcomings, the Custom worked quite well for such players as Robert Fripp (in the early days of King Crimson) and 1970s rocker Peter Frampton, who ended up with a Gibson signature model based on his Les Paul Custom.

MODEL
Gibson Les Paul Custom (humbucking pickups)

YEAR
1957

PRODUCTION
1957 to 1960, 1968 to current

70

The most important improvement to the Les Paul Model, aka goldtop, on its way to becoming a legendary model, came in mid 1957 with the introduction of Gibson's innovative double-coil "humbucking" pickups.

"Hum" – electrical interference from outside sources such as rheostats (light faders) or fluorescent lights – had been a problem for electric guitar players since the invention of the instrument. Electrical engineers had long known that two coils of wire wound in the opposite directions would have a hum-canceling effect on each other, and by 1955, Gibson engineer Seth Lover had applied the concept to guitar pickups, but Gibson did not push the pickups into production until word spread through the industry that Gretsch had developed a very similar unit.

Humbuckers provided a level of power that single-coils simply didn't have, and blues artists were among the first to take advantage. Blues great Freddie King's humbucker-equipped goldtop had a profound influence on the future of rock'n'roll; it was a photo of King that inspired Eric Clapton to buy his first Les Paul.

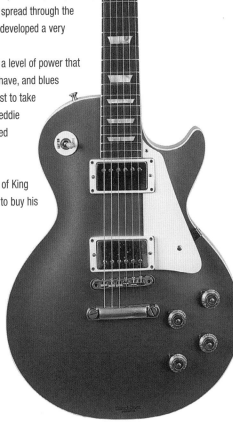

MODEL

Gibson Les Paul Model (goldtop, humbuckers)

YEAR

1957

PRODUCTION

1957 to 1958, 1983 to current

71

GIBSON

In 1958, Gibson replaced the Les Paul Model's gold top finish with a transparent cherry sunburst and began calling it the Standard. The result was the Holy Grail of electric guitars. Gibson produced around 1,500 sunburst Standards from 1958–60 before abandoning the entire design in favor of the double-cutaway SG style. But within a few years, Chicago guitarist Mike Bloomfield was using a 1959 model to create a blues-rock style so influential that it prompted British guitarist Jimmy Page to buy a sunburst Les Paul. By 1966, Eric Clapton had set aside his goldtop for a sunburst Les Paul. When he used it on an album with John Mayall's Bluesbreakers, combining the power of humbucking pickups with an overdriven Marshall amplifier, the future sound of rock guitar was set.

By the end of the 1960s, Jimmy Page, armed with his sunburst Les Paul, would become one of the era's most influential rock guitarists as a member of Led Zeppelin. And the sunburst Les Paul would become the most highly sought model in the vintage guitar world.

MODEL
Gibson Les Paul Standard

YEAR
1958

PRODUCTION
1958 to 1960,
1968 to 1969,
1976 to current

The non-sunburst cherry finish on this 1959 Les Paul Standard is also found on two examples that predate the familiar "cherry sunburst" finish. Presumably, Gibson felt in 1958 that red should be the new color of the model, but exactly what shade and pattern of red was not exactly determined.

This rich cherry shade came straight out of Gibson tradition, from guitars and mandolins of the late 1910s and 1920s. While it was certainly an attractive finish, it had two drawbacks. In 1958, the prevailing philosophy at Gibson was to break with tradition (this was the year Gibson would introduce the Flying V and Explorer), so reviving a 40-year-old finish style would be moving in the opposite direction. Additionally, the two earlier examples had a "shaded" effect on the back of the body and neck as well as on the top, which required more time to apply.

In 1958, Gibson settled on what is considered today to be the classic look – a cherry border on the top and a uniform cherry stain on the back and neck.

MODEL
Gibson Les Paul Standard (cherry finish)

YEAR
1959

PRODUCTION
1958 to 1959

GIBSON

This 1960 Les Paul Standard illustrates the wide range of hues to which the cherry sunburst can fade over time, due to exposure to light and inconsistencies in paint batches. While 1960 examples are generally thought of as having a brighter red border than those from 1958–59, the red has completely disappeared on this particular model.

To Les Paul enthusiasts today, the intensity of the cherry stain is not nearly as important as the intensity of the wood grain. Vintage 'bursts, as they are nicknamed, with heavily figured "curly" tops have inspired a plethora of descriptives – tiger-striped, ribbon flamed, quilted, etc. – and they bring a premium over those with plainer tops.

Gibson made one small change in the Les Paul Standard from 1959 to 1960 and that was to slim down the neck. The difference is significant enough that Gibson today offers its regular-production Les Paul Standards, as well as its historic reissues, with a "fat 1950s" neck or a "slim 1960s" neck.

MODEL

Gibson Les Paul Standard

YEAR

1960

PRODUCTION

**1958 to 1960,
1968 to 1969,
1976 to current**

Ironically, Les Paul had very little personal input into the design of the classic 1950s Gibsons that bore his name. That changed in 1969 with the Les Paul Personal.

Paul's first stint with Gibson had ended in 1963, but when Gibson revived the Standard and Custom in 1968, Paul returned. This time Gibson gave him free rein to design a guitar that truly represented his personal preferences, and he came up with two models. Both had the body lines of the earlier models but were larger – a full inch wider. The Personal was just that, with one of the most personalized features ever to appear on a production guitar – a microphone jack on the bass-side rim allowing the player to attach a mic to the guitar, just as Paul did in his live performances. The second model, the Professional, had more universally appealing features, such as an in-phase/out-of-phase switch and an extra tone control.

Both models featured low-impedance pickups, which Paul preferred because they were better suited for a recording studio, and, two years after they were introduced, Gibson combined the electronics of the Professional with the ornamentation of the Personal to create the Les Paul Recording.

75

MODEL
Gibson Les Paul Personal

YEAR
1969

PRODUCTION
1969 to 1970

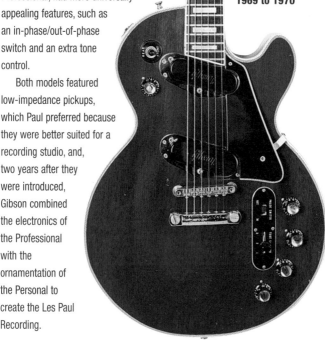

GIBSON

In Gibson's 1970s nomenclature system, "Deluxe" was applied ironically to the lowest of three model levels (the other two designations were Custom for midline and Artist for high-end models). Consequently, despite such features as a custom blue sparkle finish (available from 1975–77), the Les Paul Deluxe was *not* a deluxe Les Paul. It was a Standard with smaller, mini-humbucking pickups.

The Deluxe began as a model of convenience, the result of Gibson's decision in 1969 to send production of its second-tier brand, Epiphone, to Japan. That left Gibson with a surplus of mini-humbucking pickups (previously used only on Epis). Gibson had just revived the Les Paul Standard with the original-style "soapbar" pickups, and the minis fit perfectly in the pickup routings. Voila! The Les Paul Deluxe.

In response to players' demands, a Standard with full-size humbuckers soon returned, but some players preferred the Deluxe. The Who's Pete Townshend had several Deluxes with various modifications that he numbered. The model lasted until 1985 and has since been reissued, with standard specs as well as three Townshend signature versions.

MODEL

Gibson Les Paul Deluxe

YEAR

Circa 1975

PRODUCTION

1969 to 84, 1992, 2001

Upon Les Paul's return to Gibson in 1968, he designed two models that featured his personal preferences. In 1971, Gibson combined the Les Paul Personal and Professional into one model – the Les Paul Recording. Like the Personal and Professional, the Recording was spec'd with low-impedance pickups, along with a switch to change the pickups to out-of-phase alignment, and it had an extra tone control not found on other Gibsons.

The Recording got its name because low-impedance pickups were better-suited for the way Paul worked in a recording studio – bypassing an amplifier and plugging his guitar directly into a recording console. To accommodate guitarists who plugged into amplifiers – which were the overwhelming majority of guitarists – a transformer was added to the Les Paul Recording, allowing the player to switch between high- or low-impedance output.

Ultimately, guitarists did not want Les's guitar; they wanted the original Les Paul Standard. As the Standard made its comeback in the 1970s, the Recording faded, and it did not make it to the 1980s.

MODEL
Gibson Les Paul Recording

YEAR
Circa 1972

PRODUCTION
1971 to 1979

With renewed interest in Les Pauls in the 1970s, Gibson expanded on the original four models, exemplified by the Les Paul Artisan of 1976. The Artisan had the gold-plated hardware and multi-layer binding of the Custom, but with floral inlays on the fingerboard and peghead. This example has two additional Gibson upgrades from 1976 and 1977, respectively: the "wide-travel" or "Nashville" tune-o-matic bridge, which provided extended intonation adjustment, and the TP-6 fine-tune tailpiece. The model was also offered with three humbuckers.

The inlay pattern, including the prewar-style peghead logo, was familiar to a world of musicians as far away from Les Pauls as one can get – bluegrass banjo players. "Hearts and Flowers" had been a standard inlay pattern on Gibson's pre-World War II banjos but had only been used briefly in the postwar years on the expensive Style 800 banjo.

The upgraded inlays and hardware of the Artisan carried the Les Paul line into a higher range of ornamentation and performance, and it lasted in the line until 1981.

MODEL
Gibson Les Paul Artisan

YEAR
1981

PRODUCTION
1976 to 1981

By the mid 1970s, a tiger-striped maple top had become a coveted feature on vintage Les Paul Standards from 1958–60, and in 1976 Gibson used spectacularly figured maple as a starting point from which to build the ultimate Les Paul. It was called simply The Les Paul.

The plastic parts on a standard model were replaced with rosewood on The Les Paul, including the knobs, the pickguard, the pickup mounting rings, the selector switch cap, the washer surrounding the selector switch, and the control cavity covers on the back. Rosewood was even used for the outer layer of binding (the inner layers were colored wood) and as the center portion of the ebony-rosewood-ebony fingerboard. The fingerboard inlays were of figured abalone pearl, and the metal parts were, of course, gold-plated.

Gibson produced the model in limited numbers (less than 100 total) for only three years, but The Les Paul remains the most luxuriously appointed model of any catalog solidbody ever offered by Gibson.

MODEL
Gibson The Les Paul

YEAR
1978

PRODUCTION
1976 to 1979

GIBSON

In 1979, Gibson decided to create an Anniversary Les Paul model and then went looking for an anniversary to celebrate. The Les Paul Model, aka goldtop, had been introduced 27 years earlier, and Gibson had already celebrated the goldtop's 25th anniversary in 1977 with, ironically, a Custom 25th Anniversary model. The Custom was 25 years old in 1979, which was cause for celebration again.

Les Paul had been playing professionally since he was 13 years old, which added up to 51 years in 1979, but that was close enough to 50 for Gibson. Although the new model was officially called the 25th Anniversary Les Paul, the special 25/50 inlay on the headstock noted the double celebration.

The Anniversary sported the maple top – highly figured – of a Standard, with the ebony fingerboard and gold-plated hardware of a Custom. The slashed-block fingerboard inlays came from Gibson's most famous archtop, the Super 400. Production was limited – not in numbers but to the year 1979 – and Gibson production figures show over 3,400 sold.

MODEL
**Gibson Les Paul
25th Anniversary**

YEAR
1979

PRODUCTION
1979

A few dealers showed Gibson the way to a bright future in the late 1970s and early '80s by special-ordering Les Paul Standards as close to the original 1959 specifications as Gibson was willing to make them.

In 1983, Gibson finally "got it" and launched the Les Paul Reissue. As this 1987 example shows, the reissues typically had a more highly "flamed" or tiger-striped top than the majority of the originals. When it came down to details such as peghead shape, top contour, pickups, capacitors, control cavity routing, neck tenon, etc., the Reissue had a long way to go. To that end, in 1993, when Gibson made its Custom Shop a standalone division, the "tweaking" began in earnest and the term "replica" unofficially replaced "reissue" in the world of Les Paul aficionados.

Gibson has managed to find something new every year to make the R9, as the '59 reissue came to be called, even more accurate, and the family of Les Paul reissues – from goldtops to "plaintops" – has become the foundation of the Custom, Art & Historic division's success.

MODEL
Gibson Les Paul Reissue

YEAR
1987

PRODUCTION
1983 to current

81

GIBSON

Gibson's 1952 goldtop Les Paul Model priced at $210 (without case) competed effectively with Fender's $189.50 Telecaster, but Fender also offered the single-pickup Esquire at a significantly lower price of $149.50. In 1954, Gibson came after the Esquire with its own single-pickup model – the Les Paul Junior.

Gibson knew from experience that the least expensive models would always outsell the fancier models, as long as the essential elements were present. The Les Paul Junior did not have the Les Paul Model's goldtop finish or even its maple top cap, and the Junior had no binding, but it had the same body shape, the same neck, and the same pickup. At $99.50 it was the best value on the solidbody market.

The Les Paul Junior, especially when sold with a companion amplifier, became the "starter guitar" for thousands of young guitarists in the 1950s. And as Leslie West proved when he used his Junior to create the memorable lead part on Mountain's 1970 recording "Mississippi Queen," some guitarists never saw a need to put their Junior down.

MODEL
Gibson Les Paul Junior (single cutaway)

YEAR
1956

PRODUCTION
**1954 to 1958,
1986 to 1992,
1998 to current**

Late in 1954, Gibson offered a light-colored finish on the Les Paul Junior as an alternative to the standard, traditional sunburst. Gibson marketed it as a new model called the Les Paul TV.

Legend has it that the TV name was given because the light finish would show up better on black-and-white TV screens of the day. However, TV performers were likely to play a more expensive model than the entry-level Junior; Les Paul and Mary Ford, for example, had their own TV show beginning in 1953, and their goldtop Les Pauls looked just fine on the small screen. The TV name may well have been inspired by the light-colored TV cabinets that were part of the Fifties Modern movement in furniture design.

The Les Paul TV never seriously challenged the sunburst Junior in sales, but it brought a flair of color to the lower end of the Les Paul line and inspired Gibson to make "TV yellow" the standard finish on the Les Paul Special of 1955.

MODEL
Gibson Les Paul TV

YEAR
1957

PRODUCTION
1954 to 1958

GIBSON

The Special was the last of Gibson's four original Les Paul models. The wide gap between the entry-level Junior, with its single pickup and flat "slab" body, and the original goldtop Les Paul Model, with its two pickups and carved, contoured top, begged to be filled, and Gibson did just that in 1955 with the Les Paul Special.

The Special offered the same performance as the goldtop, with a pair of P-90 pickups, but it had the cheaper-to-produce slab body design of the Junior. Gibson appropriated the newly introduced "TV yellow" finish – soon to be known as "Limed Mahogany" – from the Les Paul TV model and made it the standard finish on the Special.

Sales of the Les Paul Special were as expected for its place in the Les Paul line – fewer than the less-expensive Junior and more than the higher-priced Model/Standard. Possibly the most famous of the single-cutaway versions is an early 1970s Special that was the main guitar of reggae legend Bob Marley.

MODEL
Gibson Les Paul Special (single cutaway)

YEAR
1955

PRODUCTION
1955 to 1959

Sales figures for every Les Paul model fell in 1958 and, towards the end of that year, Gibson modernized the Junior with a double-cutaway body and a cherry red finish. Sales picked up immediately and, not surprisingly, the Special received the same makeover in 1959 (cherry finish was optional on the Special). The results were similar, with Les Paul Special sales almost doubling from 1958 to '59.

Curiously, by the end of 1959, Gibson began calling it the SG Special (SG for Solid Guitar). This seemed to anticipate the 1961 changeover to what would become known as the SG body shape, with pointed horns, but how Gibson could drop the Les Paul designation with Les Paul still under contract, and why the company would do it on just one model, has never been explained.

Gibson revived the double-cutaway (non-SG) Special in the mid 1970s as a separate model from the single-cutaway version, and the basic model remains in production, although sometimes under the confusing name of Junior Special.

MODEL
Gibson Les Paul Special (double cutaway)

YEAR
1959

PRODUCTION
1959

GIBSON

Cheaper is better – at least when it comes to selling Gibson guitars. That was the driving thought behind Gibson's Melody Maker of 1959.

Historically, in every Gibson model line, acoustic as well as electric, the least expensive model was the biggest seller. That held true for Les Pauls, where the Junior outsold all the other models combined. It was hard to undercut the single-pickup, slab-body Junior, but Gibson managed to do it with the Melody Maker by making the body even thinner, eliminating Les Paul's endorsement, and fitting it with a pickup that had no polepieces.

The Melody Maker was successful enough that, in the 1960s, Gibson expanded it into a family, including a three-quarter-size, a two-pickup model, a three-pickup model, and even a 12-string. It changed body shapes several times before settling in on the pointed horns of the SG. Ultimately, the Melody Maker remained a student model – a starter model – but its budget appeal inspired new versions in the 1980s, 1990s (as the All American II), and in Gibson's current model line.

MODEL
Gibson Melody Maker

YEAR
1959

PRODUCTION
1959 to 1970

The Les Paul Junior was already a double-cutaway model when Gibson overhauled the entire Les Paul line in 1961 with a sleeker body and bold, pointed horns. Technically, the models were still Les Pauls until Paul's contract ran out in late 1963. Then they officially became SG models.

The Junior maintained the same position as an SG that it had held in the 1950s as a Les Paul – an entry level guitar and the best-selling model of the four. With Gibson's acquisition by the Norlin company in 1970, however, the entire SG line underwent a series of design changes (none for the better) and, despite the Junior's status as the least expensive, good-quality Gibson solidbody, it was absent from the new SG line of 1971.

While the original Les Paul Junior enjoyed a comeback, the SG version of the Junior made only brief appearances, in 1991–93 and 2000–02. Even when Gibson equipped it with a humbucker and renamed it the All American I (1995–97) or SG-X (1998–2000), the single-pickup SG guitar was short-lived.

MODEL
Gibson SG Junior

YEAR
1961

PRODUCTION
1961 to 1970,
1991 to 1993

GIBSON

When sales of Gibson's Les Paul Standard, with its recently introduced cherry sunburst finish, flattened out in 1960, Gibson changed the entire line to a new body style. Although they weren't officially called SG models until late 1953, the effect on sales was dramatic. With the more modern look and lighter weight of the SG body, Standard sales jumped from 635 in 1960 to 1,662 in 1961.

The SG Standard gained some notoriety in 1966 when George Harrison used one in The Beatles' videos for "Rain" and "Paperback Writer." In 1967, Eric Clapton began playing a custom-painted SG Standard with his new group Cream. The most enduring image of the SG Standard, however, was that of Australian guitarist Angus Young, walking knock-kneed about the stage in his schoolboy attire as his SG provided the signature sound of the rock band AC/DC.

The SG Standard remains a vital element of Gibson's solidbody legacy, and the company currently makes a Standard and a '61 Reissue as regular-production models, as well as a Historic Collection version and an Angus Young signature edition.

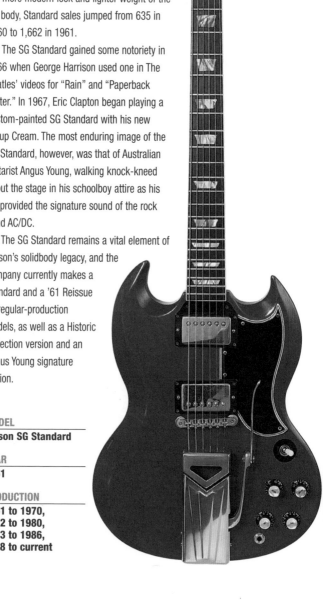

MODEL
Gibson SG Standard

YEAR
1961

PRODUCTION
1961 to 1970,
1972 to 1980,
1983 to 1986,
1988 to current

GIBSON solidbody guitars

The SG model name inexplicably debuted on what had been the Les Paul Special in late 1959, over a year before it received the SG body and more than three years before Les Paul's contract with Gibson ended.

Otherwise, though, Gibson maintained its identifying features – two single-coil pickups and bound fingerboard with dot inlays – through the changeover. The "TV" finish of the 1950s gave way to a more opaque cream or white finish, or else a cherry stain finish, and in rare cases such as this 1966 example, a Pelham Blue finish (aged to a dark green).

As it had in the 1950s, the Special occupied an awkward spot between the cheaper single-pickup Junior and the humbucker-equipped Standard. It gained its moment in the spotlight in the late 1960s when Carlos Santana appeared onstage at Woodstock with an SG Special and Pete Townshend of The Who made it his main guitar. Various versions (typically with humbucking pickups) have been in production since 1985, and Gibson replicated Townshend's guitar in a limited edition in 2000.

89

MODEL

**Gibson SG Special
(SG body shape)**

YEAR

1966

PRODUCTION

1961 to 1970

GIBSON

The Les Paul Custom switched to the SG body at the beginning of 1961 and, until late 1963, it retained the Les Paul name on a small plate at the end of the neck. Only at that point did it officially become the SG Custom.

The Custom's ebony fingerboard, large pearl block inlays, five-piece peghead inlay, and gold-plated hardware carried over from the single-cutaway, carved-top model. However, the black finish that had identified the Custom as the Black Beauty since its inception in 1954 did not survive the change, and the new SG style sported a creamy white finish. Another change was the addition of a vibrato as standard equipment. Typically a large coverplate extended from the vibrato base to the end of the guitar; the ebony block with three pearl inlays on this example is purely ornamental.

More expensive and less popular than the Standard, the Custom survived virtually intact until 1980, after which it went in and out of production several times. The Les Paul/SG Custom lives on today in Gibson's Custom, Art & Historic division.

MODEL
Gibson SG Custom

YEAR
1962

PRODUCTION
1961 to 1979,

Gibson started making doubleneck
Hawaiian guitars in 1937, within two
years of the company's first electric model, but
the concept did not take hold on conventional
"Spanish" style guitarists until the
1950s. Gibson tested the
doubleneck waters in 1958 with
several custom-order models. Any
conceivable combination of guitar
necks and banjo necks was possible,
but the six- and 12-string EDS-1275
(EDS for Electric Double Spanish)
emerged as the most popular.

The first version was an unusual
design, with hollowbody and carved
spruce top with no soundholes, but
Gibson changed it to the more practical
SG design around 1962 and put it into
regular production. Doublenecks did not
sell well, however, and Gibson
discontinued them in 1968.

As rock'n'roll players discovered
doublenecks, demand grew and Gibson
revived the EDS-1275 in 1977. Thanks to
regular use by such guitarists as Alex
Lifeson of Rush, Charlie
Whitney of Family, Steve
Howe of Yes, and Jimmy
Page of Led Zeppelin, the
EDS-1275 remains in
production today.

MODEL

**Gibson EDS-1275
(SG body shape)**

YEAR

1966

PRODUCTION

**Circa 1962 to 1967,
1977 to current**

Gibson was well-established by the mid 1950s as Fender's top competitor, but while Fender pushed solidbody guitar design to a new level with the Stratocaster, Gibson was coming up with little more than cosmetic changes. Leo Fender allegedly made remarks about Gibson being a stodgy old company, and Gibson president Ted McCarty responded in 1958 with not one but three angular solidbody shapes – the Flying V, Explorer, and Moderne – that threw traditional designs out the window.

The Flying V was the most successful (the Moderne was not produced at all), and such influential players as bluesman Albert King and early rocker Lonnie Mack became closely identified with their original Flying Vs. However, most Vs ended up as unsold attention-grabbers in dealers' windows. After shipping only 98 instruments, Gibson gave up.

The V turned out to be only a few years ahead of its time, as Gibson found out when they reintroduced it in late 1965. Within two years, Jimi Hendrix began playing Flying Vs, and the model found a permanent home on the cutting edge of rock'n'roll.

MODEL
Gibson Flying V

YEAR
1959

PRODUCTION
1958 to 1959

Few companies can resist creating a super-deluxe version of a successful model, and Gibson's Flying V, with its radical but simple design, was a perfect candidate. In 1979, Gibson went far beyond the typical cosmetic upgrades of hardware, bindings, inlays, etc., and gave the V a complete redesign.

The mahogany or walnut body featured a contrasting layer of maple that, when the edges were beveled, created a sort of accent stripe that added curves within the straight lines of body outline. Reinforcing the V-shape were a pair of pickups whose coils had been split and angled to form a V; they were quickly nicknamed "boomerang" pickups.

Gibson introduced the new model as the Flying V II (or V2, as the truss-rod cover says) in 1979, but as it turned out, the basic model needed only a boost, not a make-over. Gibson changed the body of the standard model from mahogany to alder, put hotter pickups in it, and renamed it the Flying V I in 1981; the V II was gone within a year.

MODEL
Gibson Flying V II

YEAR
1981

PRODUCTION
1979 to 1982

93

GIBSON

The Explorer was the second of Gibson president Ted McCarty's three Modernistic designs. Gibson debuted the Explorer with the Flying V in 1958, but the V made the 1958 catalog while the Explorer did not, and the Explorer lagged well behind the V in production as well as sales.

The earliest version of the Explorer featured a "split" V-shaped headstock, which was the way McCarty drew it in his patent for the model. The design required the longer strings to bend around the tuner posts, however, and the split headstock was quickly replaced by a more practical and functional "scimitar" shape with six-on-a-side tuner configuration.

The Explorer's body was essentially a distorted and angled version of a standard guitar, complete with upper and lower bouts and body waists, and in that respect it was less radical than the Flying V's, but the Explorer's huge "tail fin" made it feel heavy and unwieldy compared to the lighter Flying V, and when the Flying V failed to generate sales, the Explorer never had a chance.

MODEL

Gibson Explorer (split headstock)

YEAR

1958

PRODUCTION

1958

Gibson's quick redesign of the Explorer's headstock from the split-V to the curved "scimitar" shape could not save the model. Gibson shipping records do not list the Explorer specifically in 1958 and '59, only "Korina (Mod. Gtr)," and the total for those two years is a meager 22 instruments.

Unlike the Flying V, which Gibson successfully reintroduced in the 1960s, the Explorer remained out of production until the mid 1970s, when guitarists intent on pushing rock'n'roll to new limits began looking for an untraditional guitar to identify their music. In 1975, prompted by Hamer's introduction of a similar model and by Eric Clapton's appearance in a Music Man amplifier ad playing an original Explorer, Gibson brought back the Explorer.

James Hetfield of Metallica and Mathias Jabs of the Scorpions established the Explorer as an identification badge for heavy metal guitarists. Dave Grohl of the Foo Fighters and The Edge of U2 have also wielded Explorers. And the model received immortality of a sort when played by the character portrayed by Nigel Tufnel in the film *This Is Spinal Tap*.

MODEL
Gibson Explorer (curved headstock)

YEAR
Early 1960s (from leftover parts)

PRODUCTION
1958 to 1959

95

Ray Dietrich was an automotive designer, famous for his work with Chrysler, Packard and Lincoln, who by the early 1960s was retired and living in Kalamazoo, Michigan, home of Gibson guitars. Gibson president Ted McCarty invited Dietrich to design a guitar, and the result was the Firebird series of 1963.

The original version of the Firebird is known as "reverse body," and that is exactly what Dietrich did. He reversed the conventional solidbody shape, making the upper treble horn longer than the bass horn and extending the lower bass bout. (McCarty had gone in the same direction, but to an extreme, with his Explorer of 1958.) The peghead, too, was reversed, with all the tuners on the treble side. To make this configuration workable, Gibson used banjo-style tuners rather than the standard right-angle design.

The heart of Dietrich's design was a nine-ply neck that continued through the body. This "neck-thru"design eliminated the neck joint and provided a strong, unbroken connection between neck and body – a critical element in solidbody performance. Gibson introduced four Firebirds in 1963, with the single-pickup Firebird I as the basic model.

MODEL
**Gibson Firebird I
(reverse body)**

YEAR
1964

PRODUCTION
1963 to 1965

The Firebird V was the equivalent to Gibson's Les Paul Standard or SG Standard, identifiable by its trapezoidal fingerboard inlays. Gibson stopped making the original reverse-body style in 1965, but this version appeared in the hands of up-and-coming bluesman Johnny Winter when he made his major-label debut in 1969, and to this day, Winter has been the most visible and consistent proponent of the Firebird V.

Part of the Firebird's appeal was its smaller double-coil "mini-humbucking" pickups, which produced a more cutting tone than the thick-sounding, full-size humbuckers that Gibson had invented and introduced in 1957. Not only was it perfect for the blues that Johnny Winter played, it provided an alternative sound in the arsenal of numerous players, including Eric Clapton, Allen Collins of Lynyrd Skynyrd, Noel Gallahger of Oasis, Dave Grohl of Foo Fighters, Paul Stanley of KISS and Rolling Stones Brian Jones, Keith Richards and Mick Taylor.

When Gibson began reissuing the Firebird in 1972, the Firebird V was the base model, and it returned permanently to regular production in 1990.

MODEL
Gibson Firebird V (reverse body)

YEAR
1965

PRODUCTION
1963 to 1965

GIBSON

I n the 1950s, Gibson had successfully split the original Les Paul design into four distinct models, delineated by pickups and ornamentation, and Gibson continued the pattern with the SG-shaped Les Pauls in 1961 and the Firebirds of 1963.

The Firebird I corresponded to the Les Paul Junior, with a single pickup, unbound fingerboard and dot inlays. The Firebird III had the same features as the Special. The Firebird V was the Standard. And at the top of the line, the Firebird VII was the equivalent of the Les Paul Custom, with three pickups, ebony fingerboard, pearl block inlays and gold-plated hardware.

Although the Firebird V, like the Les Paul Standard, has been the mainstay of the line, the Firebird VII has had its share of devotees. Phil Manzanera of Roxy Music was one of the earliest, using his VII onstage and in the studio in the early 1970s. More recent Firebird VII players include Gem Archer with Oasis, Kenny Olson with Kid Rock, Andy Abad with Marc Antony, and Peter Stroud with Sheryl Crow.

MODEL

Gibson Firebird VII (reverse body)

YEAR

1964

PRODUCTION

1963 to 1965

Prior to Ted McCarty's patents on the Flying V, Explorer and Moderne, few guitar bodies varied far enough from tradition to warrant patent protection. Fender had not tried to patent the Telecaster or Stratocaster but, possibly as a result of McCarty's action, Leo Fender obtained a patent on the Jazzmaster body that Fender introduced in 1958.

Fender's patent covered one of the Jazzmaster's least noticeable features – offset waists. The typical guitar body (even Gibson's radical Explorer) curved inward at the same point on both sides, but the Jazzmaster's waists were offset to provide a more comfortable playing position for a seated guitarist. Gibson's Firebirds had slightly offset waists, and Fender complained.

Gibson used the complaint as an excuse to make the Firebird more conventional, reversing the body, giving rise to the term "non-reverse" for these models, and shortening the horns. At the same time, Gibson made the Firebird easier to produce by discarding the neck-thru-body design for a traditional set (glued-in) neck. The makeover, implemented in 1965, effectively clipped the Firebirds' wings, and they faded out of production in 1969.

99

MODEL
**Gibson Firebird I
(non-reverse body)**

YEAR
1965

PRODUCTION
1965 to 1969

GIBSON

With the Firebird's changeover from the original "reverse" body to the squatter "non-reverse" style of 1965, Gibson seemed to lose more than the innovative ideas of Firebird designer Ray Dietrich. The company lost a sense of model identification that it had established ten years earlier in the Les Paul line.

The lowest model in the Les Paul, SG, and Firebird lines had always had a single pickup. Now the non-reverse Firebird I had two pickups. The highest model had been the only one with three pickups, but now the Firebird III had three pickups as well. The Firebird V and VII did have humbuckers while the Firebird I and III had single-coils – a difference that was shared with the Les Paul and SG lines – but all four models had the lowest of Gibson's fingerboard ornamentation: pearl dot inlays and no binding.

The Firebirds simply lost their identity, along with their flair, and they were gone within five years. Gibson's Custom Shop offered a modernized reissue in 2002, but it fared even worse, lasting only two years.

MODEL

**Gibson Firebird III
(non-reverse body)**

YEAR

1965

PRODUCTION

1965 to 1969

In an effort to bring the electric guitar into the modern world of solid-state electronics, Gibson created a model series in the late 1970s with "active" electronics, including expansion and compression controls, powered by an onboard nine-volt battery. Gibson developed the circuitry in conjunction with the Moog synthesizer company, which Norlin, Gibson's parent company, had acquired in 1973.

To reflect the high-tech creative atmosphere, Gibson named them RD, the commonplace techno-scientific abbreviation for Research & Development. The RD Artist, introduced in 1979, was the most expensive of the three models (the lowest version did not have active electronics), and the Artist designation branched out to include traditional models that were fitted with active circuitry, e.g., ES-Artist, L.P. Artist and SG Artist.

While the RD models did have an intriguing body shape that looked like a softer, curvier version of the original reverse-body Firebirds, and while high-fidelity electronics seemed like a good idea on paper, guitarists ultimately wanted a Gibson simply to sound like Gibsons had sounded since the late 1950s, and the RD models were gone by 1972.

MODEL
Gibson RD Artist

YEAR
1979

PRODUCTION
1978 to 1981

GIBSON

In 1984, Gibson introduced a pair of Les Pauls with a carved top and the double-cutaway shape of Gibson's late-1950s Les Paul Special and Junior. The results were disastrous for Gibson, but when Paul Reed Smith introduced his similarly inspired, upscale PRS models in 1985, he was able to build a successful company around that design.

In 1997, Gibson moved to regain the market segment that it had lost to PRS by introducing a new pair of double-cutaway, carved-top Les Paul models that, a year later, were rolled into one model – the Les Paul DC Standard.

Curiously the double-cut DC models featured only a master tone and master volume control rather than individual volume controls for the two humbucking pickups. It was a break from tradition and may have hampered initial acceptance, but it was a change designed to give the DC model family its own identity. Though still not a serious challenge to PRS or to Gibsons single-cutaway Les Paul Standard, the DC is now well-established in Gibson's model offering.

MODEL
Gibson Les Paul DC
Standard

YEAR
1998

PRODUCTION
1998

The Goya name was well-known in the late 1950s and early '60s for high-quality acoustic guitars made by the Levin company of Sweden for Herschman Musical Instruments, a New York distributor. The first Goya solidbodies, introduced in the late 1950s, were eye-catching, sparkle-top models made by another Swedish company, Hagstrom.

Goya was purchased in 1966 by Avnet (which purchased Guild in the same year), and the Goya catalog of 1966 showed a more southern European source for electric models. Although the source was never specified, the Rangemaster models – solidbody and semi-hollow – had all the earmarks of the Italian-made Eko guitars.

This 1968 Rangemaster sports a typical Italian potpourri of features, including split pickups with six pushbutton selectors, plus three pushbuttons for tone control. It also had the typical impact – high visual, low sales – of most Italian guitars. Goya electrics faded quickly from the marketplace as production moved to Japan and Korea and ownership moved to Kustom (1970), then to Dude, and finally in 1976 to Martin.

MODEL
Goya Rangemaster

YEAR
1968

PRODUCTION
Late 1960s

GRETSCH

Gretsch initially ignored Leo Fender's solid guitars of 1950, but when Gibson jumped into the market with the Les Paul Model in 1952, Gretsch followed quickly with its first solidbody.

The Duo Jet of 1953 had a similar body to the Gibson, but its extra layers of body binding and its bound peghead gave it an extra level of ornamentation, and the black finish added a degree of elegance. It was probably no coincidence that when Gibson came with a fancier Les Paul at the end of 1953, it sported a black finish.

This 1957 Duo Jet was the first American-made guitar owned by George Harrison. He bought it in 1961 from a newspaper ad. It certainly qualifies as a "Beatles guitar" from the group's early years, but by the time the group took America by storm in 1964, Harrison was playing a Gretsch Chet Atkins model. While it was all good for Gretsch, the Duo Jet did not fare as well as the Atkins model, and it went out of production in 1971.

MODEL
Gretsch Duo Jet

YEAR
1957

PRODUCTION
1953 to 1971

Gretsch's 1955 catalog had the company's calling card right on the cover, with its high-end hollowbody electrics shown in yellow, green, and white finishes in addition to a traditional sunburst. In the solidbody line, the Gretsch Silver Jet took finish colors to the next level with a gleaming silver sparkle finish that was a step beyond the capabilities of its competitors.

In the middle years of the 20th century, Gretsch was as successful a drum maker as it was a guitar company. So when it came to creating an eye-catching guitar finish, rather than spraying lacquer with metallic particles – as Gibson did on its "goldtop" Les Paul Model – Gretsch simply "finished" its guitars with silver-sparkle drum coverings, giving them a more dramatic sparkle effect than any metallic paint.

As a company, Gretsch was even older than Gibson, but while Gibson fought its image as a stodgy traditional company, the Silver Jet had a flair that permeated the entire Gretsch line and underscored Gretsch's claim on its 1955 catalog – Guitars for Moderns.

MODEL
**Gretsch Silver Jet
(single cutaway)**

YEAR
1955

PRODUCTION
1955 to 1960

Gretsch not only followed Gibson into the solidbody market in the early 1950s, Gretsch also followed Gibson's lead in enlisting a famous guitarist to promote its solidbodies. Chet Atkins was by no means as famous as Les Paul – no guitarist was – in late 1954, but he was on the verge of his first pop success ("Mr. Sandman" in 1955), and he would go on to be far more influential than Paul.

Gretsch gave Atkins his own semi-hollow and solidbody models, and Atkins's only requests were a vibrato and, for more sustain, a metal nut. Gretsch's Jimmie Webster had just created the Gretsch Round-Up in 1954 with full western ornamentation, which seemed to be appropriate for a country artist. (Record companies treated "country & western" as a single genre at the time.) With the substitution of the metal nut and the vibrato, the Chet Atkins Solid Bbody was created.

Atkins never cared for the western features, and his later models were not western-themed, but his signature Solid Body retained the same western look until it was discontinued in 1963.

MODEL
Gretsch Chet Atkins Solid Body

YEAR
1956

PRODUCTION
1955 to 1962

Gretsch had battled with Gibson and Epiphone in the pre-World War II acoustic arena with such flashy features as cat's eye soundholes on archtops and a triangular soundhole on flat-tops. In the postwar years, Gretsch continued to attract attention with aesthetic touches, especially finish colors, illustrated by a Duo Jet style solidbody with a bright red top. Gretsch introduced it in 1955 as the Jet Fire Bird.

The red-topped Gretsch did not affect Gretsch's sales as much as it did competitors' guitars. Within three years, Gibson changed the finish on the Les Paul Junior from sunburst to a red stain, and the Les Paul Standard changed from gold to a red sunburst. At the same time, Fender added a red layer to its regular sunburst and introduced a standard palette of custom finish colors.

Unlike Gibson and Fender, however, Gretsch heightened the impact of its color options by treating each as a different model. The Jet Fire Bird, though it followed all the spec changes of the black Duo Jet, kept its own identity through to its ultimate demise in 1971.

MODEL
Gretsch Jet Fire Bird

YEAR
1960

PRODUCTION
1955 to 1970

107

GRETSCH

For all of Gretsch's flash and fanfare, when it came down to basics, Gretsch followed Gibson – in entering the solidbody market, enlisting a famous endorser, implementing humbucking pickups, and finally, adopting a double-cutaway body shape. Gibson had given its lower Les Paul Junior and Special a boost with double-cutaways in 1958 and 1959, respectively and, in 1961, Gretsch followed suit, changing all the Jet-family models to double-cutaway.

A year later, the Silver Jet became the patriarch of an unofficial sparkle family, when Gretsch officially made all their sparkle drum coverings available as guitar finishes. Champagne Jets and Gold Jets were the most popular choices after Silver; Burgundy and Tangerine were also listed.

The flash of notoriety was shortlived, however. In 1963, Gretsch stopped listing the Silver Jet as a separate model and made all the sparkle finishes optional on the basic Duo Jet models. Three years later, Gretsch stopped offering sparkle finishes officially, but this 1969 example shows that sparkles were available until the Duo Jet was discontinued in 1971.

MODEL
**Gretsch Silver Jet
(double cutaway)**

YEAR
1969

PRODUCTION
1961 to 1969

108

Gretsch's Astro Jet appeared in 1965 with a unique design that today looks like an early casualty of the drug culture that would permeate rock music by the end of the decade.

The double-cutaway body had elongated bouts on the upper bass and lower treble side, but they bulged awkwardly where the guitars of other makers had sleek, angular lines. The peghead appeared to have been left out in the sun too long, to the point that only two tuners would fit on the treble side.

Unfortunately for Gretsch, the Astro Jet was not just an aberration in an otherwise successful history of solidbody design. Instead, it was the model that, for all practical purposes, signaled the end of Gretsch's prominence in the solidbody market. Two years later, the Baldwin piano company acquired Gretsch and wisely deleted the Astro Jet, but aside from a pair of Chet Atkins solidbodies in the mid-1970s, none of Gretsch's subsequent owners ever came up with another respectable solidbody model.

MODEL
Gretsch Astro Jet

YEAR
1966

PRODUCTION
1965 to 1967

GRETSCH

The success of Gibson's budget-priced 1954 Les Paul Junior – surpassing the combined sales of the three more expensive Gibsons – could not have gone unnoticed at Gretsch. Curiously, though, Gretsch did not introduce its own inexpensive solidbody until the Corvette of 1961.

The Corvette was inspired by Gibson's 1959 double-cutaway Junior, with its slightly extended bass horn. It started with a "slab" body, like Gibson's, but within two years it sported sleek beveled edges. At the same time, Gretsch offered it with one or two pickups and with a Burns vibrato.

Around 1966, a custom version of this budget model appeared, sporting a sparkle paint finish (not the sparkling drum covers of the Silver Jet family). Gretsch had offered a custom-color, short-scale Corvette a few years earlier called the Princess, and in keeping with the courtly model nomenclature, the sparkly Corvettes were dubbed the Dukes. The Gold Duke had a yellowish finish and gold-plated hardware while the Silver Duke had a white finish with nickel parts. Neither model was catalogued and both are quite rare today.

MODEL
Gretsch Corvette Gold Duke

YEAR
1966

PRODUCTION
Circa 1966

Bo Diddley made his marks in rock'n'roll history with the rhumba-rock beat that powered his 1955 hit record "Bo Diddley" and with a rectangular-body guitar that Gretsch custom-made for him in 1958. His third most noteworthy achievement may be the more recent, but just as memorable, Gretsch design known as the Billy Bo Jupiter Thunderbird.

The original Jupiter Thunderbird was actually two different guitars that were custom made for Diddley in 1961 by Tom Holmes (best known today for his custom pickups). The Jupiter had a more squarish body shape than the curvier Thunderbird. At some point, Diddley gave his Thunderbird to ZZ Top's Billy F. Gibbons, who locked it away in his guitar vault. Years passed until one day when Gibbons was looking for something different to use on a recording session, he "rediscovered" it.

In the meantime, Gibbons had had Holmes make him some similar guitars, called the BFG models. With a little input of his own – hence "Billy" in the model name – Gibbons convinced Gretsch to revive the Jupiter/Thunderbird in 2005.

MODEL
Gretsch Billy Bo Jupiter Thunderbird

YEAR
2005

PRODUCTION
2005 to current

111

GUILD

The Guild company made a memorable first impression when it entered the solidbody electric market in 1963 with the Thunderbird. The body has been described as resembling a melted Hershey bar, and the unconventional design did not stop there. Installed in the back of the guitar was a "kickstand" – a length of metal that pivoted out so the guitar could stand on its own.

Zal Yanovsky of The Lovin' Spoonful was the most visible guitarist playing a Thunderbird in the mid 1960s. The easily recognisable model also made spot appearances in the hands of Banana (Lowell Levinger) with The Youngbloods, Jorma Kaukonen with Jefferson Airplane and blues great Muddy Waters.

The Thunderbird's splash of success did not change Guild's identity as a traditional company – a respected maker of archtop guitars in the 1950s and flat-top acoustics in the 1960s. Guild replaced the Thunderbird in 1970 with the S-100 line, which was more conventional – similar to a Gibson SG – and more successful than the Thunderbird.

MODEL
Guild Thunderbird

YEAR
1966

PRODUCTION
1963 to 1968

After languishing through the 1970s with unremarkable solidbody guitars, Guild surprised the guitar world with an eye-catching "flying star" model in 1981. The X-79 Skyhawk was one of four Guild models with the stretched, four-point body shape. It was soon joined by the X-80 Skylark (soon to be renamed Swan), the X-82 Nova (soon to be Starfighter), and the X-88 Motley Crue model, plus three more variations with bolt-on necks.

Guild equipped the X-79 with all the right features, including humbucking pickups (two or three), a coil tap or phase control, an optional Kahler vibrato, and an array of finishes ranging from traditional sunburst to black sparkle to purple.

As Guild had discovered with the Thunderbird-style solidbodies of the1960s, guitar buyers thought of tradition rather than innovation when they thought of Guild guitars. By the time a new ownership group acquired Guild in 1986, the flying stars had proven to be shooting stars, and they had all fizzled out.

113

MODEL
Guild X-79

YEAR
1984

PRODUCTION
1981 to 1985

GUILD

Guild's BHM-1 of 1984 was the company's first of several attempts to re-create the homemade guitar played by Brian May in the British group Queen. With his father's help, May had made the "Red Special," as he called it, from whatever materials were available, including body wood from a mantelpiece, vibrato arm from a knitting needle, and vibrato springs from a motorcycle engine.

The first Guild model did not exactly replicate May's guitar – as is obvious from the optional green finish color – but it did not fit any of Guild's standard tooling, either. Consequently, it was a production nightmare, and over a three-year period, only 316 were made, according to Guild records.

Guild tried again in 1993 with a more accurate version called the Brian May Signature. After a limited edition of 1,000, Guild introduced three versions – the Pro, Special, and Standard – in 1994. However, Guild was in financial trouble and the company was sold to Fender in 1995, at which point the Brian May models ended.

MODEL
Guild Brian May Signature

YEAR
1993

PRODUCTION
1993

The "Sharp 5" designation on this 1960s Guyatone may have confused those guitar buyers familiar with the "Flat 5" musical interval that was an integral element of bebop jazz. Guitarists in Asia, however, would have recognized the endorsement of the Sharp Five, a leading Japanese pop band of the era.

By 1967, when this Sharp 5 was produced, the Guyatone brand would have been recognized by fans of British guitar heroes Hank Marvin and Jeff Beck, both of whom owned Guyatones in their early years. In Japan, however, Guyatone, had been well known for years as one of the oldest Japanese guitar companies. It was founded in Tokyo in the 1930s by Mitsui Matsuki, whose nickname "Guya" meant "one who cares for his tools."

Some Guyatones, like the Sharp 5, stayed close to Fender designs, while others took off in more dramatic directions, including one 1970s model with an onboard drum machine. The brand made a resurgence in the 1990s but by the turn of the 21st century was offering only accessories and effects pedals.

MODEL
Guyatone LG350T
Sharp 5

YEAR
1967

PRODUCTION
Mid 1960s to late
1960s

HAGSTROM

Hagstrom's greatest international success came in the late 1960s, when the brand became synonymous with fast, thin necks. But, as this 1959 model P46 Deluxe shows, Hagstrom guitars had been attracting attention with innovative designs as well as flashy looks since the Swedish company entered the guitar market in 1958.

The sparkle finish and pearloid fingerboard of the P46 were standard ornamentation elements found on accordions, and Hagstrom had, in fact, started out as an accordion company, founded in 1921 in Älvdalen, Sweden, by Albin Hagstrom. The pushbutton controls of the P46 were also inspired by accordion designs, and they activated different electronic circuits as well as pickup combinations. With the use of roller controls for tone and volume, Hagstrom eliminated standard control knobs altogether from the P46.

The Les Paul-inspired single-cutaway body gave way in the 1960s to Hagstroms (marketed in the U.K. under the Futurama brand) with a Stratocaster body shape and a unique, vinyl-covered back. The company fell victim to inexpensive Asian imports in the 1980s.

MODEL
Hagstrom P46

YEAR
1959

PRODUCTION
Late 1950s to early 1960s

Hamer, based in the Chicago area, made its name in the late 1970s on the strength of Gibson-inspired models, such as the Standard (based on the Explorer) and the Sunburst (based on the double-cutaway Les Paul Special), but as soon as the company established a solid following among guitarists, Hamer began introducing its own original designs.

The Phantom A5 of 1984 – like its 1981 predecessor, the Prototype – had a fairly conventional body design that was basically a longhorn Stratocaster. "Fat Strats," with a humbucker in the bridge position, were becoming a popular modification to give Fenders a more powerful sound, and Hamer appeared to take the concept to the extreme with a triple-coil bridge pickup. A pair of switches offered conventional switching (bridge, neck or both), but the second switch allowed only a humbucker-or-single option for the triple-coil, making it effectively only a Fat Strat with a relocated middle pickup.

Andy Summers of The Police had a Phantom in his arsenal of Hamers, but it remained an obscure model and did not survive Hamer's acquisition by Kaman Music (Ovation's parent company) in 1988.

MODEL
Hamer Phantom A5

YEAR
1984

PRODUCTION
1984 to 1988

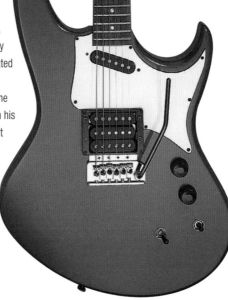

HOFNER

Hofner was founded in Germany in the 1880s by Karl Höfner, a maker of bowed instruments. The company was able to rebound after World War II and, thanks in part to the absence of American-made guitars in Britain, to establish a strong market there with electric and acoustic guitars that had the appearance, at least, of high-quality instruments.

When restrictions on American imports were lifted in 1959, Hofner enjoyed continued success in the 1960s by basing its solidbodies on the most popular American models. The body of this Galaxie from 1965 is a Fender Jazzmaster from the waist down, combined with the upper horns of a Fender Stratocaster.

When it came to ornamentation and electronics, however, Hofner did have its own style. The most obvious Hofner "signature" element on the Galaxie is found on the fingerboard in the horizontal bands that function as fret markers. And following the lead of Swedish-based Hagstrom, Hofner eliminated all conventional knobs, replacing them with an array of roller controls and switches.

MODEL
Hofner Galaxie

YEAR
Circa 1965

PRODUCTION
1960s

HOFNER

Perhaps in response to the Stratocaster-inspired, Swedish-made Hagstrom models that featured a vinyl covered back, the German-based Hofner company served up Model 175 in the late 1960s with a body completely covered in vinyl. But where the vinyl on the Hagstroms had the color-coordinated look of upscale automotive upholstery, the vinyl on the Hofner looked as if it might have been taken from a kitchen floor.

Aside from the vinyl covering, Model 175 was very similar to the Hofner Galaxie, with three pickups, numerous roller controls, a distinctive vibrato, a string mute, and Hofner's signature full-width fingerboard markers.

Hofner achieved considerable notoriety in the 1960s – not as a result of the 175 but on the strength of a violin-style hollow bass used by The Beatles' Paul McCartney. The company went through a series of ownership changes beginning in 1994, and although vintage-style Hofner instruments (primarily acoustics, hollow electrics, and basses) are still produced and distributed worldwide, the vinyl-covered 175 is mercifully not included in the current offering.

MODEL
Hofner 175

YEAR
Circa 1968

PRODUCTION
Late 1960s

IBANEZ

Ibanez is the best known brand of Hoshino Gakki Ten, a Japanese company that started in the guitar business in the 1920s as an importer. In 1962, the company broke into the U.S. market the easy way, by forming a business partnership with American dealer Harry Rosenbloom of Ardmore, Pennsylvania, who was selling guitars under the Elger brand.

Model 882 was one of the earliest Ibanez-brand solidbodies. Ironically, Ibanez was still only producing acoustic guitars at the time, so the 882 was out-sourced to other Japanese makers. It was obviously based on Fender's Jazzmaster but, with its rocker-button controls and its simple, Bigsby-like vibrato, it was not an outright copy.

Through the 1960s, Ibanez maintained its own identity with models largely inspired by Burns of London, but they fell by the wayside in the 1970s when Japanese companies began unashamedly copying classic Gibsons and Fenders. The "copy era" ended when Gibson's filed a patent infringement suit against Elger in 1977, after which Ibanez went on to become one of the most respected of Japanese makers.

MODEL
Ibanez 882

YEAR
Circa 1963

PRODUCTION
Early 1960s

The "copy era" of Japanese guitar production legally ended in 1978 when Gibson's lawsuit against Ibanez (technically against Hoshino U.S.A.) was settled by Ibanez's agreement to stop making copies of Gibsons. However, Ibanez did not immediately abandon its taste for the designs of other guitar companies. This MC 500 from Ibanez's Musician Series of 1978 is a case in point, showing a clear Alembic influence.

The seven-piece neck-thru-body design (lower Musician models had a five-piece neck), with contrasting, heavily-figured body "wings" of mahogany or ash, mimicked Alembic's signature look, although Alembic was much better-known for basses than guitars. And if there were any doubt as to the Alembic inspiration, the higher models in the Musician Series models dispelled it with active electronics – another signature feature of Alembics.

In the post-copy era, Ibanez quickly began to find greater success with its own designs – and moreover, with its growing reputation for quality – than with copies of expensive models such as the Musician Series, and the company abandoned the Alembic-based designs after 1982.

MODEL
Ibanez Musician MC 500

YEAR
1978

PRODUCTION
Circa 1978 to 1980

IBANEZ

The Iceman was conceived in the mid 1970s as a national guitar of Japan, a design that would bring the same level of respect and prestige to a Japanese guitar that the Fender Stratocaster and Gibson Les Paul carried.

Four Japanese makers collaborated and then divided up worldwide territories. Ibanez's parent company Hoshino Gakki was given the U.S. market, and Ibanez introduced the Iceman in 1975 in various configurations, including bolt-neck and set-neck versions. The Iceman's curving treble horn was inspired by Yamaha's Flying Samurai of the 1960s, but the Iceman's body was better-developed, and it featured a unique pickup design.

Steve Miller, one of Ibanez's first American endorsers, gave the Iceman wide exposure when he used it on his 1976 album *Fly Like an Eagle*, and Paul Stanley of KISS was the Iceman's most flamboyant player. While the Iceman was a success, it fell far short of its designers'goals, and Ibanez stopped making it after 1983. It did become a cult favorite, however, and a revived Iceman has been in production since 1994.

122

MODEL
Ibanez Iceman

YEAR
1979

PRODUCTION
1976 to 1983

One of Ibanez's most successful signature models does not bear the artist's name, but any guitarist familiar with the Ibanez JEM knows it was designed by Steve Vai.

In the mid 1980s, Ibanez was scrambling to compete with Kramer and Jackson's "Super Strat" designs – basically a Stratocaster with a bridge-position humbucker and a "dive bomb" vibrato. At the same time, Vai was emerging as one of the most gifted guitarists in rock'n'roll, with hotshot technique from the Berklee School of Music and eclectic on-the-job training with Frank Zappa.

Vai and Ibanez created a personalized model featuring Dimarzio pickups (including humbuckers in the neck and bridge positions) and the "monkey grip" hole in the body. However, he felt his name would not sell enough guitars, so he suggested JEM, the name of a company owned by Joe Despagni, Vai's childhood friend and longtime guitar tech. Vai introduced the JEM playing on David Lee Roth's 1988 album *Skyscraper*, and the JEM's monkey grip remains a familiar sight in Ibanez's solidbody line.

123

MODEL
Ibanez JEM

YEAR
1989

PRODUCTION
1987 to current

IBANEZ

Joe "Satch" Satriani was one of the most prominent rock guitar teachers when he introduced his virtuoso style to the masses with his 1986 solo album *Not of This Earth*. Within a year he was featured in Ibanez ads, and a year later he was an official endorser, playing Ibanez guitars onstage as the lead guitarist behind Rolling Stones singer Mick Jagger on Jagger's solo tour.

In 1990, Ibanez advertised a new JS signature model sporting a gleaming chrome finish, but when it appeared in stores, the JS1 had a standard paint finish. Like Ibanez's JEM guitars, which were designed by one of Satriani's former students, Steve Vai, the JS models featured Satriani's preferred setup – Dimarzio pickups in a humbucker-single-humbucker configuration.

In 1998, a decade after Satriani's official association with Ibanez, the company honored him with the JS 10th Anniversary. Nicknamed "Chrome Boy," the limited-edition model featured a pair of humbuckers rather than JS's typical HSH arrangement, and the twin humbuckers continue today as the standard offering on Ibanez's JS models.

MODEL
Ibanez JS 10th Anniversary

YEAR
1988

PRODUCTION
1988

The Ibanez Universe was simple enough to describe: a seven-string version of the Steve Vai-designed JEM model, without the "monkey grip" hole in the body. And it was Vai who opened up a new world to rock guitarists when he used a prototype Universe with the group Whitesnake and then on his 1990 landmark solo album *Passion and Warfare*.

Russian guitarists of the 19th century and American jazz guitarists of the 20th century made use of the extra low string to provide additional harmonic possibilities, but they could not have dreamed of the power that Vai coaxed from the lower strings.

Introduced in three different versions in 1990, several of which sported green highlights, the Universe appeared to be a flash in the pan, and Ibanez actually discontinued it in 1995, just as the group Korn was using a Universe to create the monster low-end rhythm that would help define the alternative metal and nu-metal movements. Ibanez successfully reintroduced the Universe in 1996 and has since added less-expensive seven-strings in its RG line.

MODEL
Ibanez Universe

YEAR
1990

PRODUCTION
**1990 to 1994,
1996 to current**

IBANEZ

The Ibanez S Classic or SC guitars represented one of the more upscale branches of Ibanez's large and popular family of S models. The signature features of the S-Series' were a thin, solid-mahogany, Stratocaster style body (although the S does not stand for Strat), and a fast, unfinished neck.

The originals were developed by Ibanez's U.S. design team, headed by Rich Lasner, who would go on to create guitars for Yamaha, Peavey, and Modulus, among others. The thin body with sharp edges inspired them to name the model Saber, but when the Ernie Ball company announced its intent to reintroduce its Sabre basses, Ibanez simply shortened the model designation to S.

The thin body of the S-Series guitars belied their solid, sustaining performance – a result of using mahogany rather than basswood, which had become the norm for Strat-style guitars. The Classic line took the S design a step back toward the traditional, with a maple top (and even a nylon string version), but it strayed too far from the original concept and only lasted eight years in production.

MODEL
Ibanez S Classic SC420

YEAR
1999

PRODUCTION
1997 to 2004

The 1983 Randy Rhoads model was the first guitar that Charvel owner Grover Jackson made under his own brand name. It featured an offset-V body shape, with a shorter treble-side body wing. When the long wing was mirrored on the treble side, it became a Double Rhoads.

Dave Linsk, who would become best known as the guitarist for the thrash band Overkill, had this Double Rhoads custom built for him in 1984. Robbin Crosby of RATT got his own Double Rhoads, which Jackson renamed the King V. After Dave Mustaine of Megadeth custom-ordered a King V in 1985, Jackson created a signature production model for Mustaine.

Randy Rhoads, who had gained fame in 1979 in the band of former Black Sabbath singer Ozzy Osbourne, was killed in a plane crash in 1982 at age 25, but he continues to be a strong influence on heavy metal guitarists, and his offset-V signature model remains one of the representative models of the innovative Charvel/Jackson company.

127

MODEL
Jackson Double Rhoads

YEAR
1984

PRODUCTION
1984

Grover Jackson bought Wayne Charvel's guitar company, which had been founded as a repair and parts business, in 1978 and quickly became one of the most important forces in the new wave of guitar design that emerged in the 1980s.

Jackson was the first guitarmaker to develop models with the modifications that many young players were making to their Stratocaster-style guitars – replacing the bridge pickup with a humbucker and adding a Floyd Rose vibrato. He added another important design element – neck-thru-body construction for greater sustain – that had been all but abandoned by the major makers.

Jackson began making prototypes of this "Super Strat" concept in the early 1980s and officially offered it in 1984 as the Soloist model, although he would not do actual production runs until 1990. This 1985 Soloist has only one single-coil pickup with the bridge humbucker, and it sports the bound ebony fingerboard but not the "shark fin" inlays that would eventually identify the Soloist Select Series models that are currently in production.

MODEL
Jackson Soloist

YEAR
1985

PRODUCTION
1984 to 1990

Grover Jackson merged his namesake company with International Music Corporation, a Texas-based importer, in 1986 and then left the business in 1989. IMC continued to introduce new designs, including the Stealth series in 1991.

IMC aimed at affluent buyers with the American-made Custom Shop series and a U.S. Series featuring airbrushed finishes, but the Stealth models kept Jackson's within the reach of the majority of players. They featured bodies of ash or basswood with the typical Jackson pickup and vibrato options. This Stealth TH2 from 1996 shows that IMC was not afraid of trading off one of Jackson's most identifiable elements, the angular pointed headstock, in exchange for a new headstock shape that provided straight string pull (a trademark feature of 1985 upstart Paul Reed Smith).

The Stealth Series last only until 1996, and IMC lasted only until 1997, when it sold Jackson/Charvel to the Japanese-based Akai company. Five years later Akai sold the brand to Fender, where such classic Jacksons as the Soloist, Rhoads and King V live on today.

129

MODEL
Jackson Stealth TH2

YEAR
1996

PRODUCTION
1991 to 1996

KLEIN

Based in the small town of Vineburg in northern California, Steve Klein has designed acoustic and electric instruments for clients ranging from Joni Mitchell to Joe Walsh, from Bill Frisell to the Taylor guitar company. His BF solidbody represents 12 years of collaboration with a noted guitar designer, a well-known player, and one of his best friends.

The most obvious influence is the headless neck design of Ned Steinberger. The vibrola is also a Steinberger design. Rock guitarist Ronnie Montrose contributed to the aesthetic and performance aspects.

The idea for the body came from Klein's longtime associate Carl Margolis. As a polio survivor, Margolis always had an eye out for the most efficient and comfortable physical situations, and he noticed that most guitarists held the neck too low, causing discomfort in the left hand. The treble-side body curve on the Klein guitar fixed that problem by forcing the player to raise the neck and to hold this most unclassical instrument in the position a classical player would use.

MODEL
Klein BF

YEAR
1998

PRODUCTION
1990s to current

Gary Kramer had been a partner with Travis Bean, known for metal-neck guitars, so it was not surprising that when the first Kramer-brand guitars appeared in 1976, they had a metal neck. Kramers were made by the BKL company of Neptune, New Jersey, whose name came from the initials of Dennis Berardi (one of Kramer's retail clients for Bean guitars), Gary Kramer, and former Norlin (Gibson's parent company) vice president Peter LaPlaca. Businessman Henry Vaccarro joined the company to provide additional financial backing.

The walnut-and-maple body of this Model 450 from 1977 shows a strong aesthetic influence from the contrasting woods of Alembic models, which seems incongruous with the industrial look of the aluminum neck. The synthetic fingerboard material put the neck even more at odds with the body. And despite the appearance of an Alembic-style neck-thru-body design, Kramer's aluminum necks were bolted on.

Gary Kramer accepted a buyout and left BKL within a year, and the metal necks lasted only about five years before BKL found greater success with wood-neck models.

MODEL
Kramer 450

YEAR
1977

PRODUCTION
1976 to early 1980s

131

KRAMER

While the early metal-neck Kramers attracted a lot of attention, they did not attract buyers, and management of the struggling company was taken over for a brief period (around 1980–81) by Guitar Center, the Los Angeles-based retail chain. During that time Kramer switched to more-conventional wood necks.

The elongated, four-point star shape of this Voyager Imperial, introduced in 1981, shows that not every element of Kramer's new designs was conventional. The single humbucking pickup was also unconventional, but it reflected the personal preference of the hottest guitarist of 1981, Eddie Van Halen.

The key element on this model was the Floyd Rose vibrato, which allowed extreme pitch changes while remaining in tune and consequently was becoming essential equipment for rock guitarists. In 1982, Kramer became the exclusive distributor for Floyd Rose, and that relationship helped seal the deal on an endorsement from Eddie Van Halen. Van Halen's two-handed fingerboard tapping and "dive bomb" vibrato techniques had made him the most influential guitarist of the era, and Kramer became one of the most visible guitar brands of the decade.

MODEL

Kramer Voyager Imperial (rounded tips)

YEAR

1982

PRODUCTION

1981 to 1984

132

Kramer's American Sustainer of 1989 featured a Floyd Rose vibrato (as did most Kramers) along with a Floyd Rose-designed, distortion-generating humbucker in the bridge position. The Floyd Rose connection had been the foundation of Kramer's prosperity through the 1980s, but ironically, it was also the ultimate reason for Kramer's demise at end of the decade.

Kramer simply became a victim of its own success. As Kramer sold thousands of guitars with Floyd Rose's patented vibrato system, unpaid royalties piled up. Floyd Rose sued in 1990 to collect those royalties, and that was effectively the killing blow for Kramer.

The company's original financial backer, Henry Vaccarro, tried to revive Kramer in 1995, but after a handful of guitars were produced, the company was sold out of bankruptcy to Gibson in 1997. For the better part of a decade Gibson barely kept the brand alive as a cheap import line managed by its Epiphone division. In 2006, Epiphone pumped up the Kramer line with a new wave of imported reissues as well as several U.S.-made models.

133

MODEL
Kramer American Sustainer

YEAR
1989

PRODUCTION
1989 to 1990

MELOBAR

Walt Smith of Sweet, Idaho, invented the Melobar in the 1960s so that steel guitarists – traditionally confined to a chair – could look as cool onstage as conventional guitarists. The Melobar gave them an instrument that was designed to be played standing up.

Smith took a steel guitar and rotated it 45 degrees along the axis of its strings, providing a more natural, comfortable playing position than that of a steel guitar played in the lap. The rest of the instrument's design was cosmetic but no less important. The steel guitar part was attached to a cool guitar body that ranged in shape from this generic double-cutaway Skreemr model to the angular lines of a Gibson Explorer.

Such prominent steel players as David Lindley with Jackson Browne, Rusty Young with Poco, and Cindy Cashdollar with Asleep at the Wheel have played them onstage occasionally, but Melobars never gained widespread acceptance. Walt Smith's son Ted carried on the company after Walt's death in 1990, but they were struggling to stay in business by the end of 2007.

MODEL
Melobar Skreemr

YEAR
Circa 1973

PRODUCTION
1967 to current

The signature feature of Micro-Frets guitars was not in the fretwork, as the name would suggest, but in the nut – or to be technically correct, the six individually adjustable nuts that were intended to provide better intonation.

The segmented, adjustable nut was one of three innovative features developed by Ralph Jones of Frederick, Maryland, who founded the company with financial backer Marion Huggins in 1967. Early models featured a body with a routed top and routed back that were joined at the sides. Within a year he had introduced the Calibrato, a vibrato designed to provide better intonation by taking into account the differences in string gauges.

The bodies of Micro-Frets models typically had a modern element, like the pointed horns of this 1968 Signature, but with a body that looked a little overweight. And the micro-nut adjustment looked more useful than it actually was; it affected only the interval between the open string and the string played at the first fret. Jones died in 1973, and Micro-Frets guitars were gone within a year.

MODEL
Micro-Frets Signature

YEAR
Circa 1968

PRODUCTION
1967 to 1973

MOSRITE

The Ventures introduced "surf music" to America in 1960 with their No. 2 hit "Walk Don't Run," but within a year, their instrumental singles were not even breaking into the Top 50. Consequently, Semie Moseley, a well-known southern California custom guitar maker may not have been especially excited when, in 1963, Ventures guitarist Nokie Edwards asked to borrow one of Moseley's Mosrite-brand guitars.

Moseley had already built around 25 of the reverse-Stratocaster guitars as a signature model for flashy country star Joe Maphis, but when Edwards proposed a Ventures signature model, Moseley accepted.

The timing could not have been better. The Ventures re-released "Walk Don't Run" in 1964 and it went to the Top Ten. They noted on the back of an album cover that their guitars were distributed by Mosrite of California, and Mosrite production went from 20 or 30 a month to 1,000 guitars a month – until the Ventures endorsement ended in 1967. Moseley continued the Ventures model as the Mark series, but he never recaptured the success of the Ventures period.

MODEL
Mosrite Ventures

YEAR
Circa 1966

PRODUCTION
1963 to 1967

It doesn't look much like a Ventures model, or any other Mosrite guitar, but the notches in the peghead forming the letter M clearly identify this oddball as one of Semie Moseley's creations.

Moseley used this skateboard-with-cutouts framework to create a green six-string, a red 12-string and a purple bass for the West Coast psychedelic band Strawberry Alarm Clark, a one-hit-wonder group who had a No. 1 record in 1967 with "Incense and Peppermints." Despite the odd, cumbersome-looking frame, the essentials were all there, including a pair of Mosrite pickups and (on the six-string) a Mosrite vibrato unit.

The finish work on the Strawberry Alarm Clock instruments was done by legendary hot-rod and motorcycle painter Von Dutch (the professional name of Kenny Howard), who was the first custom-builder to paint stripes and flames on motorcycles in the 1940s and '50s. Although Moseley fell on hard times shortly thereafter, the oddball guitars did not hurt Von Dutch's career, and his legacy continues today as Von Dutch Kustom Motorcycles.

MODEL
Mosrite Custom for Strawberry Alarm Clock

YEAR
Circa 1967

PRODUCTION
Circa 1967

MOSRITE

Semie Moseley and his Mosrite company had a somewhat nomadic history, as illustrated by this Model 88 from 1988, which was made in the mountains of North Carolina. Born in Oklahoma, Moseley established Mosrite in Bakersfield, California. After the company bankrupted in 1969, he was able to reacquire the name, and he split his time in the 1970s between guitar making and performing gospel music while he moved production to Oklahoma in 1976, back to California in 1977, to Nevada in 1979, and then to Jonas Ridge, North Carolina, in 1981. He stayed in Jonas Ridge for ten years before making his final stand in Booneville, Arkansas, in 1991.

While he experimented with numerous designs, Moseley's most popular were essentially Ventures reissues without the Ventures name. Model 88 had the familiar shape – which Moseley developed in the early 1960s by flipping over a Fender Stratocaster – but it lacked the pickguard and "German carve" (the elegant "lip" around the top edge) of the originals.

Semie Moseley died in 1992, and his widow Loretta continues the business today.

First man. Ⓜ **mōsrite**

MODEL
Mosrite Model 88

YEAR
1988

PRODUCTION
1988

The Music Man Stingray of 1976 marked the official return of Leo Fender to the guitar world after a ten year absence. Actually, he had been working with Music Man on amplifier designs for several years, but in secret, due to a non-compete clause in his 1965 agreement to sell the Fender company. The Stingray was his first post-Fender guitar.

Ex-Fender employees Forrest White and Tom Walker had formed their own company in 1971, calling it Tri-Sonic and Musitek before settling on Music Man in 1974. In 1975, they announced Leo Fender as president. A separate company owned by Fender, CLF Research, designed and built the instruments for Music Man.

The Stingray had an improved three-bolt neck system, but the rest of the design lacked the flair that players might have expected. The body was a little fatter than a Stratocaster and the headstock was smoother. Two humbucking pickups were standard fare on Gibsons, but never on one of Leo's models. Business disagreements led to Leo's departure in 1978, and the Stingray guitar disappeared four years later.

MODEL
Music Man Stingray

YEAR
Circa 1978

PRODUCTION
1976 to 1982

MUSIC MAN

When Leo Fender left Music Man in 1978, the company was left without a production arm, as Fender's CFL company had been contracted to supply instruments to Music Man. Grover Jackson stepped in for a short time, but his attention was focused on his growing Charvel/Jackson company. After several years of difficulties, the owners decided to sell.

One of Music Man's employees, Sterling Ball, was the son of Ernie Ball, a musician, music store owner, string designer, and the maker of Earthwood acoustic basses in the early 1970s. In 1984 Ball became the new owner of Music Man, and he opened a new plant in San Luis Obispo, on the coast of California.

Ball was able to continue Music Man's success with the Sabre and Stingray basses, and in 1986 introduced his first new guitar, the Silhouette. Although it was basically a "Super Strat," it also featured such innovations as the four-and-two tuner arrangement, a Teflon-coated truss-rod for easier adjustment, and quick-change solderless pickup assemblies.

MODEL
Music Man Silhouette

YEAR
1988

PRODUCTION
1986 to current

With his fast fingerboard-tapping technique and dive-bomb vibrato effects, Edward Van Halen was the most influential guitarist of the 1980s and the foundation of the Kramer company's success. In 1990, Ernie Ball/Music Man scored a major coup when Van Halen came aboard with a signature model.

The Music Man's rather traditional single-cutaway body with a bound, bookmatched maple top was a far cry from Van Halen's original homemade "Frankenstrat" or his earlier Kramer signature models, which featured a Stratocaster-style body with a red-and-white crisscrossed finish pattern. The pair of humbucking pickups was also a departure, as Van Halen was known for using only a single humbucker. The single knob is actually a volume control, although EVH specified it to be labeled "Tone." The signature model also featured the Floyd Rose vibrato that no Van Halen guitar would be complete without.

When Van Halen moved his endorsement to Peavey in late 1995, Music Man renamed his model the Axis, and its distinctive body shape and bound maple top are still featured in the Music Man line.

MODEL
Music Man Edward Van Halen

YEAR
1992

PRODUCTION
1990 to 1995

MUSIC MAN

Albert Lee has never had a hit record, but a generation of country guitarists have been influenced and inspired by his lightning-fast licks. Appropriately, his Music Man signature model looks like it was designed for speed.

The English-born virtuoso first gained widespread recognition when he joined Emmylou Harris's band in 1976. He moved on to Eric Clapton's band in 1978, where he remained until 1993, when he became music director for the reunited Everly Brothers.

Music Man designed a sort of angular Strat-shaped guitar in 1987, and when Lee tried out the prototype he put down the Telecaster that he had been identified with throughout his career and began using the Music Man onstage as well as in the studio. In 1993, Music Man made it the official Albert Lee Signature model. Standard features included three Seymour Duncan single-coil pickups, a maple neck and a non-vibrato bridge. The original color was a pinkburst. Optional finish colors and a vibrato were added in 1996, and the model remains in production.

MODEL
Music Man Albert Lee

YEAR
1994

PRODUCTION
1993 to current

Steve Lukather was already an in-demand session player when his melding of jazz and blues-rock influences gained national attention in 1978 as lead guitarist in the band Toto.

Through the 1980s, Lukather split his time between the group, session work, and a solo career, eventually participating in over 800 No. 1 albums as a guitarist, arranger or writer.

Lukather teamed up with Music Man in 1993 to create a signature model called the Luke. The body style was an elongated Stratocaster-inspired shape. The neck featured a deep-V profile, and the headstock sported the four-and-two tuner arrangement that had become a signature of Music Man's Ernie Ball era. The active pickups are in a humbucker-single-single "Super Strat" configuration, and they are Lukather's design, too – a signature set made by EMG. The Floyd Rose vibrato completed the Super Strat features.

As Toto reached its 30th anniversary in 2008, Lukather was still the band's lead guitarist and the Music Man Luke was still in production.

143

MODEL
Music Man Luke

YEAR
1998

PRODUCTION
1993 to current

PARKER

The name Fly is a reference to boxing's lightest division, flyweight, but the Parker Fly represents a redesign of every element of the electric solidbody guitar.

Ken Parker began developing his ideas while repairing and customising instruments in a New York City guitar shop. His goal of minimising weight led not only to the minimalist shapes of his horns and headstocks but also to the use of carbon/glass fiber as a strengthening material. He also believed guitarists should be able to mix acoustic as well as traditional sounds, and to that end he partnered with acoustic pickup designer Larry Fishman. The Korg company (best known for synthesizers) financed the venture, and the Parker Fly debuted in 1992.

This Parker Nitefly from 1996 features three single-coil Dimarzio pickups in a traditional Stratocaster configuration, plus a Fishman piezo pickup in the bridge. The wood body – in this case maple – reflects Parker's belief that wood is as vital to the tone of an electric guitar as it is in an acoustic, and all Parker Fly models have a wood body.

MODEL
Parker Fly Nitefly

YEAR
1996

PRODUCTION
1992 to current

The Parker Fly could not have been made without such modern materials as carbon fiber and epoxies, but Ken Parker felt that a wood-body was an integral part of a solidbody guitar's sound.

The Sitka spruce body of the Fly Artist model gave it the same tone-wood base as an acoustic guitar. An array of controls provided traditional volume and tone controls for the two humbuckers and the piezo. There was even a roller knob (below the bridge) for players to dial in their preferred tension on the vibrato unit.

The Fly shape debuted in 1992 and soon expanded to over three dozen models featuring every conceivable combination of pickups, woods, set or bolt-on neck, vibrato, or hardtail, etc. Although few guitarists embraced the Fly as their primary instrument, artists in virtually every style of music made good use of the Fly. Parker's endorsement list ranges from rockers Adrien Belew (David Bowie) and Joe Walsh (Eagles) to jazzers Phil Keaggy and Larry Coryell, and includes such diverse artists as bluesman Corey Harris, singer/songwriter Joni Mitchell, and country legend Merle Haggard.

MODEL
Parker Fly Artist

YEAR
1996

PRODUCTION
1996 to 2002

145

PRS

While dive-bomb vibrato units and dramatic body shapes carried a wave of upstart guitar companies through the 1980s, a new company called PRS introduced itself in 1985 with elegant refinements of traditional designs.

Paul Reed Smith, now based in Stevensville, Maryland, took his inspiration from the short-horn, asymmetrical double-cutaway shape of Gibson's low-end Les Paul Junior and Special of the late 1950s. His calling card was a contoured top of highly figured maple, the unbound edges of which gave his guitars the appearance of being bound with curly maple, but he redesigned almost every element of the traditional design. The result was a high-end instrument that appealed to guitar connoisseurs as well as to players.

Appropriate to Smith's ten-year background as a custom builder, he named the maple-top PRS model the Custom. He introduced his new guitar at the winter NAMM trade show in January 1985 and took orders. By the summer show his production team had made their first 20 instruments. Less than a year later, on June 16, 1987, the company celebrated its 1,000th guitar.

MODEL
Paul Reed Smith Custom

YEAR
1985

PRODUCTION
1985 to present

The PRS Standard, initially called simply the Paul Reed Smith Guitar, debuted along with the Custom in 1985. It had an all-mahogany body rather than the maple top of the Custom, but otherwise it sported all of the features that instantly identified a PRS guitar, including the "half-moon" figuration of the fingerboard inlays, the straight string-pull headstock shape, and a vibrato that stayed in tune.

The PRS pickup configuration was a standard two-humbucker setup, but the controls on the early models were anything but standard. The toggle switch, which, on most guitars of the day, would be a pickup selector, was actually a tone control – nicknamed the "sweet switch" – that rolled off high-end frequencies. One of the knobs was dedicated to a rotary pickup selector switch, and the other was a volume control; a tone control knob replaced the sweet switch in 1991.

147

MODEL
**Paul Reed Smith
Standard (24-frets)**

YEAR
1986

PRODUCTION
1985 to current

PRS

Not long after the successful launch of PRS guitars in 1985, dealers began asking for a less expensive model. In 1988, the company responded with the Classic Electric, whose name was shortened to CE after Peavey complained about infringement on its Classic model name.

The body of the CE had the same elegant shape of PRS's initial models, and the neck had the full 24-fret, two octave range. The cost-saving feature was a bolt-on neck. Because a bolt-on neck is a Fender feature, Paul Reed Smith made the CE more Fender-like with an alder body and a maple neck and fingerboard.

The Fender look did not fly, so a rosewood fingerboard, which had been an option, became standard in 1989, and the CE found a market. The other Fender-inspired feature, the alder body, lasted longer, but it was replaced by mahogany in 1995. A maple top option and 22-fret version secured the CE's position as a vital model of the PRS line.

MODEL
Paul Reed Smith CE (CE 24)

YEAR
1988

PRODUCTION
1988 to current

The expensive look of the original PRS models created a demand for even more expensive guitars and, within two years, Paul Reed Smith was making Signature models featuring the best woods available. He personally signed each one, but as the business grew he found himself traveling at times when guitars needed to be signed, so, in 1991, after 1,000 Signature models, he retired the Signature and replaced it with the Artist.

The Artist, standardized the Signature's high-end appointments. By this time, the optional "10-top" – a highly figured maple top cap – had become PRS's calling card, and the Artist went a step beyond, with a "10-plus" top. Bird inlays, another popular option, were standard on the Artist's Brazilian rosewood fingerboard. The only thing missing was Paul Reed Smith's personal signature, but he made up for it by inlaying the headstock signature with abalone pearl.

The Artist was not totally about cosmetics. The longer neck heel and the "wide fat" neck profile signaled Smith's dissatisfaction with his original design and were the first steps toward PRS's 22-fret models.

MODEL

Paul Reed Smith Artist I

YEAR

1991

PRODUCTION

1991 to 1994

149

PRS

After less than 500 Artist models, Paul Reed Smith felt it was ready for an upgrade. PRS ads introduced the new version in 1993 as the Artist Series II guitars (thereby making the original Artist the Artist I).

Except for the curly maple binding around the fingerboard – a significant difference in the context of PRS ornamentation – the II was cosmetically similar to the I, with a "10-plus" top, bird inlays, abalone peghead signature, and wraparound stopbar tailpiece. However, there was an important change in the neck design. As the PRS ad noted, Smith had picked the stiffest mahogany neck blanks for the Artist I, and now the Artist II took the next step. Its 22-fret neck, combined with a more substantial neck heel, gave it a fundamentally different tone.

The Artist II (along with the PRS Dragon) led the way for 22-fret versions of the Custom (1993) and the Standard (1994). After less than 500 Artist II models, the Artist Series moved on successfully to the Artist III, Artist IV and an Artist Limited version.

MODEL
Paul Reed Smith Artist Limited

YEAR
1995

PRODUCTION
1993 to 1996

The CE (nee Classic Electric), with its bolt-on neck, was an instant success when it was introduced in 1988, thanks to its status as an "affordable" PRS. However, with an alder body, it lacked the maple top that was fast becoming a PRS trademark, and only a year into production, the CE Maple Top appeared.

The tops on the CEs were figured, but not as highly figured as those of the Custom. (Paul Reed Smith said that in earlier years they would have thrown away the tops that ended up on the CEs.) Nevertheless the maple-top version seemed to bring the CE up to the standards set by other PRS models.

In the meantime, Smith had become dissatisfied with the performance of the guitars and to improve tone, as well as sustain, he began to redesign the neck joint to make the neck stiffer. The result was a 22-fret neck, and PRS offered the set-neck Custom with the new neck in 1993. A year later the 22-fret neck came to the set-neck Standard and the bolt-neck CE.

MODEL
Paul Reed Smith CE 22 Maple Top

YEAR
1998

PRODUCTION
1994 to current

PRS

The PRS Dragon guitars were the realisation of a dream Paul Reed Smith had when he was 16. The first dragon model, introduced in 1992, was more than a showpiece, however. It featured several small but fundamental changes in the standard PRS design.

If anyone got past the dragon inlays on the neck, they would have noticed that it had only 22 frets, which was two less than all the other PRS guitars. It was one result of Smith's desire to improve on the 24-fret neck. The shorter neck (though not shorter scale length) made it stiffer, which provided a fatter sound and more sustain. A longer heel added support for the neck. A new Stop-Tail bridge/tailpiece provided further sustain. A "wide fat" neck (though not as fat as some vintage guitars) added even more.

PRS created a new dragon each year for three years. For 1994, the dragon had deep blue wings folded much more smoothly than previous creatures. The fourth dragon did not appear until 2000, at which time it took over the body of the guitar.

152

MODEL
**Paul Reed Smith
Dragon III**

YEAR
1994

PRODUCTION
1994

The CE model of 1988 was created to offer guitarists a less expensive PRS, and to that end it featured a bolt-on maple neck and alder body. A year later, PRS made it more PRS-like with a maple top/mahogany back version, but the figuration of the CE tops would have been graded in the 5–6 range – less curly than the 7–8 top that was standard on the Custom, and much less dramatic than the optional "10 top" or the "10 plus" top of the Artist.

However, despite the company's best intentions, the bolt-neck CE gained a following in its own right – not as just a downgraded PRS Standard. It deserved, and received, a version with a 22-fret neck in 1994, and as this 1998 CE 22 Maple Top illustrates, a spectacular, quilted-maple top was *not* too good for a CE.

The CE Maple Top continues today as a mainstay of the PRS line, with 22 or 24 frets, a nicely figured maple top, and optional gold-plated hardware.

MODEL
Paul Reed Smith CE 22 Maple Top

YEAR
1998

PRODUCTION
1994 to current

153

PRS

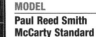

154

The Gibson-like plastic toggle-switch cap identifies a PRS McCarty model. McCarty presided over Gibson from 1948–66, a golden era highlighted by the first Les Pauls and the invention of the humbucking pickup. McCarty was personally responsible for such influential designs as the semi-hollow ES-335 and the radical solidbody shapes of the Flying V and Explorer.

McCarty was in his 70s and semi-retired when, in 1986, Paul Reed Smith called him to ask about glues and pickups and other production issues. McCarty became not only a consultant but a friend and mentor to Smith, and Smith thanked him by creating the PRS McCarty model in 1994.

Like the PRS Custom (and the first Gibson solidbody, the Les Paul Model), the McCarty featured a carved maple top, but it was delineated from other PRS models by a mahogany back that was one-eighth-of-an-inch thicker than standard. A year later, the McCarty Standard joined the line, following the same progression as Gibson's Les Paul models (from Standard to Custom) with a solid mahogany body and no maple cap.

MODEL
Paul Reed Smith
McCarty Standard

YEAR
1998

PRODUCTION
1995 to 2006

From the first PRS models of 1985, Paul Reed Smith's designs have been described as having evolved from the best features of traditional Gibsons and Fenders. The CE models of 1988, with bolt-on maple necks and alder bodies, strengthened the appeal to Fender fans. Finally, in 1996, PRS introduced a model with an unmistakably direct connection to classic Fender models.

The body shape of the new model was the tried-and-true PRS shape, but the wood was important enough to be incorporated into the model name – the Swamp Ash Special. Although the first PRS CEs had an alder body, which most Fender Stratocasters of the "pre-CBS" period (1965 and earlier) had, the earliest Stratocasters had an ash body and all of the blond-finish Broadcasters/Telecasters and Esquires had bodies of the wider-and deeper-grained ash.

The maple neck/fingerboard added to the Fender look of the Swamp Ash Special, and a third pickup – a middle-position single-coil, controlled by a push-pull tone knob – sealed the deal on its Fender appeal.

155

MODEL
Paul Reed Smith Swamp Ash Special

YEAR
1997

PRODUCTION
1996 to current

PRS

In 1998, four years after PRS introduced the McCarty model, the company added two model variations with an obvious link back to the Ted McCarty era at Gibson – white "soapbar" pickup covers. The McCarty Soapbar featured two of the single-coil pickups (made by Seymour Duncan) and the Custom 22 Soapbar sported a trio.

As most guitarists with a sense of history knew, "soapbar P-90s" made their debut on Gibson's "goldtop" Les Paul Model – the company's first solidbody – and were used until the advent of metal-covered humbuckers in 1957. By the late 1990s, the P-90 was once again in demand.

The maple fingerboard – a Fender feature – on this Custom 22 Soapbar seems incongruous with the soapbars' strong identification with Gibson, and this version of the Custom 22 lasted only through 2001. The McCarty model, however, provided a fitting home for the pickups, and the McCarty Soapbar remains in production. By the time of McCarty's death in 2001, PRS had honored the legendary Gibson president with over a dozen model variations.

MODEL
Paul Reed Smith Custom 22 Soapbar

YEAR
1999

PRODUCTION
1998 to 2001

Mark Tremonti was the founder and lead guitarist of the mainstream rock group Creed, best known for their 1999 hit "Higher." While he did not have the influence of some of the "guitar gods" whose names were on signature models, he gave PRS guitars unique exposure due to the controversy among Christian music fans over whether or not Creed was a Christian rock band.

For his 2001 signature model, Tremonti chose PRS's Singlecut as a starting point. The Tremonti model featured the four-knob and three-way toggle switch controls that PRS had introduced on the Singlecut only a year earlier, but Tremonti went with a thicker mahogany back than the regular model. The pickups were wound to his personal specifications. Cosmetic touches included bird inlays on the fingerboard, a pearl-trimmed truss-rod cover, and Tremonti's signature inlaid at the 12th fret. pickups

Like the Singlecut model, Tremonti production was suspended while litigation between PRS and Gibson was settled. His signature model returned to production in 2005 and continues in PRS's signature line today.

MODEL
Paul Reed Smith
Mark Tremonti

YEAR
2001

PRODUCTION
2001 to current

"Single cutaway" would not seem to be a controversial issue. After all, guitarmakers have been "cutting away" or cutting into the upper treble bout to give players easier access up the neck for decades – long before anyone ever thought about an electric guitar. But in 2000, when Gibson pulled its dealership authorisation from the giant Guitar Center retail chain, PRS seized the opportunity to capture some of the Les Paul market with its own single-cutaway solidbody.

PRS already had a single-cutaway model in development but, unlike the prototype, which featured McCarty-style, two-knob electronic controls, the production model had a selector switch on the upper treble bout and four control knobs – the same general setup of Gibson's Les Paul Standard. Gibson thought the Singlecut looked too much like the Les Paul shape (which Gibson had patented), and Gibson sued.

In 2005, after a lengthy trial and appeal, during which Singlecut production was suspended, PRS was declared the winner. The basic Singlecut model was discontinued after 2006 but the Singlecut design continues in several standard and artist signature model.

158

MODEL
Paul Reed Smith Singlecut Trem Satin

YEAR
2006

PRODUCTION
2002 to current

In the late 1990s, Paul Reed Smith began looking for a way to put the elegant design of a PRS guitar in the hands of beginning players and players on a budget. The answer lay in overseas production, and PRS created the SE (Student Electric) line for the import models.

The original EG series, introduced in 1990, had been an attempt to offer a U.S.-made PRS at an even lower price than the CE models. Like the CEs, the EGs had bolt-on necks, but their bodies were *not* the familiar PRS style. Instead, they had a shallower edge bevel that gave them a Stratocaster-inspired look. The connection was accentuated by a large, Strat-like pickguard and, on some models, Strat-like pickup configurations. The SE EG took the Strat look a step farther with a beveled lower bass bout.

While the original, U.S.-made EGs lasted only until 1995, the 20th-century versions, like most of the models in the SE import line, accomplished what the originals could not do – they brought PRS guitars to the masses.

MODEL
Paul Reed Smith SE EG

YEAR
2004

PRODUCTION
2003 to current

PRS made a limited run of 100 guitars in 1996 with a rosewood neck. That feature alone would have been intriguing enough to those guitarists – Paul Reed Smith, among them – who believe that wood is as important as electronics in shaping the sound of a solidbody electric. However, when PRS put a rosewood-neck model into regular production in 2004, the esoteric neck material turned out to be a relatively minor refinement compared to the electronic system introduced on this new model.

What appeared to be a humbucker-single-humbucker setup was really five single-coil pickups. The two blade-style selector switches created a total of 13 different pickup combinations. The system five-pickup, 13-selection system was sufficiently innovative for PRS to incorporate it into the model name of the 513 Rosewood. Newly designed bird inlays also received the designation "513 birds."

Introduced in 2004, the 513 Rosewood lasted only a few years, but the 513 electronics remained viable, and in 2007 PRS answered the increasing demand for this system with the more conventional mahogany-neck Model 513.

MODEL
_____
Paul Reed Smith 513 Rosewood

YEAR
_____
2004

PRODUCTION
_____
2004 to 2006

PRS was a year short of its 20th anniversary when it introduced its first 12-string production model, but the company was hardly new to the neighborhood. Through their Custom Shop and their elite Private Stock models, PRS had made plenty of 12-strings through the years.

Consequently, the Custom 22/12 hit the market in 2004 as a fully developed model, with humbucking pickups designed specifically for a 12-string, a bridge with 12 individually adjustable saddles, and even a headstock with the straight string-pull that had been a hallmark of PRS guitars from the first models in 1985. The Custom 22 design provided the stiffer neck required to handle the extra string tension, along with the elegant aesthetic features of the Custom model.

The Custom 22/12 had an extra added attraction in the form of a single-coil middle pickup made by Lindy Fralin. With a coil-tap on the bridge pickup, the 22/12 had tonal capabilities unmatched by any of the classic 12-strings made by Fender, Gibson or Rickenbacker.

MODEL
Paul Reed Smith Custom 22/12

YEAR
2004

PRODUCTION
2004 to current

PRS

Mark Tremonti, lead guitarist with the rock band Creed, was only the second artist to have a PRS signature model (the first was the legendary Carlos Santana), and he was the first to embrace the PRS Singlecut design. The PRS Mark Tremonti model of 2001 was successful enough for PRS and Tremonti to create a limited-edition model in 2004.

The Mark Tremonti Tribal featured a large graphic design on the top of the guitar, along with a condensed version on the peghead. Although it had the general look of a ceremonial mask from a primitive culture, the specific inspiration was never noted. The basic specs of the Tribal were the same as Tremonti's regular model, built on a slightly-thicker-than-standard Singlecut body.

The PRS Custom Shop was around halfway through the announced limited run of 100 Tribals when production was suspended due to a lawsuit over the Singlecut design. More were made in 2006. In the meantime, Creed broke up in 2004 and Tremonti continued his career with the band Alter Bridge.

MODEL

Paul Reed Smith Mark Tremonti Tribal

YEAR

2004

PRODUCTION

2004 to 2006

Rickenbacker brought the first viable electric guitar to market in 1932. Moreover, its horseshoe-shaped pickup was the only pre-World War II pickup from any maker that, to today's ears, still needs no improvement. Surprisingly, though, the company all but ignored the "Spanish style" electric until 1953, when founder Adolph Rickenbacker sold his share to F.C. Hall (founder of Radio-Tel, Fender's exclusive distributor at the time).

Hall immediately switched focus from the fading Hawaiian models to the new solidbodies and introduced the Combo 800 and 600 in 1954. They featured a carved top, like the Gibson Les Paul that preceded them by two years, but with a more pronounced "lip" that would come to be known as the "German carve." The term was accurate; Roger Rossmeisl, the son of a German guitarmaker, brought it to Rickenbacker in 1954.

The Combo 800, with a double-coil pickup, and the Combo 600, with a single-coil horseshoe, lasted only until 1959, giving way to thinner bodies with more dramatic cutaway lines, but the German carve became a Rickenbacker signature feature on hollow as well as solidbody models.

MODEL
Rickenbacker Combo 800

YEAR
1955

PRODUCTION
1954 to 1959

163

RICKENBACKER

Model 900, 950 and 1000

I n contrast to the carved top and "sliced" cutaways of Rickenbacker's first solidbody models, the new Combo models of 1956 featured a thinner, flat body with upper bouts that curved symmetrically to their points – inspiring the nickname "tulip shape."

The Combo 1000 had the highest model number but was actually the lowest of the tulip-shapes, with a single pickup, three-quarter scale length (one of three short-scale models in the group), and three fewer frets than the higher models. The group's most important design element was revealed by a bit of light-colored wood peeking out just below the pickguard. It was the end of the neck – evidence of neck-thru-body construction – which made these Combo models unique in the guitar world at that time.

The tulip shape proved to be limiting for players, and shortly after this 1957 Combo 1000 was made, Rickenbacker widened the treble-side cutaway. Most of the models in this series changed to another new body known as the "cresting wave" in 1958, but the 1000 retained the modified tulip shape and was discontinued the next year.

MODEL
Rickenbacker Combo 1000

YEAR
1957

PRODUCTION
1957 to 1970

This Rickenbacker Combo 450 from 1957 still featured the tulip-shape body, but it already sported several upgrades. The pickup covers have two openings, earning them the nickname "toaster tops." And the old, pre-World War II knobs (aka "flying saucers") have been replaced by a larger, flashier style, affectionately known as "cooker" or "kitchen stove" knobs. An anodized aluminum pickguard set off the Jet Black finish – one of three eye-catching options, the other two being a golden Montezuma Brown and a blue-green Cloverfield Green.

Jean "Toots" Thielman played a tulip-shaped 450 with the George Shearing quartet and, in 1960, a photo of Thielman appeared on the cover of the American magazine Accordion and Guitar World. Although the tulip shape was two years out of date by then, the photo nevertheless inspired future Beatle John Lennon to one day own a Rickenbacker.

With the Combo 450's change in 1958 to the "cresting wave" body, characterized by a curled bass horn, it went on to become one of Rickenbacker's most popular and enduring solidbody models, lasting until 1984.

165

MODEL

Rickenbacker Combo 450 (tulip shape)

YEAR

1957

PRODUCTION

1957 to 1958

SHERGOLD

Jack Golder and Norman Houlder left the Burns company when Baldwin bought it, and they started Shergold in 1967. They did contract work for Burns London, among others, until one of their clients, the Hayman company, went out of business, leaving them with a surplus of guitar parts. They put the parts together and put the Shergold logo – a man carving a guitar – on an instrument for the first time in 1975.

The Custom Masquerader appeared in 1977, featuring innovative string "trees" to provide straight string-pull. Their Modulus model offered an array of interchangeable electronics. Their most famous guitar was played by Mike Rutherford of Genesis, and it was actually two guitars – a 12-string and a bass that could be put together to form a doubleneck.

In a slumping guitar market, Shergold scaled back to custom orders only in 1982, and Houlder left the business a year later. Jack Golder brought Shergold back for a moment in 1991 with a limited-edition Masquerader, but he died in 1992, ending the Shergold guitar.

MODEL
Shergold Custom Masquerader

YEAR
1980

PRODUCTION
1977 to 1981

Supro was the budget brand of the Valco company (originally National-Dobro) and, with the exception of a few resonator-equipped acoustics, Supro was strictly electric. Supro's first solidbody models, the Ozark series of 1952, looked like cheap, thrown-together instruments, but the Dual Tone, introduced in 1954, sported a Gibson-inspired, single-cutaway body shape, a pair of pickups, and the striking look of a gleaming white plastic body wrap.

By the time of this 1958 Dual Tone, the original dot fingerboard inlays had been replaced by large plastic blocks, undoubtedly to simulate the large mother-of-pearl blocks on Gibson's Les Paul Custom. The Dual Tone also simulated the classy look of gold-plated hardware with lacquered brass parts. The pickups were the size of Gibson's humbuckers, but under the covers there was just a single coil, typically wrapped around a cheap cardboard bobbin.

Like most of Supro's solidbody line, the Dual Tone received a makeover in 1962 and emerged with a molded fiberglass body that looked solid but was actually hollow.

MODEL
Supro Dual-Tone (wood body)

YEAR
1958

PRODUCTION
1954 to 1961

SUPRO

Supro's calling card in the 1950s was celluloid, particularly the simulated mother-of-pearl pattern that appeared on kitchen tables of the period and is affectionately known today in the guitar world as "mother of toilet seat." The Belmont, with its "sherry maroon" pearloid covering, replaced the lowly Ozark models in 1954.

Supro was owned by Valco, which evolved from the National and Dobro companies of the late 1920s. Although there were no Supro acoustics, this 1960 Belmont sports a piece of the company's acoustic history with its flared tailpiece, a style that originated on the earliest National and Dobro resonator guitars.

The Supros have a kitschy appeal today, and, true to their appearance, they were not very sturdily made. In addition, their pickups were weaker than those of other major makers. They did, however, maintain their aesthetic flair, as the celluloid look gave way to molded fiberglass in the early 1960s. The Supro brand also supported Valco's amplifier line, and the budget line lasted until 1967, when Valco acquired the Kay company and promptly went bankrupt.

168

MODEL
**Supro Belmont
(wood body)**

YEAR
1960

PRODUCTION
1955 to 1961

The Teisco Spectrum 5 is the Holy Grail of Japanese guitars – the Teisco SD-4L shown here was produced at the same time and is also considered a classic by collectors. However the Spectrum 5 with a dramatic body shape incorporating the "German carve" (the contoured lip around the edge), six pickup coils, a lot of knobs and switches, and finish choices of sunburst, red or blue, represents the pinnacle of "kool kitsch" in 1960s guitar design.

The Teisco brand debuted in 1948 on amps and lap steels, and the first Teisco solidbodies appeared in 1954. By the early 1960s, Teisco offered a variety of models in the U.S. under its own brand, as well as contract instruments under such brands as Kingston and Kent; in the U.K. they were branded Top Twenty, among other names.

The Spectrum 5 debuted in 1966, but a year later Teisco was taken over by Kawai, the piano giant, and the Spectrum 5 disappeared. It grabbed the attention of guitarists again in the early 1990s when Eddie Van Halen appeared with one on the cover of *Guitar Player* magazine. Since the mid 1990s, Kawai has made a series of Spectrum 5 reissues for the Japanese market.

MODEL
Teisco SD-4L

YEAR
1963

PRODUCTION
1962 to 1964

TOKAI

The pointed horns of this 1968 Tokai Humming Bird were inspired by Gibson's SG models, but the rest of the body shape, including the "German carve" (the contoured "lip" around the top edge), was copied directly from Mosrite of California's most famous guitar – the Ventures signature model. It was available only to Japanese buyers, who also got such Mosrite features as the diagonally mounted neck pickup, the configuration of control knobs and selector switch, and the "zero fret."

Tokai, based in Hamamatsu, Japan, made its first electric models in 1967 and entered the U.S. and British markets in the 1980s. While Tokai was one of the leaders in copying classic American designs, the company was also at the forefront of a movement toward better quality from Japanese makers, and in 1982 the Houston-based Robin company contracted with Tokai to build its first guitars.

With rising labor costs in Japan and increasing competition in the global market, Tokai retreated to the Japanese market in the mid 1990s.

MODEL
Tokai Humming Bird

YEAR
1968

PRODUCTION
Late 1960s

Henry Vaccaro was a real estate entrepreneur when he brought financial backing into the partnership that created Kramer guitars in 1976, but after Kramer closed its doors in 1990 he couldn't get guitars out of his system. After a failed attempt to revive Kramer in 1995 (culminating in the sale to Gibson), he and his son formed the Vaccaro Guitar Company in 1997.

Vaccaro had held onto the patent for the aluminum neck with split headstock that the original Kramer's had featured. Henry Jr. worked on new body styles, and they launched their line in 1998. This Stingray from 1999 exemplifies Henry Jr.'s models, which by his own description he created by "sampling" various designs "from '50s modern, '60s mod, '70s kitsch and '80s new wave."

Vaccaro signed Peter DiStefano of Porno for Pyros as its first endorsee and amassed a list of artists that ranged from The Edge of U2 to Dave Grohl of the Foo Fighters. Based in Asbury Park, New Jersey, Vaccaro still offers the Stingray under a new name, the X-Ray.

MODEL
Vaccaro Stingray (X-Ray)

YEAR
1999

PRODUCTION
1999-current

VALLEY ARTS

A Valley Arts Custom Pro is just what its name suggests – an instrument custom-built for the professional-level guitarist.

Valley Arts started in the 1970s as a music store in Los Angeles owned by guitarists Mike McGuire and Al Carness. As they branched into repair and custom building, their store became a hangout for L.A. studio guitarists, and the Valley Arts client list for custom guitars grew to become a who's who that included Larry Carlton, Tommy Tedesco, Steve Lukather, Robben Ford, Mitch Holder, Mundell Lowe, Al Viola, Duane Eddy and Lee Ritenour.

After a store fire, for which McGuire and Carness were underinsured, they sold controlling ownership to a Korean company and eventually left Valley Arts. By 2003 they were both working for Gibson – McGuire as Custom Shop production manager and Carness in sales – when Gibson acquired Valley Arts. The Custom Pro, available in full-size or 7/8-size, with numerous wood and hardware options, continues to be the showcase model for Valley Arts.

MODEL
Valley Arts Custom Pro

YEAR
1993

PRODUCTION
Late 1970s to current

John Veleno of St. Petersburg, Florida, began hand-making guitars out of carved aluminum around 1970. Although the very first commercially viable electric guitar, Rickenbacker's "Frying Pan" of 1932, was made of cast aluminum, Veleno chose aluminum for the simple reason that he knew nothing about woodworking and a lot about shaping metal. As a machinist, he had worked on components for space vehicles, including the Lunar Excursion Module.

Veleno's engineering expertize also extended to the guitar's electronic parts, all of which were connected with a single, thin strand of copper wire. Veleno had noticed that telephones used single-strand wiring, and a telephone engineer told him that it provided a purer signal than multi-strand wires.

An estimated 145-185 Velenos were made from 1970–75, and the list of Veleno players included Mark Farner of Grand Funk Railroad and studio wizard Todd Rungren (whose Veleno had a body in the shape an ankh, an Egypitian hieroglyphic for "life"). John Veleno began making aluminum-body guitars again in 2003, in the symmetrical double-cutaway shape called the Original and also in the ankh shape.

MODEL
Veleno The Original

YEAR
Circa 1972

PRODUCTION
1970 to 1975,
2003 to current

With a body featuring a prominent "lump" that begged to be removed, the Apache was the first of a series of oddly shaped Vox solidbody guitars, but it represented the fourth genre of musical instruments that the Jennings Musical Instrument company offered.

Like many European guitar brands of the 1960s, JMI had roots in the accordion business – not a multi-generational family company but as a British import business founded by accordion player Tom Jennings in 1945. By the end of the 1940s, Jennings was in the electronic organ business with a model called the Univox. In the mid 1950s, as rock'n'roll was bringing the electric guitar to the forefront of pop music, Jennings began adapting organ amplifiers to guitars, and he teamed up with an Army buddy, Dick Denny, to create the first Vox amplifier in 1958.

A year later, JMI entered the guitar business with cheap models made by a British woodworking company. In 1961, the company added an in-house design team to create models worthy of the Vox brand name, and the Apache led this new wave of Vox guitars.

MODEL
Vox Apache

YEAR
Circa 1961

PRODUCTION
1961 to 1966

In early 1964, Vox designers rounded out the blob body shape of the Apache into a symmetrical teardrop shape – similar to that of a lute. Its official names were Phantom Mk III, then Mk VI, but guitarists around the world knew it as the Vox Teardrop that Brian Jones plays in The Rollings Stones.

By the mid 1960s, Vox was on top of the world – on top of three worlds, actually. Jones was one of several guitarists in "British Invasion" groups who were playing Vox's attention-grabbing guitars. Vox combo organs were featured in the sound of The Dave Clark Five and The Animals. And Vox amps were used by The Beatles.

Vox's fast growth led, ironically, to production and financial challenges that, in 1964, prompted JMI founder Tom Jennings to outsource Vox guitars to the Italian-based Eko company and to sell a controlling interest to the Royston group, a British holding company. It marked not only a high point for Vox guitars, but the beginning of the end. Vox guitars would be gone by the end of the decade.

MODEL
Vox Mk VI

YEAR
Circa 1965

PRODUCTION
1964 to 1967

175

In contrast to the classy, conventional
look of Vox amps, with their diamond-
stitched grille cloths, Vox guitars were
among the most modernistic
instruments of the early 1960s, and they
fit the musical attitude of the era perfectly.
The angular polygonal body of the Phantom
series made it difficult, if not impossible, to
play in a sitting position – a sign that Vox
designers recognized the solidbody guitar as
the instrument of rock'n'roll, where no
guitarist would even think of sitting down.

Introduced in late 1961, the Phantom line
grew to include a 12-string in 1963 and this
stereo 12-string in 1966. The Phantom XII's
three pickups were split, and each coil had its
own volume and tone control. The 12 knobs
of the stereo Phantom XII may have set a
record, but the guitar did not find its way *onto*
many records, and it was last made in 1968.

In 1969, Vox's parent company, Royston,
folded, and while amplifier production
continued under future owners, it was
the end of the original Vox guitars.

MODEL

**Vox Phantom XII
(stereo)**

YEAR

1966

PRODUCTION

1966 to 1968

Vox was better-equipped than any musical instrument company of the 1960s to combine a guitar with an organ. After all, JMI (Vox's parent company) had been making electronic organs since the late 1940s and electric guitars since the late 1950s. When Robert Moog demonstrated his first synthesizer in 1964 at the Audio Engineering Society convention, the timing must have seemed perfect for electronic sounds on a guitar.

Vox engineers wired the guitar's frets to tone generators from its highly successful Continental model combo organ. In addition to Octave, Organ Tone and Flute sounds, they also provided the guitarist with onboard rhythm sounds. Six pushbuttons controlled individual strings. The angular body of Vox's Phantom guitars provided aesthetically appropriate lines for the rows of controls.

The result was a modernistic instrument with which a guitarist could theoretically play a guitar along with a supporting organ part and a rhythm section (as well as in various other combinations), but in practice, the Phantom Guitar Organ was simply an electronic mess. It was introduced in 1966 and didn't last a year.

MODEL
Vox Phantom Guitar Organ

YEAR
1966

PRODUCTION
1966

WASHBURN

Darrell Abbott, aka Dimebag Darrell, was associated with Dean guitars through most of his career, starting as a hotshot contest guitarist in his home state of Texas and continuing for over 20 years (1981-2003) with the heavy metal band Pantera. Washburn's growing reputation as a maker of heavy metal guitars was enhanced considerably when Dimebag Darrell switched his allegiance in 1996.

Washburn made nine different "Dime" models with body shapes based on a Flying V or a four-point star. The cherry stain finish on this 1999 model, the Dime Culprit, has one of the series' more subdued treatments; others featured green slime and lightning-bolt finish effects. Dimebag also had his own special humbucking pickups, called Dimebuckers made by the Seymour Duncan company.

In December 2004, just a few months after he renewed his association with Dean guitars, Dimebag Darrell was shot dead onstage at a concert in Columbus, Ohio. In 2004 Dean put a new line of Dimebag tribute guitars into production.

MODEL
Washburn The Dime Culprit

YEAR
1999

PRODUCTION
1996 to 2000

Washburn is one of the oldest guitar brands, dating back to 1887, and in the late 19th century its parent company Lyon & Healy was the largest musical instrument maker in America. The brand name was the middle name of founding partner George Washburn Lyon.

In the late 20th century, under ownership of the Chicago-based Fretted Industries Inc. (now called Washburn International), the Washburn brand returned to prominence with models endorsed by heavy metal guitarists.

Paul Stanley, founding member and rhythm guitarist of the rock band KISS, came over to Washburn in 1998 after a career of playing Ibanez guitars. In an ironic turn of events, an American company copied a Japanese guitar – and it wasn't just any model, it was the Ibanez Iceman, conceived as a sort of national guitar design of Japan – to create the Washburn Paul Stanley model of 1998. Although the model only lasted two years, Stanley and Washburn got back together in 2006 for a new line of seven signature models, none of which had the Iceman shape.

179

MODEL
**Washburn Paul
Stanley PS-500**

YEAR
1999

PRODUCTION
1998 to 1999

WATKINS

Many aspiring British guitarists of the early 1960s learned to play on a Watkins Rapier. The London-based company was headed by Charlie Watkins, who specialized in amplifiers, while his brother Sid handled guitars. The Watkins Rapier line was easy to understand: Model 22 had two pickups, 33 had three pickups and 44 had four.

The Watkins brand debuted in the solidbody market in 1959 with Gibson-inspired models, but their inspiration switched to Fender in 1961. This Rapier 33 looks like a poor-man's Stratocaster, with its inelegant headstock shape and square-cornered pickups.

In 1965 the brandname changed to WEM (for Watkins Electric Music), and the company found greater success with amplifiers, P.A. systems, and effects than it had with guitars. The brand changed again by the end of the 1960s to Wilson (the maiden name of Watkins' mother), and Sid Watkins focused on semi-acoustic guitars, the inexpensive Ranger solidbody, and another Strat-inspired model, the Hand Made Mercury. Watkins/WEM/Wilson guitar production finally ended in 1985.

MODEL
Watkins Rapier

YEAR
Circa 1964

PRODUCTION
Mid 1960s

L ike several other Italian guitar makers, Welson began as an accordion company. Founded in the town of Castelfidardo by Orlando Quagliardi in 1921, Welson introduced its first solidbodies in 1962. They were typical Italian guitars, featuring an array of pushbutton controls.

In the mid 1960s Welson switched its design themes to more conventional styles, such as the Jazz Vedette. The name was undoubtedly intended to connect with Fender's Jazzmaster, and the three-tone sunburst finish and tortoiseshell celluloid pickguard were typical Fender features. The three-piece pickguard design, however, was a clear nod to Londoner Jim Burns.

In French, "vedette" is an entertainment term for a star (it is also a small boat), and it underscoresd Welson's success outside of Italy. In addition to its own brand, the company made a full line of guitars under the Dynacord brand for the German market, while the U.S.-based Wurlitzer company marketed Welson instruments under the Wurlitzer and Orpheum brands. In the 1970s, the company gravitated toward copies of Gibson models before going out of business in 1981.

MODEL
Welson Jazz Vedette

YEAR
Circa 1967

PRODUCTION
Late 1960s

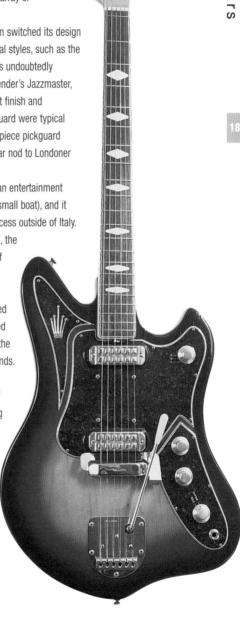

181

YAMAHA

Yamaha was founded in Japan in 1887 as a piano company, and after World War II it branched out into guitars, as well as motorcycles and electronics. The company got a relatively late start in the solidbody market in 1964, but within a few years Yamaha made an unforgettable impression with models such as this 1967 SG-5A.

The Flying Samurai, as this body style is affectionately called, doesn't appear to be particularly airworthy. The upper part of the body is a reverse image of Rickenbacker's "cresting wave" shape, while the lower bass bout seems to be pulling against the rest of the body. The headstock appears to have come from a different designer, but it does provide straight string-pull in a most economical and minimalist way.

The SG-5A's three single-coil pickups did not generate the level of power or sustain that players would expect from a samurai, and it did not cause fear in the hearts of Western guitarmakers. But in the era of "copy" imports, it represented a new wave of original designs from Japanese makers.

MODEL
Yamaha SG-5A
"Flying Samurai"

YEAR
1967

PRODUCTION
Mid 1970s

In the 1970s, Yamaha joined other Japanese makers in copying American designs, but in the case of this SG-60T from 1973, they picked an unlikely model.

The body did feature a routed "lip" around the top edge that was known as the "German carve," in part because it had been introduced in America on Rickenbacker guitars designed by German-born luthier Roger Rossmeisl. However, the Yamaha SG 60T (T for tremolo; it was also available without tremolo) did not copy the Rickenbacker so much as the cheap National and Supro guitars made in the early 1960s by the Chicago-based Valco company. National had gone out of the business in 1967, unable to compete with inexpensive Japanese imports; perhaps Yamaha somehow thought the National/Supro designs still viable.

While the SG 60T did not raise Yamaha to the level of Fender or Gibson, it was part of a second wave of Yamaha solidbodies that sported better tuners and more powerful humbucking pickups, and it served notice that Yamaha might soon be a formidable player in the solidbody market.

MODEL
Yamaha SG 60T

YEAR
Circa 1973

PRODUCTION
Early 1970s

YAMAHA

I n 1976, Yamaha changed the reputation of Japanese-made guitars with the SG2000. Most players familiar with the original models, made from 1976–88, consider the workmanship as well as the performance of the guitar to be superior to anything Gibson offered at that time.

The body design looks Gibson-esque, and the shape did come from a somewhat obscure double-cutaway version of the Gibson Melody Maker, made from 1963–64. The top cap was three-piece maple, like that of Gibson's Les Paul in the 1970s, but under the top was a fundamental difference. Where the Gibson had slab of mahogany, the Yamaha had a neck-thru-body design. The extra rigidity of the three-piece mahogany and maple neck gave the SG2000 more sustain than any other popular guitar on the market, a factor that won over Carlos Santana for a brief period (before he endorsed Gibson's L-6S).

Yamaha moved production of most of its models to Taiwan in 1984 but kept the SG2000 in Japan until it was discontinued in 1988. It was reissued as the SBG2000 in 2007.

MODEL
Yamaha SG 2000 (SBG 2000)

YEAR
Circa 1984

PRODUCTION
1976 to 1988

The metal front plate is the most familiar sign of a guitar by British maker Tony Zemaitis. He was already a well-known maker of acoustic guitars when, around 1970, he was shielding some pickups on an electric guitar with aluminum foil and decided to take the concept to the extreme.

His first guitar with a full metal top went to bluesman Tony McPhee. His next was the first of many made for Ronnie Wood (then of The Faces, later of The Rolling Stones). He enlisted the help of gun engraver Danny O'Brien for the elaborate ornamentation of the metal top plates, and his clients quickly grew to include Keith Richards, Ronnie Lane and Eric Clapton.

Zemaitis also made instruments with intricate pearl and mosaic inlays, and he was known as the father of the "boutique" guitar by the time he retired in 2000. He died two years later, but his designs are carried on today by his son, Tony Zemaitis Jr.

MODEL
Zemaitis Metal front

YEAR
Circa 1975

PRODUCTION
Circa 1970 to current

classic electrics

HOLLOWBODY GUITARS

ELECTRIC HOLLOWBODY

Within a few years of the earliest attempts at electrifying stringed instruments, guitar makers and players realized that the amplification system – not the volume produced by the vibration of the top nor the tone shaped by the body – was the key element to the sound of the electric guitar. In 1950, Leo Fender seemed to drive that point home decisively with his innovative solidbody guitars. However, not everyone bought into the concept that a hollowbody was no longer necessary to the electric guitar.

Given the personal relationship that guitarists have with their instruments, it's not surprising many players feel that a guitar, like any living being, needs air. The effect that hollow areas of the body have on the sound of an electric guitar is subtle but, to the ears of players, critical. Adding or subtracting the right amount of air, finding the perfect degree of natural resonance to temper and shape the electric sound, is much like creating an alloy to make a base metal stronger or more malleable. Opinions vary widely as to the optimal configuration, and the debate is played out in these pages, from traditional body styles that are essentially all-acoustic with an unintrusive "floating" pickup, to bodies that are functionally solid with only the perception of hollowbody construction.

Just as the human voice extends over a wide range, so does the voice of the electric guitar. As these classic guitar models illustrate, there is no single perfect combination of acoustic and electric qualities, but in pursuit of that goal, guitar makers have created a fascinating spectrum of hollowbody models, some of them influential, some simply interesting, all classics.

While the guitars of John D'Angelico in New York and the Strombergs in Boston dominated the East Coast jazz scene, in Chicago a Swedish immigrant named Carl Albanus Johnson quietly emerged in the late 1950s with carved-top guitars that rivaled those of the more legendary makers.

Albanus guitars featured a carved ebony tailpiece that was a carryover from Johnson's training as a violin maker, and it preceded the more widely publicized ebony tailpieces of James D'Aquisto by as much as a decade. His distinctive, asymmetrical headstock, inspired by Gibson's "dove-wing" design, proved to be perfect for the extra tuner on this seven-string model. Seven-string guitars were popularized by jazz stylist George Van Eps, who tuned the seventh string to a B below the standard low-E. When rockers discovered the seven-string in the 1980s, thanks in large part to Steve Vai, they tuned down to A to get a powerful root-fifth-octave configuration on the lower strings.

Johnson died in 1973. His total production is estimated at less than 100 guitars.

MODEL
Albanus 7-string

YEAR
Late 1950s

PRODUCTION
Late 1950s to 1973

ANTORIA

The Antoria brand appeared in England by the late 1950s on guitars imported by distributors J.T. Coppock Leeds Ltd. and later CSL Charles Summerfield. Some Antorias looked very much like Ibanez models; not coincidentally, they came from the same Japanese factory – Fuji Gen-Gakki.

The Rockstar drew its inspiration from two classic Gibsons. The most obvious influence was the double-cutaway body of the ES-335, the original semi-hollow electric, although Antoria claimed the Rockstar had a "double sustain block" rather than the one-piece center block of the 335. The two humbuckers, four knobs, placement of the controls, dots on the fingerboard – all signs pointed to the 335. And to ensure a Gibson connection in the mind of the buyer, the Rockstar sported a cherry sunburst finish – not found on the ES-335 but the signature look of Gibson's most famous electric, the Les Paul Standard.

The Rockstar design was appealing enough that in later years, after production moved to Korea, the supplier pitched the same model to other importers, and a similar guitar appeared in the line of the Chicago-based Harmony company.

MODEL
Antoria Rockstar
EG1935

YEAR
1989

PRODUCTION
Late 1980s

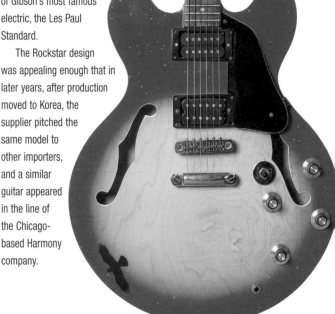

In the 1980s, a time when the quality of Gibson guitars was slipping and the quality of Japanese guitars was rising, the Aria Pro II TA60 offered guitarists all of the features of Gibson's semi-hollowbody ES-335 at a lower price.

The Aria company was founded by Japanese classical guitarist Shiro Arai in the early 1950s and made its first electrics in 1960. By the end of the decade Aria was leading Japanese makers into the "copy era," where the most successful Japanese guitars looked very much like the most successful American guitars. By the end of the 1970s, however, Aria had begun developing its own designs, and the brand name was upgraded to Aria Pro II in 1975.

The Titan Artist semi-hollow series appeared in 1981. The TA-60's double-cutaway shape with rounded horns was a slightly elongated and sleeker version of Gibson's ES-335, which had been introduced in 1958 and by this time would qualify as a traditional style. The headstock shape was distinctive, but otherwise the TA60 appealed strictly to the Gibson crowd.

MODEL
Aria Pro II TA60

YEAR
1989

PRODUCTION
1981 to 1999

BARKER

William Barker began his guitar-making career in the employ of Carl Albanus Johnson, the Chicago maker whose archtops rivaled the legendary D'Angelicos and Strombergs in the 1950s and 1960s. By the late 1960s, Barker and his brother had set up their own shop in Peoria, Illinois, a few hours southwest of Chicago.

Barker died in 1991 at age 66, after making somewhere between in 105 and 120 instruments, only a handful of which were seven-string guitars, and only one of which – this one – was a seven-string with an 18-inch body. Barker's headstock, with a slightly longer bass side, shows an Albanus influence, but curiously, Barker chose to put the extra tuner on this seven-string guitar on the treble side.

In the same manner that John D'Angelico passed the torch in New York to his assistant James D'Aquisto, the guitarmaker's torch was passed two times in northern Illinois – from Johnson (Albanus) to Bill Barker and then to Barker's longtime assistant Bill Hollenbeck, who went on to become a respected archtop maker in his own right.

MODEL
Barker 7-string

YEAR
1985

PRODUCTION
Late 1960s to late 1980s

By the end of the 1980s, established companies such as Fender and Gibson had difficulty selling anything but reissues of classic models, but upstarts like Charvel could have fun – and success – with an "off the wall" model like the Charvel Surfcaster.

The Surfcaster's retro-cool look combined several iconic designs of the 1950s and '60s – the body shape of Fender's Jazzmaster, the slash soundhole and triangular fingerboard inlays of Rickenbacker's Capri models, and the "lipstick tube" pickups of the Danelectro/Silvertone budget-line guitars.

Charvel had been founded in 1974 by Wayne Charvel as a supplier of guitar parts, but was taken over in 1979 by employee Grover Jackson, who began making guitars under his own brand as well as the Charvel brand. The foundation of his success in the 1980s was the "Super Strat" – a solidbody design inspired by Fender's Stratocaster and equipped with a bridge-position humbucker and "dive bomb" vibrato. Charvel's ride came to an end in 1997 when the company was sold to Aria in Japan.

MODEL
Charvel Surfcaster

YEAR
1991

PRODUCTION
1991 to 1993

CORT

Jazz-fusion guitarist Larry Coryell's signature model helped the Chicago-based Cort company to rise above the typical image of an importer, to become known in the 21st century for its elite group of guitar designers and signature artists.

Cort was founded in 1973 by Chicago importer Jack Westheimer, and although the company's products have always been made overseas, Cort built its own factory in Korea rather than out-sourcing production. In addition to the typical import copies of traditional favorites, Cort began commissioning designs from noted U.S. luthiers in the 1990s and assembling a signature artist line that included Matt "Guitar" Murphy, Hiram Bullock and Larry Coryell.

Coryell's eclectic career encompassed jazz, rock and classical music, starting in the late 1960s with a stint in jazz vibraphonist Gary Burton's band and a U.S. tour with ex-Cream bassist Jack Bruce and ex-Henrix drummer Mitch Mitchell. He spent the 1980s playing acoustic guitar and returned to jazz in the 1990s. His Cort model has a traditional design with a rounded Venetian cutaway and pickups by Seymour Duncan.

194

MODEL
Cort Larry Coryell

YEAR
1999

PRODUCTION
1998 to current

D'ANGELICO

hollowbody guitars

Born in New York City in 1905, John D'Angelico learned the luthier's trade from a grand-uncle who made violins, mandolins and flat-top guitars. He established his own shop in 1934, and his earliest archtop guitars were modeled on Gibson's 16-inch L-5 model – the first f-hole archtop. When Gibson increased the size of its guitars, D'Angelico did, too. By 1936 he had three 17-inch models and, at the top of the line, the 18-inch New Yorker, and by the end of the 1940s, only the Excel and New Yorker remained.

This New Yorker features the most easily identifiable mark of D'Angelico's high-end models – the oversized headstock with the "broken-scroll pediment" (the squashed cutout) framing an ornamental cupola (the button).

The truss-rod cover took its inspiration from the skyscrapers of New York. The slashed-block fingerboard inlays distinguished the New Yorker from the Excel, which had solid pearl blocks on its fingerboard. The body of a D'Angelico had its own identifying features, too, including a massive tailpiece with a stairstep motif that was repeated in the pickguard design.

195

MODEL
D'Angelico New Yorker

YEAR
1955

PRODUCTION
1936 to 1964

D'ANGELICO

D'Angelico's model offering of the 1930s encompassed five basic models. The plainer A, A-1 and B models appeared often in his ledger book and were apparently a favorite of music store clients. As the maker's reputation grew, more and more individual players ordered guitars, and by the end of the 1940s, the Excel had emerged as the most popular D'Angelico model. The larger, fancier Excel New Yorker may have produced a bit more volume, but as guitarists began putting pickups on their instruments, acoustic volume became less of an issue, and the comfort of the smaller Excel made it more attractive to many players.

D'Angelico was somewhat of a latecomer to the cutaway. Although Gibson offered its first cutaway guitars in 1939, it was 1947 before D'Angelico first noted a cutaway in his ledger book. Among his cutaways, the Excel maintained its popularity over the New Yorker.

John D'Angelico died September 1, 1964, leaving ten guitars unfinished. His apprentice James L. D'Aquisto finished those ten and carried the art of the carved-top guitar to even greater heights.

MODEL
D'Angelico Excel Cutaway

YEAR
1950

PRODUCTION
1947 to 1964

Working out of a small shop in New York, John D'Angelico made archtop guitars for some of the greatest musicians from the late 1940s through the early 1960s. He was the first individual luthier to gain a legendary reputation, and he established the idea that fine archtop guitars required the focused attention of an individual artisan, who could make guitars to a higher standard of quality than a factory.

Although D'Angelico had standardized models, every guitar was, in effect, a custom order, and this Excel cutaway is a case in point, with a smaller body than the Excel's typical 17-inch width.

Except for some electrics with laminated bodies, D'Angelico's guitars were acoustic. However, many players fitted them with a "floating" pickup, so-called because it was installed with no drilling or routing into the top. The DeArmond Rhythm Chief on this Excel cutaway model was the most popular aftermarket pickup in the 1940s and '50s. It attached by way of an extension arm to the side of the fingerboard, and the controls (including a jack) attached to the pickguard.

197

MODEL
D'Angelico Excel Cutaway

YEAR
1950

PRODUCTION
1947 to 1964

D'ANGELICO

Although many D'Angelico instruments were fitted with floating pickups, not one of the 1,164 guitars entered into his ledger book was noted as being electric. Nevertheless, a fair number of true electric guitars – with electronics mounted directly into the top – appeared in the 1950s and early 1960s with D'Angelico's name prominently engraved on the tailpiece and inlaid in the headstock.

This left-handed example shows the distinctive wood grain of a maple top, and it lacks a center seam – clear evidence that the top was laminated rather than solid and was pressed into an arched shape rather than carved. It seemed beneath D'Angelico – and it was. The body was made by United Guitars or Codé, both located across the river from New York City in New Jersey.

D'Angelico made the neck and the tailpiece, but the knobs and toggle switch look as if they came off a Harmony or some other inexpensive model. The pickups, however, were the best available at the time – Gibson humbuckers.

MODEL
D'Angelico Electric (left-handed)

YEAR
Late 1950s

PRODUCTION
1950s to early 1960s

New York luthier John D'Angelico never felt his electric guitars were worthy of entry into his ledger book, but they helped him through chronic hard times. His apprentice James D'Aquisto (who would become a renowned maker in his own right) said that D'Angelico felt lucky if he could get $500 for one of his carved-top acoustics, so the electrics – which required him to make only the neck and then to assemble and finish the instrument – were quick jobs for quick cash.

This D'Angelico electric has several upgrades over the typical example with a D'A neck and a body by United or Codé. The spruce top is undoubtedly laminated but is a higher-quality element than the typical laminated maple top on these models. And the pickguard has the stairstep shape and multi-layered binding of a "real" D'Angelico. The pickups may have come from Magna Electronics, makers of budget-line Magnatone guitars and amplifiers.

These laminated-body electric D'Angelicos are fairly rare though not nearly as prized by collectors or players as those with bodies actually made by D'Angelico.

199

MODEL
D'Angelico Electric

YEAR
Circa 1955

PRODUCTION
**1950s to early
1960s**

D'ANGELICO

Like D'Angelico's legendary acoustic archtops, his more mundane, laminated-body electrics were typically built to order for individual customers, so they, too, varied in specifications.

This 1960 guitar is 16.75 inches wide, which is a quarter-inch larger than many others. Unlike the two-pickup examples, which typically had only two control knobs, this one has four knobs providing individual volume and tone controls for each of the humbucking pickups. The "Rhythm/Treble" ring around the pickup selector switch on the cutaway bout, along with the mottled-pattern pickguard, suggest that D'Angelico grabbed parts from wherever he could find them. The switch ring was probably lifted directly from a Gibson Les Paul solidbody and the pickguard from a Gibson Super 400 archtop.

D'Angelico had kept a close eye on Gibsons in the 1930s, and it's likely that his production of laminated models peaked in the mid 1950s along with the popularity of Gibson's laminated-maple ES-175 and ES-5 models. Examples with humbuckers would be among the last of his true-electric guitars.

MODEL
D'Angelico Electric

YEAR
Circa 1960

PRODUCTION
1950s to early 1960s

In carrying on the tradition of John D'Angelico, James D'Aquisto continued with the model names that his mentor had established, and the very first guitar logged into D'Aquisto's book was a New Yorker.

However, while the name remained the same, the appearance changed considerably, as exemplified by this 1986 New Yorker. It does have the 18-inch wide, single-cutaway body of D'Angelico's model, but D'Angelico would have had to read the engraving on the peghead to recognize this guitar as a New Yorker. The S-shaped soundholes, ebony bridge, narrow pickguard, and circular peghead cutout were all D'Aquisto's signature touches.

The dark-colored pickup cover was a sign of D'Aquisto's move away from traditional metal parts, but the most non-traditional element may be the finish – which has a light, natural, almost bleached look that stands out as a sharp contrast to the aged, amber hue that most guitars had featured. Like the pickup cover, it was a sign that D'Aquisto was about to shake off all the conventional concepts of archtop guitar design.

MODEL
D'Aquisto New Yorker

YEAR
1986

PRODUCTION
1964 to late 1980s

D'AQUISTO

L ike D'Angelico, D'Aquisto made many custom models, and one of his most popular – a New Yorker with a 17-inch body rather than the standard 18-inch width – became a standard model called the New Yorker Special.

Although D'Aquisto continued the basic construction and, to some degree, the ornamentation of D'Angelico guitars, he quickly began adding his own design touches, and by the time of this 1978 New Yorker Special, there was no mistaking a D'Aquisto for a D'Angelico. The S-shaped soundholes replaced traditional f-holes. A sleek, narrow pickguard, made of ebony, replaced the tortoiseshell celluloid style with the stairstep design. A large ebony tailpiece replaced the metal stairstep design. The peghead cutout of D'Aquisto's 1970s guitars was the only conceptual feature that linked him to tradition, and the ebony tailpiece and pickguard were a signal of more radical departures ahead.

D'Aquisto called his regular, 18-inch model the New Yorker Deluxe, and unlike D'Angelico, whose production was fairly evenly divided between Excels and New Yorkers, D'Aquisto's clientele overwhelmingly preferred the New Yorker models.

MODEL
D'Aquisto New Yorker Special

YEAR
1978

PRODUCTION
1965 to 1995

James L. D'Aquisto started working for John D'Angelico as a teenager in the 1950s, and he had D'Angelico's legacy suddenly thrust upon him when his mentor died in 1964. Ten guitars were left as works in progress, and by the time D'Aquisto finished them, the apprentice had established himself as a master luthier.

In addition to following in D'Angelico's footsteps as the premier maker of traditional archtop guitars, D'Aquisto also followed D'Angelico's lesser-known habit of making a less-expensive, true electric guitar, with pickups and controls mounted directly in the top of a ready-made, laminated maple body.

The tailpiece on this example (believed to be one of the earliest made by D'Aquisto on his own) appears to be the same as those on D'Angelico's electrics, except that it's engraved *D'Aquisto*. However, the S-shaped soundholes (without the central points of traditional f-holes) and the circular peghead cutout, show that D'Aquisto was already adding his own signature design features. With the engraving on the pearl scroll peghead, D'Aquisto christened this model with the unimaginative name "D'Aquisto Electric."

MODEL
D'Aquisto Electric

YEAR
Circa 1965

PRODUCTION
Circa 1965

D'AQUISTO

As James D'Aquisto was becoming America's premier maker of traditional archtop guitars, he was also stretching his designer wings with electric hollowbody models created for Hagstrom in the late 1960s (put into production in the mid 1970s) and for Fender in 1984. In the meantime, he brought what were essentially mass-market design ideas into his own shop with such models as the Jazz Master.

The Jazz Master's lack of soundholes indicated that acoustic qualities were of no concern to the maker. That alone was a departure for D'Aquisto; even his true electric models had had soundholes. The figured maple top reflected the growing market for vintage reissues of Gibson's Les Paul Standard or the newly introduced PRS solidbodies. (The Jazz Master was not solid, however; it had only a solid center block.)

The Jazz Master name was familiar, of course, as a Fender model, but Fender had dropped its Jazzmaster in 1980. Not only did the D'Aquisto bear no resemblance to the solidbody Fender, it was more appealing to jazz players than the Fender had ever been.

MODEL
D'Aquisto Jazz Master

YEAR
1987

PRODUCTION
Late 1970s to late 1980s

Before seven-string guitars were embraced by heavy metal guitarists in the 1980s, they were most often found in the hands of jazz players. George Van Eps (son of classical banjo great Fred Van Eps) had the Epiphone company put a seven-string neck on an Epi archtop in 1938 and gained enough notoriety to have his own signature Gretsch model in the late 1960s.

In the 1970s, musicians who wanted the best seven-string jazz guitar naturally went to the premier maker of archtop jazz guitars, and that was James L. D'Aquisto in New York. Beginning in 1973, he made around a half-dozen seven-strings, including this New Yorker Special (which, despite the term "Special" in the model name, was a standard D'Aquisto model – a 17-inch version the New Yorker).

D'Aquisto had abandoned conventional f-holes for curved, S-shaped holes, but on this guitar he went farther afield from tradition with a pair of elliptical holes that were more in-tune aesthetically with his narrow pickguard. These avant-garde soundholes would appear in the late 1980s on a D'Aquisto model named, appropriately, the Avant Garde.

MODEL
D'Aquisto New Yorker Special 7-string

YEAR
1975

PRODUCTION
1973 to 1984

D'AQUISTO

I n the late 1980s, James D'Aquisto began reinventing the archtop guitar, and his innovations were most obvious on acoustic models, such as the Avant Garde, Solo, and Centura, which featured experimental soundhole shapes. A larger goal was to create a more organic instrument, with components that were more closely related than ever before in the history of the guitar. To that end, he eliminated celluloid, which had been used for binding, pickguards, and other ornamental features for almost a century. He also minimized the use of metal.

This Centura Electric illustrates the new concept with wood knobs, wood truss rod cover, wood tuner buttons, and even a wood pickup cover. Moreover, D'Aquisto used boldly striated ebony rather than the traditional black ebony so that the wood grain could be aligned to create a unified appearance.

D'Aquisto's revolutionary designs brought him – and archtop guitars in general – unprecedented notoriety in the 1990s. He died 1995 at age 59, ironically the same age at which his mentor John D'Angelico died.

MODEL
D'Aquisto Centura Electric

YEAR
1991

PRODUCTION
Circa 1991 to 1995

Domino guitars were made in Japan and imported into the U.S. by the New York-based Maurice Lipsky Music Co. In the mid-to-late 1960s, Dominos copied popular Fender and Vox models, but they also featured some original designs, exemplified by the Californian Rebel.

Domino never specified what it was rebelling against, but the enemy would appear to be aesthetically appealing guitar designs. Domino's basic Californian model copied the five-sided body of Vox's infamous Phantom, but the Rebel's design stretched that body to the point that it looked like a giant tuner button. In the process, it gained curves in its cutaway lines and a klunky six-sided shape. Perhaps the body reworking was intended to make room for the oversized f-hole; or vice versa, the f-hole was used to fill the vast space on the bass side of the body.

This two-pickup version was model 80E2, and the three-pickup 80E3 was also offered. A 1967 Domino ad featuring the Californian Rebel claimed "Domino imagination leads the rock generation," but no one followed the Californian Rebel.

MODEL
Domino Californian Rebel

YEAR
1967

PRODUCTION
Circa 1967

ELECTAR

The Epiphone company created a new brand, Electar, to introduce its first electric model in 1935. Not coincidentally, the name was similar to the Electro brand on the very first viable electrics made by Rickenbacker (which was officially the Electro String Instrument company).

The term "Spanish" distinguished guitars played in the conventional position from those played Hawaiian style (in the lap). While Rickenbacker had offered a Spanish-electric along with its original "Frying Pan" Hawaiian in 1932, the Rick bodies were cheap instruments furnished by the Harmony company. National's Electric Spanish model, introduced in early 1935, was also built on a budget guitar, in this case made by Regal. Epiphone was the first company to offer a pickup on a guitar that was made by the company whose name was on the headstock.

Among the most successful aspects of the Electar Model M and the smaller-bodied Model C that was introduced with it, was the simple fact that Epiphone beat its arch-rival Gibson into the electric Spanish market by a full year.

MODEL
Electar Model M Spanish

YEAR
Circa 1935

PRODUCTION
1935 to 1937

By 1939, Epiphone had dropped the Electar brand and introduced three new models under the Epiphone name. The top model of 1939 was the Zephyr, available in a striking natural finish that showed off its maple top.

A laminated maple top, bent into an arched shape, was a departure from the carved spruce top of acoustic archtops – a sign that guitarmakers were beginning to recognize the fact that an electric guitar need not have a great acoustic sound. Although the laminated top was cheaper to make, Epiphone was willing to invest some money in the electric guitar, as evidenced by the Zephyr's triple-bound body and bound fingerboard.

Epiphone also invested in an electrical engineer – Herb Sunshine, who was shown in literature dressed in a white lab coat. Sunshine's greatest contribution was the pickup that the Zephyr sported. It was the first with height-adjustable polepieces, and although these pickups did not have the power of Rickenbacker's or Gibson's pickups, Sunshine's screw-polepiece concept would become an industry standard that endures today.

MODEL
Epiphone Zephyr

YEAR
1939

PRODUCTION
1939 to 1956

EPIPHONE

Epiphone and Gibson had engaged in a battle of one-upsmanship in the acoustic market prior to World War II, and the rivalry resumed in the postwar years. Following close on the heels of Gibson's ES-5 (a three pickup version of Gibson's venerable L-5), Epiphone introduced a three-pickup, six-pushbutton version of its top model, the Emperor.

Epiphone already had a Zephyr model, but the company also used the term to signify an electric version of any acoustic model. "Regent" was used in a similar manner to denote any model with a cutaway. So the new electric cutaway model was called the Zephyr Emperor Regent.

Although in name as well as appearance, this model appears to be an acoustic Emperor with pickups, the Zephyr Emperor Regent was in fact designed with a laminated maple top – like Gibson's ES-5 and *not* like Gibson's electric Super 400 and L-5 models, which would be introduced a year later. It was an electric guitar from the very beginning and was never intended to be played acoustically.

MODEL

Epiphone Zephyr Emperor Regent

YEAR

1950

PRODUCTION

1950 to 1956

The Epiphone Emperor of 1958 looked very similar to the early-1950s version, but its "thinline" body depth marked the end of family ownership for the New York-based Epiphone company and the beginning of Gibson ownership.

Epaminandos "Epi" Stathopoulo, who had led Epiphone since the 1910s, died of leukemia during World War II, and his brothers Orphie and Frixo were unable to bring the company back to its prewar prominence, so in 1957 they sold the company to Gibson.

New Epiphone models debuted in 1958, with the Emperor at the top of the electric line, but Gibson used up existing stocks of Epiphone necks and pickups before implementing Gibson parts. Although the pickups on this 1958 Emperor are the same size as the "mini-humbuckers" on later Epis, these "New York" pickups, as they came to be known (later pickups were made by Gibson in Kalamazoo, Michigan), were an unusual single-coil design with the coil turned on its side so that the edge-mounted poles crossed the top of the coil instead of going through it in the conventional manner.

211

MODEL
Epiphone Emperor

YEAR
1958

PRODUCTION
1958 to 1968

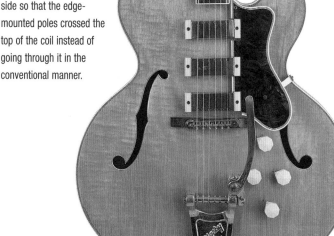

EPIPHONE

With its 18-inch body width and three pickups, the Emperor was the unchallenged king of the Gibson-made Epiphone line in the 1960s, and in kingly fashion, it made few public appearances. It is one of the rarest of Epiphone electric models from that era, and natural-finish examples are the rarest of the rare.

Gibson made only thirteen Emperors in the model's first year of production, 1959, a high-mark that was only matched again in 1961. In 1963, demand for this unusual, super-wide, thinbody design was so low that Gibson offered it only by special order, and after 1963 it was only made with sunburst finish. In 1969, as Gibson began pondering sending Epiphone production to Japan, the Emperor was discontinued. Total production for its ten-year run was 42 in sunburst and only 20 in natural.

The Emperor name, which dated back to Epiphone's rivalry with Gibson in the archtop acoustic arena of the 1930s has since been revived in various versions, but none with the size nor the prestige of the 1960s model.

MODEL
**Epiphone Emperor
E-112TN**

YEAR
1963

PRODUCTION
1959 to 1968

EPIPHONE

hollowbody guitars

Although the Epiphone line was intended to be almost-but-not-quite equal to the Gibson line, models such as the Sheraton gave Epiphone its own distinct identity. Not only was there no equivalent to the Sheraton's ornamentation in the Gibson line, some of the Epis – like this 1961 Sheraton – featured an improved vibrato design that was never available on a Gibson. On the Epi unit, the strings wrapped around a tapered bar – thinner for the bass strings, thicker for the treble – that compensated for the differences in string diameter and made for a more uniform pitch change.

Non-vibrato models had Epi's traditional Frequensator tailpiece, whose double-trapeze design also took into account the different vibrating qualities between treble and bass strings. Like the Epi vibrato, the Frequensator was unavailable on a Gibson.

By 1961, high-end models such as the Sheraton sported "humbucking" pickups. They were probably designed to have the same size and look as the earlier Epiphone "New York" pickups, but they were smaller than the humbuckers on Gibsons, and the Epi pickups got the diminutive nickname "mini-humbuckers."

213

MODEL
Epiphone Sheraton E-212T

YEAR
1961

PRODUCTION
1959 to 1969

EPIPHONE

The Sheraton's semi-hollow, double-cutaway body and high-end ornamentation pumped new life into the Epiphone line in 1958 and served notice that although the company was now owned by Gibson, the Epiphone brand still had its own unique personality.

Gibson had bought Epiphone in 1957 to gain Epiphone's acoustic bass production capabilities, but Gibson quickly applied the well-known brand name to a new line of guitars. The Epis carried the prestige of being made in Gibson's factory in Kalamazoo, Michigan, and were, for the most part, near-equivalent to Gibson models, but they could be sold by a new dealer network that would not dilute the territorial exclusivity that Gibson's established dealers enjoyed.

While some of the new electrics continued with such familiar and traditional Epiphone model names as Zephyr and Emperor, the Sheraton was new – based on Gibson's ES-335 semi-hollowbody (introduced the same year). The Sheraton's multi-ply binding, fancy inlays, and gold-plated hardware put it a step above the 335, but Gibson always kept the Epiphones in their place by reserving full-sized humbucking pickups for Gibsons only.

214

MODEL
Epiphone Sheraton E-212TN

YEAR
1962

PRODUCTION
1959 to 1969

The Epiphone Sorrento of 1960 appeared to adhere to Gibson's philosophy of keeping the Epiphone line slightly below the Gibson line by equipping Epis with "mini-humbuckers" – slightly smaller in size and less robust in sound than the full-size humbuckers on Gibson's top models. However, in the case of the Sorrento, the equivalent Gibson had single-coil pickups and was, in that respect, inferior to the Epiphone.

The Sorrento illustrates how quickly Gibson's new Epiphone line of 1958 was accepted. Gibson expanded the archtop electric line in 1959 with a model called the Wilshire, which was basically the Epi version of Gibson's popular ES-125CT, a fully hollow thinbody with a single cutaway. The Sorrento, initially offered with dot fingerboard inlays, sported mini-humbuckers and quickly replaced the Wilshire, adopting the Wilshire's oval fingerboard inlays.

Throughout the 1960s the Sorrento held a unique spot in the Gibson and Epiphone lines as the only thinline hollowbody with a pointed cutaway and humbucking pickups. A similar model did not appear under the Gibson brand until the ES-175T of the 1970s.

215

MODEL
Epiphone Sorrento

YEAR
1968

PRODUCTION
1960 to 1969

EPIPHONE

The Casino has gained the most fame of any of the Epiphone electric models of the 1960s, thanks to Beatles John Lennon, Paul McCartney and George Harrison, who each owned one.

Surprisingly, in light of the fact that The Beatles could afford any guitar in the world by the end of 1964, the Casino was only a midline model. It had been introduced in 1961 as the Epiphone version of Gibson's ES-330, a fully hollow, double-cutaway model with single-coil pickups. McCartney bought this Casino – a right-handed model that he re-strung for left-handed play – because it was the only hollowbody in the dealer's inventory that had a Bigsby vibrola. The model was offered in sunburst or natural finish, but all three of The Beatles' instruments were originally sunburst.

Among The Beatles' many uses of their Casinos were McCartney's lead part on "Paperback Writer," Harrison in the video promo for "Hello Goodbye," and Lennon with his stripped-finish Casino on the rooftop of Apple headquarters for The Beatles' last performance together in 1969.

MODEL
Epiphone Casino

YEAR
1962

PRODUCTION
1961 to 1969

216

The Epiphone Professional appears to have far more controls than a single-pickup guitar would need, and indeed, the volume and tone knobs on the treble side of the pickguard are the only actual controls for the guitar. All of the other knobs and switches are for the guitar's amplifier.

With Gibson's purchase and makeover of Epiphone in the late 1950s, Epiphone was less bound by tradition than Gibson, and the Professional represented a continuing effort within the Epiphone division to use imaginative designs to circumvent the one-step-below-Gibson status that Epiphones were supposed to maintain.

While it was a great idea, in theory, to give a guitarist a remote control over his amplifier settings, in practice the Epiphone Professional severely limited the guitarist's choices of amplifiers to the matching Professional amplifier. The control-less amp was useless without the guitar, and the guitar cord would only connect with the matching amp. Consequently, the Professional only lasted until 1966 and was a rare failure in the Epiphone line of the 1960s.

217

MODEL
Epiphone Professional

YEAR
1962

PRODUCTION
1962 to 1966

EPIPHONE

Prior to its acquisition by Gibson, Epiphone had been based in New York, so it was only natural that New York-based guitarist Al Caiola would become Epi's first signature artist of the 1960s.

Caiola began his career after World War II as a staff musician for CBS radio, and through the 1950s he played numerous recording sessions in Manhattan. He became one of the best-known guitarists in America in 1961, when his recording of the theme song from the film *The Magnificent Seven* hit the Top 40 of the pop charts, followed by his Top 20 single of the theme from the TV show *Bonanza*.

Within two years Caiola had his own Epiphone signature model, which featured a 25.5-inch scale length (most Gibsons and Epis were 24.75 inches) and five tone switches. The Caiola model was unique among Gibsons and Epis of the period in that it had only a single humbucker (a mini, as all Epis had). It became the Caiola Custom when the Caiola Standard, a plainer version with two single-coil pickups, appeared in 1966.

MODEL
Epiphone Caiola Custom

YEAR
1967

PRODUCTION
1963 to 1969

The Epiphone Sheraton filled the semi-hollowbody slot in the original Gibson/Epi offering of 1958, but the Sheraton's fancy ornamentation put it far above the "equivalent" Gibson – the ES-335. A year later, Gibson introduced a fancier model, the ES-355, that brought the Gibson line almost to the level of the Sheraton, but it wasn't until 1962 that a true equivalent of the 335 appeared in the Epi line, in the form of the Riviera.

The Riviera had the 335's single-ply binding and nickel-plated (later chrome-plated) hardware, and although it had slightly better fingerboard inlays – parallelograms compared to the 335's dots – it had the mini-humbucking pickups that kept it in line, a step below a Gibson.

When a 12-string version of the ES-335 appeared in the Gibson line in 1965, Epiphone kept apace with a 12-string Riviera. It would be the only 12-string electric among the American-made Epiphones of the 1960s, and it would last until Gibson moved Epiphone production to Japan in 1970. Epiphone reissued the Riviera 12-string in 2003 in its high-end, Japanese-made Elitist Series.

219

MODEL
**Epiphone Riviera
12-string**

YEAR
1968

PRODUCTION
1965 to 1969

EPIPHONE

As lead guitarist and primary songwriter for the English group Oasis, Noel Gallagher was so influential in the late-1990s Britpop movement that the British magazine *New Musical Express* coined the term "Noelrock" to describe the bands that he inspired and promoted.

Oasis's rise coincided with the rise in quality of Epiphone's guitars. Made in Japan and Korea since 1970, Epiphone had been just another cheap import brand until the 1990s, when parent company Gibson began authorizing Gibson copies under the Epi brand. Quality improved significantly, and Epiphone attracted its own roster of signature artists. Gallagher, who was as well known for his public snipes at other rock stars (particularly Phil Collins) as he was for his playing, gave Epiphone's prestige a huge boost when the Noel Gallagher Super Nova debuted in 1997.

Gallagher's model was essentially a Gibson ES-335 (or Epi Sheraton) semi-hollowbody with the split-parallelogram inlays of the stepped-up ES-345. This light blue metallic finish was the most popular, but it was also available with a Union Jack graphic like the custom-built guitar Gallagher used onstage.

MODEL
Epiphone Noel Gallagher Super Nova

YEAR
1997

PRODUCTION
1997 to 2005

By the 1990s, Epiphone's origin as one of the great American guitar makers was decades in the past, and Gibson, which had owned Epiphone since 1957, began to take full advantage of Epiphone's status as an established import brand. Epiphone allowed Gibson to offer inexpensive copies of Gibson's most popular models, made under Gibson's complete control but under a different brand, so that the made-in-U.S.A. prestige of the Gibson name would not be diluted.

As the Les Paul ES illustrates, Epiphone could also be used as a testing ground for such seemingly incongruous concepts as a semi-hollow version of Gibson's iconic solidbody model. "ES" was a 1930s term for Electric Spanish as opposed to Electric Hawaiian, so technically all Les Pauls were ES, but by the 1990s, ES was synonymous with Gibson's hollow and semi-hollowbody electrics.

Actually, Gibson's Custom Shop had put soundholes on Les Pauls with little success in the mid 1990s, so the concept wasn't altogether original to Epiphone, but the Epi Les Paul ES fared no better than the high-end Gibsons, lasting only two years.

MODEL
Epiphone Les Paul ES

YEAR
1999

PRODUCTION
1999 to 2000

FENDER

For the entire period of Leo Fender's ownership (until January 1965), Fender made solidbody electrics exclusively. Shortly after the CBS broadcasting conglomerate bought Fender, however, the new owners tried to tap into the archtop electric market. To that end the Fender Coronado was created.

German-born designer Roger Rossmeisl, who had been designing Fender acoustics since 1962, designed the Coronados. Their laminated top did not have the elegant "German carve" that was Rossmeisl's signature on his earlier Rickenbackers and his later Fenders, but his touch was evident in the Coronado's smoothed-out peghead shape and thin f-holes. The Coronado II had two pickups; the Coronado I had a single pickup and a dot-inlaid fingerboard.

The Coronado's pickup (made by DeArmond), bridge, and tremolo designs were distinct from Fender's solidbodies. In addition, they were available in Wildwood colors. Wildwood was actually beechwood with dye injected into the tree before it was cut. Fender organized the colors, which ranged from green to orange to blue, under a Roman-numeral system, and the greenish Wildwood II was the most commonly seen.

MODEL
Fender Coronado II Wildwood II

YEAR
1966

PRODUCTION
1966 to 1969

222

Electric 12-string guitars appeared to be the "next big thing" in rock'n'roll music after The Beatles used a Rickenbacker on "A Hard Day's Night" in 1964 and the Byrds made it the signature sound of "Mr. Tambourine Man" in 1965. Gibson introduced semi-hollow 12-strings under the Gibson and Epiphone brands in 1965, and when Fender announced its forthcoming semi-hollowbody electrics late in that year, the new series included a Coronado XII 12-string.

Introduced in 1966, the Coronado XII did not fare as well as Fender's solidbody Electric XII (introduced in mid 1965), and 12-string electrics in general quickly became more of an effect rather than a vital element of rock'n'roll music.

Perhaps it was the DeArmond pickups – Fender's first out-sourced pickups – or maybe it was the incongruity of Fender's standard bolt-on neck on a traditional-style archtop electric, but something about the Coronados did not sit right with guitarists, and all the Coronados were gone by the end of 1970.

223

MODEL
Fender Coronado XII

YEAR
Circa 1968

PRODUCTION
1966 to 1969

FENDER

Roger Rossmeisl had been with Fender for seven years, designing acoustic flat-tops as well as the Coronado semi-hollow electrics, before Fender gave his creative talent free rein in 1969. The result was the LTD model.

Fender's first hollowbody electric featured a spruce top that was personally carved by Rossmeisl. It sported the elegant "German carve" – the pronounced "lip" around the edge of the top that Rossmeisl had brought with him from his native Germany (where his father was a noted guitarmaker). The neck-position pickup with controls in the pickguard, the height adjustable ebony bridge, the gold-plated tailpiece, the ebony fingerboard with fancy inlays, the flared headstock – everything about the LTD (except, significantly, the bolt-on neck) exuded traditional artisanship in a way no Fender ever had before.

Unfortunately, no matter how great a designer Rossmeisl may have been, guitar buyers were still hesitant to buy a Fender that didn't have a solidbody. The LTD's name proved prophetic. Production was quite limited, estimated at no more than a dozen guitars.

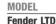

MODEL
Fender LTD

YEAR
1968

PRODUCTION
1968 to 1975

Fender's Telecaster was the first commercially successful electric solidbody guitar, but despite its historical importance, it languished in the shadow of the Stratocaster and other more modern Fenders in the 1960s.

One of the Telecaster's problems was the weight of the ash body that Fender still used for the Tele's standard "blond" finish (most other Fenders had a lighter alder body).

The solution to the weight problem was simply to remove some of the wood from the body, and rather than hide the cavity, Fender designer Roger Rossmeisl called attention to it with an f-hole. He also redesigned the Telecaster's pickguard into a flowing shape that encompassed the controls, eliminating the need for a separate control plate. A pearloid pickguard added flair to what was, by the late 1960s, the Telecaster's dated look. Most Thinlines had a natural-finish ash body but mahogany was also offered.

In 1971, Fender replaced the Thinline's single-coil pickups with humbuckers. It was reissued in Japanese production in 1997, featuring a mahogany body and the model name '69 Thinline.

MODEL
Fender Telecaster Thinline (single-coil pickups)

YEAR
1968

PRODUCTION
1968 to 1971

FENDER

Except for its lighter weight, the Telecaster Thinline of 1968 was essentially no different than the standard Telecaster that Fender had been making since 1950, and most Telecaster buyers stayed with the tried-and-true version. Consequently, after three years of unimpressive Thinline sales, Fender created a fundamentally different guitar by abandoning the Tele's traditional single-coil pickups for a pair of humbuckers.

One humbucker on a Fender was good. The Rolling Stones' Keith Richards, for example, installed a neck-position humbucker in his Telecasters, as did bluesman Albert Collins, and many Stratocaster players of the 1980s would add a bridge-position humbucker. But two humbuckers were one too many. In the 1970s, and still today, dual humbuckers were associated with Gibson (the company that invented the humbucker), and most guitarists who wanted a semi-hollowbody – or solidbody, for that matter – with two humbuckers simply bought a Gibson.

The humbucker-equipped Thinline lasted through 1979, and like the original, single-coil version, it was reissued in Japanese production in 1997, featuring an ash body and the model name '72 Thinline.

MODEL
Fender Telecaster Thinline (humbucking pickups)

YEAR
1977

PRODUCTION
1971 to 1979

The failure of Roger Rossmeisl's Coronado series in the late 1960s did not deter Fender from mounting another invasion of Gibson semi-hollow territory in the late 1970s with a new model called the Starcaster.

The Starcaster appeared to have been better thought-out, combining Fender and Gibson features in a way that gave it a better chance at success than the Coronados. Designer Gene Fields took the familiar – by this time traditional – double-cutaway, arched-top body of Gibson's ES-335 and make it more Fenderlike by stretching it diagonally, giving it the offset waist of Fender's Jazzmaster, a design that Leo Fender had patented in 1958. Fields also redesigned the peghead, giving it softer lines and an elegant beveled edge.

Functionally the Starcaster had a pair of humbuckers so it could compete directly with the Gibson ES-335. Ultimately though, just as before, guitarists preferred the original Gibson – they perceived the asymmetrical body of the Starcaster as being simply misshapen – and the Starcaster fell out of sight as the 1980s began.

227

MODEL
Fender Starcaster

YEAR
1976

PRODUCTION
1976 to 1980

FENDER

In 1984, after almost 20 years of disappointment with in-house archtop designs, Fender went outside the company and enlisted James D'Aquisto, the legendary maker of acoustic archtop guitars, to create a new Fender model.

D'Aquisto's design hand was obvious in the massive ebony tailpiece and sleek pickguard shape, along with soundholes that had a traditional f-shape on one edge and D'Aquisto's S-shape on the other. The large headstock was a refinement of Roger Rossmeisl's design on the Fender LTD of the late 1960s (which itself had been a refinement of the large headstocks of D'Angelico and D'Aquisto). Because the top was laminated, there was no pretense of equipping it with a floating pickup; the humbucker and control knobs were mounted directly into the top.

The original Fender D'Aquistos – a Standard and an Elite – were produced only briefly by the newly formed Fender Japan division. In 1994, a year before D'Aquisto's death, Fender's Custom Shop revived the design in the form of the D'Aquisto Deluxe. In 2002, Fender's agreement with D'Aquisto's estate ended and the name was licensed to Aria.

228

How Tommy Tedesco gets a date.

MODEL
Fender D'Aquisto Deluxe

YEAR
1995

PRODUCTION
1994 to 2002

Although Japanese makers became infamous for copying successful American guitars in the late 1960s, this Framus Hollywood 5/132 shows that German makers were blazing that trail a decade earlier. The general body shape and the cherry sunburst finish of this guitar were obviously intended to appeal to players who aspired to own a Gibson Les Paul Standard.

The Framus differed from the Les Paul in many obvious ways, including its three pickups, large pickguard, tailpiece, and control knobs. And under the top, the difference was even more significant, as the Framus was actually a semi-hollowbody rather than a solidbody guitar.

Framus, founded in Germany in 1946, was the leading European maker of electric guitars by the mid 1950s, and the Hollywood series of simulated solidbodies – available with one, two, or three pickups – appeared in 1958. Although Framus guitars never gained a strong international following, they were still considered in the U.S. to be a quality import, a step above the flashier but more cheaply made guitars from Japan and Italy.

MODEL
Framus Hollywood 5/132

YEAR
1959

PRODUCTION
1958 to mid 1960s

GIBSON

Gibson's ES-150 was not the first electric guitar, but it might as well have been. It was the first professional-quality model, and moreover, it was the guitar Charlie Christian played when he revolutionized the role of the electric guitarist as a member of Benny Goodman's band from 1939 until his death in 1942.

Gibson employee Walt Fuller, an amateur radio enthusiast, developed a distinctive hexagonal pickup for the company's first model, the EH-150, introduced in late 1935. E stood for Electric, and H stood for Hawaiian (as opposed to conventional "Spanish" style guitars); 150 denoted the $150 price of guitar and its companion amplifer. It took a year for Gibson to gain enough confidence in electrics to introduce an Electric Spanish version, the ES-150.

Any doubt about the future of electric guitars was smashed by Charlie Christian, who used an ES-150 and later a fancier Gibson ES-250 to free the electric guitar from a rhythmic role, establishing it as a lead instrument with its own unique voice.

MODEL
**Gibson ES-150
(pre-WWII version)**

YEAR
1937

PRODUCTION
1936 to 1942

In a technical sense, the "wings" from a conventional Epiphone hollowbody guitar made this homemade instrument a semi-hollowbody, but Les Paul built it to demonstrate the viability of a hollowbody guitar.

Paul was one of America's best-known guitarist by the 1940s, thanks to a stint on Chicago radio in the mid 1930s as country artist Rhubard Red and then with his trio as a featured part of the Fred Waring band. Although the public knew him as an acoustic player, Paul was a firm believer in the electric guitar – not just any electric guitar but a solidbody electric. An inveterate tinkerer, he built his own guitar in 1941, mounting the neck and electronics on a four-inch-square piece of wood and attaching sides from a conventional archtop.

Through the 1940s, Paul played "The Log," as it was nicknamed, in numerous public settings, but it was viewed more as a gimmick than as the future of guitar design. His main guitar remained a customized Epiphone hollowbody until Gibson signed him to endorse its first solidbody electric in 1952.

MODEL
Gibson "The Log" custom built by Les Paul

YEAR
1941

PRODUCTION
1941

GIBSON

The 18-inch wide Super 400, introduced in 1934, was not merely Gibson's top archtop model in the 1930s, it was an industry leader in a movement toward larger-bodied guitars – acoustic guitars, that is. On the electric side, the first Gibson electrics, which appeared in 1936, were not as big, not as highly ornamented, and did not require the same level of craftsmanship as the acoustic models.

A standard Gibson electric was apparently just not good enough for the player who custom-ordered this Super 400 with a pickup in 1940. Gibson had recently developed its first pickup with height-adjustable polepieces for the ES-300 model, and it was easy enough to rout the top of a Super 400 for the electronics. The model name on the label, Super 400 Premier EN, includes all of this guitar's special features: Premier for cutaway body, an option introduced in 1939; E for Electric; and N for Natural finish, introduced in 1938.

Despite the obvious potential, it would be over a decade before Gibson offered an electric Super 400 as a catalog model.

MODEL
Gibson Super 400
Premier NE

YEAR
1940

PRODUCTION
1940

Gibson's original pickup, nicknamed the "Charlie Christian," is still prized by some jazz guitarists today, but its one-piece bar polepiece had severe limitations. To allow players to adjust the signal level for each individual string, Gibson appropriated a concept from its arch-rival Epiphone and developed a pickup with height-adjustable screws for polepieces.

The new pickup got a new housing – an oval, tortoiseshell-pattern celluloid cover – as well as a new model to introduce it. The ES-300 of 1940 featured this new design in what may be a record for pickup length: over seven inches. The slanted configuration made the low strings more bassy sounding and the treble strings more brilliant, but amplifiers of the day weren't equipped to exploit the increased tonal spectrum, and a more economical-sized pickup quickly appeared.

The ES-300 introduced two new visual elements to the Gibson line: double-parallelogram fingerboard inlays and the "crown" inlay on the peghead. It continued in the postwar years but was soon overshadowed by a cutaway version, called the ES-350.

233

MODEL
**Gibson ES-300N
(pre-World War II)**

YEAR
1941

PRODUCTION
1940 to 1942

Despite Gibson's electric line expansion and pickup development in the late 1930s, the company was still cautious about betting its future on the electric guitar. Evidence of that was clear in 1939, when Gibson introduced cutaway bodies only on its top acoustic models, the Super 400 and L-5. Not until the end of World War II would a Gibson electric be offered with a cutaway.

Gibson emerged from the war with a new pickup, the P-90, and a cutaway version of the 17-inch electric ES-300 called the ES-350. The ES-300 debuted in 1947 and a year later became the first Gibson electric with two pickups.

Bebop jazzman Tal Farlow played an ES-350 before he received his own Gibson signature model, and Danny Cedrone used the non-cutaway version, the ES-300, to play the wild solo with Bill Haley and the Comets on their 1954 recording "Rock Around The Clock." Although the ES-350 was supplanted by a thinbody version in 1956, the P-90 pickup that it introduced remains in production today

MODEL
Gibson ES-350

YEAR
1952

PRODUCTION
1947 to 1956

Gibson moved fast in the post-World War II electric guitar market, introducing in quick succession an improved pickup (the P-90, with its distinctive "dog-eared" black plastic cover), its first cutaway electric (the ES-350), and its first two-pickup guitar (again, the ES-350). The versatility of a neck pickup and a bridge pickup quickly won over many guitarists, and the next step was obvious – if two pickups were good, three would be better.

In 1949, Gibson began building ES-350s with three P-90s. The two-pickup ES-350 had individual volume controls for each pickup but only one master tone control, and that concept was extended on the experimental three-pickup models, which featured three volume controls and one master tone.

Gibson put together a dozen of these models, labeled "ES-350 Sp.," in June and July of 1949 and then decided that a three-pickup guitar deserved a fancier look and more sophisticated controls. Although the ES-5 that debuted later in 1949 would be a step above the ES-350 Specials, Gibson nevertheless went back in serial number logbooks and ink-stamped "ES-5" over the original ES-350 entries.

235

MODEL

Gibson ES-350 Special (3 pickups)

YEAR

1949

PRODUCTION

1949

GIBSON

Gibson's ES-5 might seem to have had a lowly model designation in the company of Gibson's other postwar electrics – the ES-125, 150, 300 and 350. But in Gibson tradition, Style 5 signified one of the highest levels of importance as well as ornamentation. The L-5 acoustic, introduced in 1922, had been the first archtop with f-holes, and an ES (Electric Spanish) version of the L-5 would command instant recognition and respect.

The ES-5 was the first guitar – by Gibson or anyone else – with three standard pickups, each with its own volume control, plus a master tone control on the cutaway. The neck ornamentation was similar to that of an L-5, but instead or the L-5's flowerpot peghead ornament, the ES-5 had a "crown" inlay.

The beautiful wood grain of the top of this natural finish ES-5 from 1952 illustrates another fundamental difference between the ES-5 and the L-5. Like all of Gibson's postwar electrics, it had a laminated maple body rather than the carved spruce top and solid maple body of the acoustics.

MODEL
Gibson ES-5

YEAR
1952

PRODUCTION
1949 to 1955

In 1949, two years after Gibson added a cutaway to its 17-inch ES-300, making it the ES-350, Gibson did the same with its 16-inch ES-125. For the cutaway version, Gibson once again added 50 "points" to the model number and called the new guitar the ES-175. The model's pointed "Florentine" cutaway made it unique among Gibson's electric archtop models of the 1950s.

Continuing to follow the ES-350's example, Gibson introduced a two-pickup version of the ES-175 in 1951, and this comfortable, 16-inch, laminated-maple electric hollowbody quickly became one of Gibson's more successful electrics. The two-pickup ES-175D has been in continuous production longer than any other Gibson.

In the meantime, the single-pickup ES-175 gained a reputation as the workhorse guitar of the jazz guitar world. Some of the most prominent jazzmen of the 1950s, such as Kenny Burrell and Jim Hall, played single-pickup ES-175s, and Herb Ellis was so closely identified with his single-pickup ES-175 that it became the ES-165 Herb Ellis signature model in 1991.

237

MODEL
Gibson ES-175

YEAR
1953

PRODUCTION
1949 to current

GIBSON

Gibson's ES-5 was modeled after the company's legendary L-5 acoustic – but only to a point. Despite such high-end features as three pickups and gold-plated hardware, it had a laminated maple body that left some guitarists longing for a true electric version of the L-5. And that's exactly what Gibson gave them in 1951.

The L-5CES (Cutaway Electric Spanish) was built as an acoustic guitar, complete with carved spruce top and solid maple back and sides. Gibson simply cut holes in the top for pickups and controls. The holes severely compromised the guitar's acoustic qualities, but players did not seem to care.

Although the L-5 had always been a favorite of big band and jazz players, the L-5CES gained a higher level of notoriety in the hands of Elvis Presley's guitarist Scotty Moore. Moore bought a natural finish L-5CESN in 1955, just as Presley was leaving Sun Records for RCA, and Moore played it the biggest hits from the biggest pop star of the era, including "Hound Dog," "Heartbreak Hotel," "Blue Suede Shoes" and "Don't Be Cruel."

MODEL
Gibson L-5CES

YEAR
1951

PRODUCTION
1951 to current

In 1951, Gibson introduced electric versions of its two most famous acoustic archtop guitars, the Super 400 and L-5.

From a practical point of view, it made little sense to go to the trouble and expense of carving a solid spruce top and then cutting holes in it for pickups and controls, but guitarists who bought the Super 400CES didn't really care about its performance quality as an acoustic; they simply wanted a Gibson electric that was as fancy and prestigious as any Gibson acoustic model.

Like the L-5, the 18-inch Super 400 had been a favorite of big band jazz players since its introduction in 1934, but like the L-5CES, the Super 400CES gained its greatest exposure in the hands of the most influential rock'n'roll player of the 1950s – Scotty Moore, Elvis's guitarist. Moore bought a natural-finish model in January 1957 and used it into the 1960s, a period that encompassed such No. 1 Elvis hits as "All Shook Up," "Teddy Bear," "Hard Headed Woman," and "Good Luck Charm."

MODEL
Gibson Super 400CES (P-90s)

YEAR
1953

PRODUCTION
1951 to 1957

As Gibson was introducing its first solidbody electric, the "goldtop" Les Paul Model of 1952, the company also offered the expensive-looking gold finish to players of hollowbody electrics with the ES-295.

Essentially a gold version of the ES-175, the ES-295 took the concept a step beyond the gold top of the Les Paul by sporting gold finish on the neck, back, and sides, as well as the top. The connection to the solidbody model was evident in the ES-295's combination bridge tailpiece, which was invented by Les Paul and featured on his signature guitar as well (but never on the ES-175).

One musician who couldn't resist the allure of an all-gold guitar was Memphis guitarist Scotty Moore, who was playing in a country band in 1953 when he saw an ES-295 in a store window and had to have it. In 1954, Moore brought it to a session with Elvis Presley and played it on "That's All Right," and popular music was never the same again.

MODEL
Gibson ES-295

YEAR
1952

PRODUCTION
1952 to 1958,
1990 to 1994

The Super 400CES never set any sales records for Gibson, but the 18-inch archtop electric has remained in production since its introduction in 1951 as a symbol of the highest level of the guitarmaker's art. If a guitarist wanted the best guitar Gibson made – in terms of price – it had to be a Super 400.

Scotty Moore, Elvis Presley's guitarist, bought his first Super 400, which was equipped with single-coil P-90 pickups, in the mid 1950s during Elvis's "Hound Dog" era. Gibson upgraded the Super 400 (and all its other high-end electrics) with humbucking pickups in 1957, and in 1963 Moore upgraded to the newer version, which had also received a Florentine pointed cutaway.

The Super 400CES may have gotten its greatest exposure of the 1960s on Elvis's 1968 "comeback" TV Special when Elvis took the black-finished guitar from Moore's hands to accompany himself solo on "One Night With You." The Super 400 was Moore's main guitar well into the 1980s, and it remains the flagship of Gibson's high-end electric archtop line today.

MODEL
Gibson Super 400CESN (humbuckers)

YEAR
1958

PRODUCTION
1957 to current

GIBSON

While Gibson's L-5CES and Super 400CES, with their carved spruce tops, represented the highest level of artisanship in the Gibson electric line of the mid 1950s, the three-pickup ES-5 was Gibson's showcase for electronic advancement.

The original version of the ES-5 had a single volume control for each pickup, plus a master tone control, which allowed the player easily to "dial in" a preferred pickup combination but made it difficult to switch quickly and accurately to other settings. In 1955, Gibson added a tone control for each pickup, along with a slotted switch with four settings that let the player select each pickup alone or all three together. The ES-5 Switchmaster, as the new version was named, did not allow any combinations of two pickups, but the six knobs and large switch made it appear, at least, as if it could outperform any other electric guitar.

Gibson changed the cutaways on its electric models to a pointed Florentine shape in 1961, and a handful of Switchmasters were made with the new shape before production ended in that same year.

MODEL
Gibson ES-5 Switchmaster

YEAR
1957

PRODUCTION
1955 to 1961

The name Byrdland on a new Gibson in 1955 may have seemed confusing to guitar buyers who knew of the famed New York jazz club B*i*rdland, because the guitar was a signature model for two Nashville musicians, combining the names of Billy *Byrd* and Hank Gar*land*. The jazz reference was appropriate, as Byrd and Garland were among the best jazz guitarists in Nashville in the early 1950s, but the country ties were stronger. Garland was nicknamed "Sugarfoot" for his solo on Red Foley's hit "Sugarfoot Rag," and Byrd was featured in the band of traditional country singer Ernest Tubb.

The Byrdland's unique features were a shorter, 23.5-inch scale length, which catered to the wide hand stretches of jazz chording, and a body that was an inch thinner than a typical archtop. The first examples had "Alnico V" pickups, with rectangular polepieces, before humbuckers appeared in 1957.

The versatility of Byrd and Garland was reflected in the Byrdland's use by such diverse artists as country entertainer Roy Clark, hard rocker Ted Nugent, and free jazz innovator James "Blood" Ulmer.

243

MODEL
Gibson Byrdland

YEAR
1957

PRODUCTION
1955 to current

GIBSON

There's an old saying: Gibson made at least one of everything. And this custom-ordered double-cutaway Byrdland proves it.

Willie Luedecke, whose name is engraved on the tailpiece where "Byrdland" would normally be, was a guitarist in the small west Texas town of Lufkin. He played in local bands, sometimes fronting a group featuring fellow Lufkin native J. Frank Wilson of "Last Kiss" fame.

In the 1960s the Byrdland's original rounded Venetian cutaway was changed to a pointed Florentine style, so a double-cutaway with pointed horns was not a radical idea. Gibson already had full-depth double-cutaway hollowbodies available – the Barney Kessel (two models) and Trini Lopez Custom – by the time Luedecke custom-ordered this guitar. Kay had offered similar thinline double-cutaways, too, in the early 1960s that may have been the inspiration for this guitar. Luedecke apparently liked the Byrdland's shorter 23.5-inch scale and its 2.25-inch body depth – halfway between full-depth and thinline. All he had to do was to tell Gibson what he wanted, and Gibson put it all together.

MODEL
Gibson Byrdland Special

YEAR
Circa 1967

PRODUCTION
Circa 1967

For players who wanted the prestigious look of a large-bodied archtop but wanted a more comfortable instrument, Gibson introduced several models in 1955 with "thinline" bodies only one-and-five-eighth inches deep. The ES-350T appeared to be simply a slimmer version of the 17-inch cutaway ES-350, but it had the shorter, 23.5 inch scale length that Gibson had introduced that same year on the Byrdland model.

Although the shorter scale was intended to appeal to jazz players, the ES-350T will forever be remembered as the guitar Chuck Berry used as he "wrote the book" on rock'n'roll guitar licks on such hits as "Maybellene," "School Days" and "Roll Over Beethoven." Berry's natural-finish ES-350T was immortalized in early photos of the artist in a crossed-knees stance or duck-walking across a stage.

After Gibson's introduction of semi-hollowbodies in 1958, Berry switched to the ES-355, and the ES-350T never recovered. Gibson dropped it after 1962, and although Gibson reintroduced it several times (beginning in 1977), the newer versions always had a standard scale length.

245

MODEL
Gibson ES-350T
(23.5-inch scale)

YEAR
1957

PRODUCTION
1955 to 1962

GIBSON

With a 16-inch body, the ES-175D (D for Double-pickup) was barely even a midline model, but Gibson gave it an important, high-end upgrade in 1957 by replacing the ES-175's single-coil P-90 pickups with the new double-coil humbuckers.

Gibson engineer Seth Lover invented the humbucker to literally "buck the hum" that plagued single-coil pickups whenever they were near a rheostat, fluorescent light or some other source of electrical interference. The greater power of humbuckers would not be exploited until the 1960s, but they were nevertheless welcomed by players as soon as they were introduced.

While the ES-175 had been the preferred model of many jazz players in the 1950s, the humbucker-equipped model was attractive to rock'n'roll players in later decades. The jazz and rock appeal made it especially suitable for the eclectic musical output of Steve Howe, guitarist with the British group Yes. This 1964 ES-175 is his personal instrument. He became so closely identified with it that Gibson gave him a signature ES-175 (albeit fancier) in 2001.

MODEL
Gibson ES-175D

YEAR
1964

PRODUCTION
1951 to current

Doubleneck Hawaiian electric guitars appeared within a few years of the first electric guitars, but it was another 20 years before the doubleneck concept migrated to conventional electrics. In 1958, prompted by the popularity of hot-picking southern California guitarists Joe Maphis and Larry Collins (who both played custom-made doublenecks), Gibson began offering guitars with any combination of guitar, banjo, mandolin, and bass necks. The most popular was the 6/12 configuration of the EDS-1275.

The most remarkable aspect of these first Gibson doublenecks was the body. It was hollow, with a top carved spruce top, like Gibson's acoustic archtops. It was unique in that it had no soundholes – a design that had only been used on two electric basses made by Gibson in the pre-World War II years.

Within a few years, Gibson decided that the subtle tonal differences of the spruce top and hollow design were not as important as bringing the cost within the range of more guitar buyers, and by 1962, the EDS-1275 had become a solidbody based on the design of Gibson's SG series.

MODEL
Gibson EDS-1275 Double 12

YEAR
Circa 1959

PRODUCTION
1958 to 1961

247

GIBSON

More than any other guitarist of the 1950s and '60s, Barney Kessell easily moved back and forth between jazz to pop music. In the jazz world, his Charlie Christian-inspired style gained him recognition as a member of the Oscar Peterson Trio, and in pop music, he played a prominent solo on Julie London's 1955 hit "Cry Me a River."

Gibson thought enough of Kessel to give him two signature models in 1961. Both featured a new body style – a full-depth archtop body with double cutaways that came to a point. The body was laminated maple, but through the first few years of production the tops were laminated spruce. The Kessel Regular had double-parallelogram inlays while the Kessel Custom sported bowtie inlays and a musical note on the peghead.

In the 1960s, Kessel was a member of the "The Wrecking Crew," who played on hits by the Beach Boys and the Monkees, but by the end of the decade, he was spending more time running a music store and refocusing on jazz. Gibson last produced his models in 1973.

248

MODEL
Gibson Barney Kessel Custom

YEAR
1961

PRODUCTION
1961 to 1973

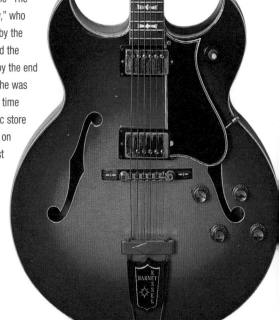

Johnny Smith brought an impeccable reputation to Gibson's artist roster in 1961, and his signature model featured the classic jazz setup – an acoustic archtop guitar with a "floating" pickup.

Smith's 1952 album *Moonlight in Vermont* set the standard for "chord melody" style, and he gained even greater fame from writing "Walk Don't Run," which was covered first by Chet Atkins and then in 1960 by The Ventures, whose version became a surf music classic.

After an endorsement agreement, and then a disagreement, with Guild, Smith signed with Gibson in 1961. The Gibson Johnny Smith model was based on Smith's personal D'Angelico guitar, which had a non-standard 25-inch scale length. It featured a smaller "mini" version of Gibson's humbucking pickup. It remained a symbol of class at the top of Gibson's archtop electric line until Gibson moved headquarters from Kalamazoo, Michigan, to Nashville, Tennessee, in 1984. Smith remained loyal to the Kalamazoo workers who stayed behind to form the Heritage company, and he left Gibson in 1988, although Gibson continued to offer the same model as the LeGrand.

249

MODEL
Gibson Johnny Smith

YEAR
1962

PRODUCTION
1961 to 1988

GIBSON

Following close on the heels of the Johnny Smith and Barney Kessel models, Gibson's Tal Farlow model secured Gibson's image as the preferred guitarmaker for elite jazz musicians. Farlow was inspired by the recordings of Charlie Christian, who practically invented electric jazz guitar, and pianist Bud Powell. The speed, accuracy and complexity of Farlow's style – demonstrated on a series of solo albums in the mid 1950s – put him in the upper echelon of bebop jazz guitarists.

Farlow's signature model was built on the familiar single-cutaway body of Gibson's 17-inch ES-5 model but with some unconventional features, including a scrolled cutaway bout (simulated with inlaid binding material), fingerboard inlays that were the "crest" of the J-200 flat-top turned upside-down, and a double-crown peghead ornament.

Ironically, Farlow (like Johnny Smith) had gone into semi-retirement shortly before Gibson debuted his signature model, not to emerge until the late 1970s. In the meantime, his namesake guitar sold less than 100 units, making it the rarest of Gibson's artist models of the 1960s.

MODEL
Gibson Tal Farlow

YEAR
1964

PRODUCTION
1962 to 1970

Despite the invention of powerful
humbucking pickups in 1957 and the
availability of a "floating" humbucker like
the one Gibson used on its Johnny Smith
model in the 1960s, some players
preferred to stick with the old ways. The
classic electric jazz guitar of the 1940s
and early 1950s was a fully acoustic
archtop with a DeArmond pickup, and that's
how the owner of this 1969 Gibson Super 400
set up his guitar.

The unusual feature of this guitar, signified
by "WAL" in the model designation, is a walnut-
stained finish on the back, sides and neck.
Numerous low-end Gibson models – solidbody
as well as hollow – with a sunburst top finish
had the dark brown stain over the rest of the
guitar, but it was unheard of on any maple-
body electric model with a natural top finish.

On the other hand, this guitar was made in
1969, and Gibson was struggling in
a market overrun with cheap
Japanese-made imports.
Any new variation might
have attracted attention
to traditional Gibsons, but
the walnut finish did not
catch on.

MODEL

**Gibson Super 400
CN WAL**

YEAR

1969

PRODUCTION

1969

GIBSON

The model name of the Gibson's ES-135 of 1991 might have been vaguely familiar to veterans of the guitar industry – it had been a full-depth, non-cutaway archtop that made a brief appearance in the mid 1950s – but the single-cutaway body of the 1991 version was something new for Gibson's semi-hollowbody line. Until that time, all of the semi-hollows had had the ES-335's double-cutaway shape.

With a center block of lightweight – but strong – balsa wood, the ES-135 was Gibson's first new idea in archtop electric design since the 1970s, and Gibson's CEO Henry Juszkiewicz (whose ownership group had acquired the company in 1986) added a touch of mystique by coining the term Chromyte for the balsa wood.

The ES-135 was moderately successful and led to two offshoots, the all-black, humbucker-equipped ES-135 Gothic (1998–99) and the Swingmaster ES-135 (1999), which featured dog-eared P-90s and such "hip" finishes as Outa-Sight White and Daddy-O Yellow. Although the ES-135 was last made in 2003, the basic model style continues in Gibson's ES-137 series.

252

MODEL
Gibson ES-135

YEAR
1993

PRODUCTION
1991 to 2003

In the 1970s, the Super 400CES provided a much-needed symbol of stability at the top of Gibson's electric line, as the company failed with one new model after another.

At the end of the 1960s, Gibson's parent company, Chicago Musical Instrument, had suffered setbacks with its Lowery organ division, and an Ecuadorian company took advantage of CMI's depressed stock and took it over in 1970. The new corporation, called Norlin, had the misfortune of getting into the guitar market at the beginning of what would be known as The Great Synthesizer Scare of the '70s, and none of its new models "stuck" in the soft guitar market of the era.

Norlin consistently lost money for 15 years, and Gibson's reputation eroded along with sales. Through it all, the Super 400CES reminded the guitar world of all that Gibson could be. Aside from the rarely offered Wine Red finish and the "witch hat" knobs on this 1976 guitar, this Super 400 could have been made any time from the 1950s to the present.

MODEL
Gibson Super 400CES WR

YEAR
1977

PRODUCTION
1976 to 1980

253

GIBSON

Gibson's original Super 400 of 1934 was designed to blow the competition out of the water. Its huge, 18-inch body width (at a time when the largest Gibson was 16 inches wide) accomplished that goal acoustically, but it also made for an uncomfortably large guitar for some players.

With the advent of electric guitars, the size of the guitar became more of a visual feature than a performance advantage, and many players preferred the L-5's 17-inch body. However, players still enjoyed the prestigious and instantly recognisable look of the Super 400's slashed-block fingerboard inlays and split-diamond peghead inlay, and in 1978 Gibson combined the comfort of the L-5 body with the look of the Super 400 neck by creating the Super V CES (CES for Cutaway Electric Spanish).

The Super V had one feature that neither of its parent models had, and that was a six-finger tailpiece, allowing the player to fine-tune the string pressure on the bridge by adjusting each string up or down.

MODEL
Gibson Super V CES

YEAR
1984

PRODUCTION
1978 to 1992

Gibson opened a new facility in Nashville in 1974, intending to move solidbody electric production there. The craftsmen who made Gibson archtops – a style of guitar that Orville Gibson had invented in the 1890s – stayed in Kalamazoo, Michigan, and in 1978 they demonstrated their skills with an elaborately ornamented creation called the Kalamazoo Award.

The pickguard alone set the Kalamazoo Award apart from all previous Gibsons. Instead of celluloid, it was birdseye maple, inlaid with an abalone flying bird and branch. The figures were repeated on the peghead and tailpiece insert, and the large block fingerboard inlays were also abalone. The floating mini-humbucking pickup, with controls mounted in the pickguard, indicated that this guitar was designed to perform equally well as an acoustic or an electric.

Made in very limited numbers during a period when Gibson quality was falling fast, the Kalamazoo Award offered the guitar world a glimmer of reassurance that the tradition of fine, hand-crafted guitars was still alive and well at Gibson.

255

MODEL
Gibson Kalamazoo Award

YEAR
1979

PRODUCTION
1978 to 1984

GIBSON

Wes Montgomery gained fame in the mid 1960s for recording popular songs, such as "Goin' Out of My Head," in a smooth, mellow style that featured the melody played in octaves, but few pop fans knew that the Indianapolis native was a highly respected jazz guitarist who had carried the standard for bebop guitar in the early 1960s.

The classic jazz guitar of the 1950s was an archtop with a single pickup, but after the introduction of the humbucking pickup in 1957, Gibson only offered the 16-inch, laminated-body ES-175 with that configuration. Montgomery preferred the larger, fancier Gibson L-5, with its carved spruce top, and he custom-ordered several L-5s with a single humbucker.

Montgomery died unexpectedly from a heart attack at age 43 in 1969, but he remained closely identified with the single-pickup L-5, and Gibson's Custom Shop introduced it as a Wes Montgomery signature model in 1993. The Custom Shop also restored a fire-damaged Montgomery guitar that had his name engraved on a heart-shaped pearl inlay, and that version was offered in a limited edition in 1997.

MODEL
Gibson Wes Montgomery

YEAR
1997

PRODUCTION
1993 to current

In 1958 Gibson president Ted McCarty melded modern solidbody design with traditional hollowbody features to create the ES-335. The thinline archtop body had f-holes, as Gibsons had had since 1922, but McCarty put a solid center block down the middle of the guitar to give it the greater sustain and reduced feedback of a solidbody.

Unlike so many concepts that looked good on paper, the semi-hollow guitar worked perfectly. The ES-335 not only bridged solid and hollow designs, it bridged musical genres from blues to rock to jazz. Eric Clapton and Alvin Lee (of Ten Years After) were among the influential rockers of the 1960s who played a 335. In jazz, Larry Carlton was so closely identified with the model that he became known as "Mr. 335." And iconic artists Chuck Berry and B.B. King are well known for playing fancier versions of the ES-335.

Of all the models introduced in the McCarty era – a Golden Era that includes Les Pauls, SGs, Firebirds, the Flying V and the Explorer – only the ES-335 has remained in continuous production.

257

MODEL
**Gibson ES-335
(dot inlay)**

YEAR
1959

PRODUCTION
**1958 to 1962,
1981 to current**

GIBSON

In 1959, only a year after Gibson had introduced the concept of a semi-hollowbody guitar, the ES-335 was well-established as the basic model, and the fancier ES-355 had found a market among more affluent buyers. Still, Gibson saw room in the middle for a third model, and the company filled that spot in 1959 with the ES-345.

Where the 335 had single-ply binding around the top, the 355 had seven-ply binding, so the 345's top was triple-bound. The 335 was nickel-plated, the 355 was gold; there was no middle ground so the 345 was given gold plating and the 355 was given a vibrato unit to make up for it. In between the dot fingerboard inlays and the large pearl blocks, the 345 sported double-parallelograms, a well-established inlay pattern on midline Gibsons.

Like the ES-355, the ES-345 was equipped with stereo output, which was a seldom-used but benign feature. However, the Varitone control ultimately made the 345 less desirable than the basic 335, and many players had their 345s rewired to bypass the Varitone.

MODEL
Gibson ES-345

YEAR
1959

PRODUCTION
1959 to 1982

258

Among the new features of Gibson's 1958 thinline, semi-hollowbody ES-335 was its double-cutaway body, a first for Gibson f-hole archtop models. It was so well-received that, a year later, Gibson tried the double-cutaway on a fully hollow thinline model.

The model number of the hollow version, ES-330, showed that, from the very start, Gibson considered it to be a little below the semi-hollow 335. And the 330's single-coil pickups secured its place as "poor relation" to the humbucker-equipped 335. The hollowbody precipitated another fundamental difference; without the support of the 335's center block, the neck had to extend farther into the body, leaving ES-330 players with less access to the upper register than the ES-335 provided.

The ES-330 did initially have one feature that the 335 lacked – a single-pickup version – but that only lasted through 1962. Not all musicians thought the hollowbody and shorter neck were too limiting. The ES-330 was reasonably successful, and the Gibson-made Epiphone version, the Casino, gained considerable fame in the hands of The Beatles.

MODEL
Gibson ES-330

YEAR
1961

PRODUCTION
1959 to 1971

GIBSON

Eric Clapton's 1964 Gibson ES-335 shows that despite the unqualified success of the ES-335, Gibson could not resist "upgrading" its basic semi-hollowbody model.

Late in 1959, little more than a year after the ES-335's introduction, Gibson added an optional cherry stain finish. Early in 1961, the pickguard was shortened by a few inches. Also in 1961, white nylon saddles replaced the metal saddles in the tune-o-matic bridge. And in mid 1962, small pearloid block inlays replaced the original dots on the fingerboard. For the most part, the changes were small and insignificant from a player's point of view, and they did not impede Clapton's performance with this guitar on Cream's recording of "Crossroads."

Gibson continued to meddle with the 335. Unlike the cosmetic upgrades, the replacement of the stopbar tailpiece with a trapeze in late 1964 was detrimental, and the addition of a coil tap in 1977 was gratuitious. Gibson finally came to its senses in 1981 and reverted to the original "dot-neck" version, and the ES-335 DOT continues to be a mainstay of Gibson's electric lineup.

MODEL
**Gibson ES-335
(block inlays)**

YEAR
1964

PRODUCTION
1962 to 1980

Gibson started making acoustic 12-string guitars in 1961 in response to the Folk Boom, but there was no demand for an electric 12-string until 1965, when The Beatles' George Harrison used one on "A Hard Day's Night" and then The Byrds used a 12-string to bring folk and rock music together with "Mr. Tambourine Man."

Gibson responded quickly. The semi-hollow ES-335, with its solid center block, was better suited than a hollow archtop to support the extra string tension of 12 strings, and the ES-335-12 debuted by the end of 1965.

ES-335-12 sales were respectable for two years, but despite the familiarity of the 12-string's unique sound, the market was apparently driven almost entirely by The Byrds. In 1968 The Byrds took a turn toward country music, and the era of the electric 12-string ended as suddenly as it had started. Sales of the ES-335-12 dropped by more than two-thirds that year and then by an even greater amount in 1969. Gibson shipped the last ES-335-12s in 1970.

261

MODEL
Gibson ES-335-12

YEAR
1965

PRODUCTION
1965 to 1970

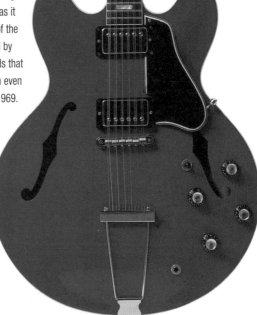

GIBSON

From the front, the ES-340 was indistinguishable from Gibson's classic semi-hollowbody model, the ES-335, but a back view would reveal a three-piece maple neck on the 340, where the neck of the 335 was mahogany during the 340's production run.

The real difference between the two models was in the wiring. Gibson's traditional wiring system for two pickups was simple: separate tone and volume controls for each pickup plus a three-way switch that selected neck pickup alone, bridge pickup alone, or both pickups. That was more than enough for most players, but for those who liked a certain blend of the two pickups together, a seemingly simple adjustment in volume would cause both pickups to be changed by the exact same amount. It was difficult, if not impossible, to maintain the same pickup mix at different volumes.

Gibson solved the problem by rewiring the two individual volume knobs to function as a pickup blend control and a master volume. As it turned out, there really wasn't such a great demand for the ES-340's system, and the model only lasted in production for five years.

MODEL
Gibson ES-340

YEAR
1969

PRODUCTION
1969 to 1973

Ironically, in light of Gibson's phenomenal success with Les Paul's endorsement, Les Paul himself had very little input into the design of his classic 1950s models. That changed in the late 1960s when Gibson revived the solidbodies and brought Paul back into the fold.

This time around, Paul's ideas were implemented in every style of electric guitar, including a solidbody, an electrified flat-top acoustic, and an oddly shaped semi-hollow model – the Les Paul Signature. Paul had intended for the Signature to have neck-thru-body construction – essentially a continuation of the ideas he had introduced in 1941 with his homemade guitar, The Log. However, when it went into production, Gibson gave it a conventional set neck and a T-shaped center support block.

The Signature also sported the low-impedance humbucking pickups preferred by Paul but, unfortunately, not by most other guitarists. The bass version gained a cult following (and was eventually reissued in Gibson's Epiphone line as the Jack Casady signature model), but the Les Paul Signature guitar barely lasted five years in production.

263

MODEL
Gibson Les Paul Signature

YEAR
1976

PRODUCTION
1973 to 1977

GORDON-SMITH

Gordon Whittam and John Smith built their first guitars in 1975. They made their mark with solidbody designs inspired largely by Gibson's double-cutaway Les Paul Junior and Special of the late 1950s. Never flashy, Gordon-Smith guitars gained a high level of respect in England as dependable workingman's instruments that matched the performance of a Gibson.

This semi-hollow Gypsy model takes its inspiration from the single-cutaway Les Paul Standard. There is also a distinctive Fender touch in the prominent wide grain of the top, which is reminiscent of a classic ash-body Telecaster or Stratocaster. The soapbar pickup covers and the electronic configuration are straight out of Gibson's design book, but the pickups themselves, along with the vibrato and the f-holes, are Smith's own design.

Whittam left the partnership in 1984 to make guitars under the Gordy brand. Smith still continues to make guitars, mostly solidbodies, still with simple but effective designs. Based in the small town of Partington, near Manchester, Gordon-Smith is now the longest-running British guitarmaker.

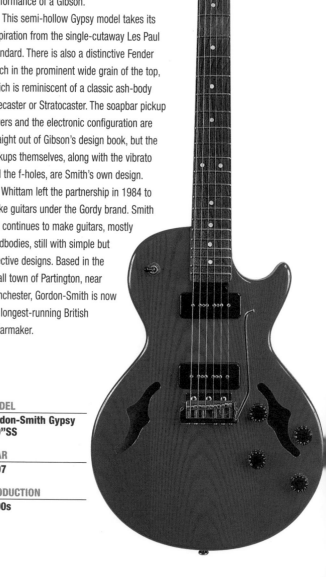

MODEL
Gordon-Smith Gypsy "60"SS

YEAR
1997

PRODUCTION
1990s

Founded in the New York borough of Brooklyn in 1883, Gretsch started as a manufacturer of tambourines, which led to drums and banjos, which led to guitars. By the end of the 1930s, Gretsch was a major player in the acoustic guitar market with its Synchromatic series of large-bodied archtops.

Gretsch was a little late in entering the electric arena, with only one model prior to World War II. The Electromatic of 1940 played on the Synchromatic name, but it wasn't until 1951 that Gretsch introduced a truly competitive electric – the Electro II. With a cutaway body and two DeArmond pickups, and with "Synchromatic" on the peghead to tie it in with Gretsch's high-end acoustics, the 17-inch Electro II went head-to-head against Gibson's ES-350 and Epiphone's Zephyr Deluxe Regent.

Although the Electro II model name was short-lived, the guitar – officially Model 6192 in sunburst finish and 6193 in natural – was renamed the Country Club in 1955, and it continued to be a mainstay of Gretsch's archtop electric line for the next 25 years.

MODEL
Gretsch Electro II

YEAR
1954

PRODUCTION
1951 to 1954

GRETSCH

Tenor guitars were prevalent in the 1930s as they provided tenor banjo players with an easy way to switch to the increasingly popular guitar. By the 1950s most companies would still make almost any model as a tenor, but only by custom order.

This Gretsch electric tenor is a Synchromatic 6031, featuring the cat's eye soundholes that appeared on the Synchromatic acoustic series in 1939 and were the first of many design flairs that would set Gretsch apart from its competitors. Although this instrument is technically an acoustic model with an added pickup, the pickguard has the shape and tortoise pattern of a standard Gretsch guard, and the cutout for the pickup is bound, indicating that it was probably original, factory-installed equipment on this guitar.

As part of Gretsch's across-the line overhaul in 1955, the Synchromatic 6030 (sunburst finish) and 6031 (natural) received a new name – the Constellation – but Gretsch's focus was almost completely on electrics by that time, and the Constellation only lasted to the end of the decade.

266

MODEL
Gretsch Synchromatic 6031 electric tenor

YEAR
Circa 1954

PRODUCTION
1951 to 1954

Gretsch's Corvette hollowbody model was never as famous as the later solidbody Corvette, and with good reason. It was really just a re-named version of Gretsch's original electric model, introduced in 1940 just before World War II brought a halt to electric guitar production, and until 1955 it was still known by its unimaginative, generic but typical prewar model name: Electromatic Spanish.

The Corvette retained the earlier model name on the peghead. The "matic" part tied it in with Gretsch's high-end Synchromatic acoustics, but the 16-inch Corvette was a step below Gertsch's prestigious archtop line. The DeArmond pickup on the Corvette also tied it to an established tradition; DeArmond made the most popular add-on pickups that electric guitarists used to convert acoustic archtops to electric.

The DeArmond pickup, featured on all early- and mid-1950s Gretsch electrics, was (theoretically, at least) a step above Gibson's P-90, with height-adjustable magnet-slug polepieces rather than the simpler screw-poles used by Gibson. It didn't help the Corvette, however, which was left in the dust of Gretsch's more modern designs of the late 1950s.

MODEL
Gretsch Corvette

YEAR
1955

PRODUCTION
1955 to 1959

GRETSCH

The Country Club started life with the generic name Electromatic II in 1951, but in 1954, it received a new name that was the first sign of an across-the-line upgrade in store for the Gretsch line a year later.

The 1955 Grestch catalog abandoned its traditional slogan – That Great Gretsch Sound – and replaced it with the hipper-sounding "Guitars for Moderns." The cover was printed in full color to show off what was, for the time, a radical selection of finish colors, including a Country Club in Cadillac Green.

Jimmie Webster, a pioneer of the fingerboard-tapping technique (that Eddie Van Halen would later appropriate for rock'n'roll), was the man responsible for the vibrant colors, as well as various electronic features and eye-catching ornamentation, that would set Gretsch apart from the competition in the late 1950s. To enhance the special treatment represented by a colorful finish, Gretsch gave each color its own model number. The Country Club in Cadillac Green was Model 6196.

MODEL
Gretsch Country Club

YEAR
1955

PRODUCTION
1954 to 1981

The Streamliner was essentially an upgraded version of Gretsch's original Electromatic Spanish (aka Corvette). In fact, its original model name was the boring but accurate Electromatic 16″ Cutaway. In addition to the cutaway, it was distinguished from the basic Electromatic by its block inlays, and it was available with one or two DeArmond pickups.

The Streamliner name was adopted in 1955, although a sign of its Electromatic origins remained on the headstock. In keeping with other new colors of 1955, such as the White Falcon or the Cadillac Green Country Club, Gretsch offered the Streamliner not only in sunburst and natural finish but also in exotic – exotic-sounding, at least – Jaguar Tan. Although it was listed as being available only by special order, Jaguar Tan had its own special model number, Model 6189.

In 1958, Gretsch celebrated its 75th anniversary by appropriating the basic Streamliner for a new model called the Anniversary. Most of the Streamliner features continued, but the Jaguar Tan finish option did not survive the transition.

MODEL
Gretsch Streamliner

YEAR
1955

PRODUCTION
1955 to 1959

GRETSCH

In 1955, Gretsch abandoned its established image as a maker of traditional archtops and gave itself a complete makeover. The new and improved guitarmaker introduced itself with a splashy array of finish colors and new models. At the top of the line, in gleaming white with gold trim, was the White Falcon.

Gretsch literature explained that this "luxurious styling" was created for the player "who is willing to pay the price," and at $600, the White Falcon was $200 more than the next most expensive model. But no other Gretsch matched its features, starting with a unique "Cadillac" tailpiece, so nicknamed because its V-shaped motif was similar to the V used with the automotive logo. The V was repeated in the truss-rod cover design, the headstock shape, and the gold sparkle wings framing the logo.

The Falcon is one of the more desirable Gretches on today's vintage guitar market, due in part to its use by rockers Stephen Stills and Neil Young and also due to the rarity that its high price ensured.

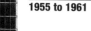

MODEL

Gretsch White Falcon (single cutaway)

YEAR

1955

PRODUCTION

1955 to 1961

The Gretsch Convertible was a classic archtop electric jazz guitar – almost. It had a 17-inch cutaway body with a spruce top, and it appeared to have a floating pickup with controls mounted in the fingerboard so as not to impede the acoustic vibrations of the top. The DeArmond pickup was not secured to the top, but the top was nevertheless cut out to make room for the extended pickup polepieces. Depsite the hole in the top, it lived up to its "convertible" billing as a guitar that could be played acoustically or electrically.

Introduced with other "Guitars for Moderns" in 1955, the Convertible was deemed worthy of the catalog cover (the back cover), thanks to its color scheme of Lotus Ivory top and Copper Mist back (sunburst was available only by special order).

When Gretsch replaced the single-coil pickup with a new Filter'Tron humbucker in 1959, jazz guitarist Sal Salvador was enlisted as an endorser, and with a little cosmetic improvement and the more conventional sunburst as the standard finish, it lasted in the line for another decade.

MODEL
Gretsch Convertible

YEAR
1957

PRODUCTION
1955 to 1959

GRETSCH

In 1952, when Gibson signed Les Paul to an endorsement agreement, Gretsch signed its first endorser, folksinger Burl Ives, for a flat-top acoustic model, and the results couldn't have been more disparate. By 1954, Les Paul's star was still rising, carrying Gibson guitar sales along with it, and Gretsch went looking for their own guitar star. They found Chet Atkins.

Atkins had been playing his distinctive, smooth, country-influenced style on a D'Angelico archtop equipped with a floating DeArmond pickup and a vibrato. For his Gretsch model, all he asked for were a brass nut, Bigsby vibrato and heavier bracing under the top (for more sustain). Gretsch staffer Jimmie Webster, the man responsible for the aesthetic flair that took over the entire Gretsch line in the mid 1950s, came up with the Western ornamention.

From this first Chet Atkins model, commonly known today simply as Model 6120, Gretsch expanded the Atkins line as Atkins's fame grew – to the point that his models carried Gretsch through the 1960s and well into the 1970s.

MODEL
Gretsch Chet Atkins Hollow Body (single cutway)

YEAR
1957

PRODUCTION
1955 to 1961

Even without the Chet Atkins signature signpost on the pickguard, this Custom Hollow Body is easily identifiable as some sort of an Atkins model.

The horseshoe inlay on the peghead is the same as that on Gretsch's Chet Atkins Hollow Body (Model 6120), having replaced the steer head in 1956. The body is the same size (15.75 inches wide) and shape as the Chet model. The Bigsby and metal bar bridge are features that Atkins specified on all his models.

This guitar not only has Atkins features, it was made for Atkins himself. Its most unusual feature is the addition of pickup polepieces under the bass strings in the upper register of the fingerboard. They were designed to run a signal through an octave effect to enhance the bass tones. The innovative electronics did not take, but the simulated f-holes of inlaid gold-sparkle material were precursors of the f-hole inlays (and the painted f-holes) that would appear in 1961 on the earliest versions of the Chet Atkins Country Gentleman model.

MODEL
**Gretsch Hollow Body
Custom**

YEAR
1956

PRODUCTION
1956

classic electrics

GRETSCH

The Gretsch Clipper was quite a "plain Jane" in the midst of large-bodied White Falcons, Cadillac Green Country Clubs and Amber Red Chet Atkins guitars, but the single-pickup, thinbody model held its own against Gretch's leading ladies for over a decade.

The Clipper's success was simple – it was a bona fide Gretsch, but without the frills and without the added expense. After starting in 1956 with just a sunburst finish and a cheap pickup (probably made by Harmony), the Clipper got an optional natural finish in 1959 and Gretsch's standard single-coil HiLo'Tron pickup in 1960. The natural finish was quickly discontinued, but the sunburst Model 6186 thrived at the bottom of the line. It was never deemed worthy of the "neo-classic" thumbprint inlays or even the zero fret that other Gretsches had, although for a short time, it had a palm-operated vibrato that was unavailable on any of the higher models.

In 1972 Gretsch discontinued the original Clipper but replaced it with a two-pickup Clipper that lived on as the entry-level Gretsch until 1975.

MODEL
Gretsch Clipper (single pickup)

YEAR
1957

PRODUCTION
1956 to 1971

274

Within a year after Gretsch introduced the Chet Atkins Hollow Body, Atkins had a Top 20 pop hit with "Mr. Sandman." In 1957, Gretsch capitalized on Atkins's fast-growing fame by creating a new model and naming it after another Atkins recording whose title fit the man playing the guitar – Country Gentleman.

Aside from the rural signpost on the pickguard, the Country Gentleman left all the Western appointments of the earlier Atkins model behind. It featured a larger, 17-inch body, and most early examples had simulated f-holes that were actually black plastic inlays (later examples had paint or inlaid binding material to simulate the holes). Gretsch was close behind Gibson in developing double-coil "humbucking" pickups, and the Country Gentleman was fitted with these new units, called Filter'Trons because, according to Gretsch literature, they filtered out *all* electronic hum.

With a rich mahogany-stained finish, gold-plated hardware and a small plaque on the headstock with the model name and serial number, it looked expensive, and was – second only to the White Falcon.

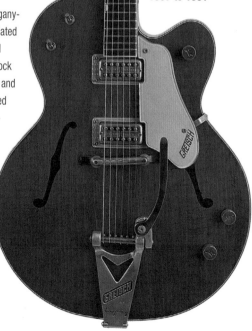

MODEL

Gretsch Chet Atkins Country Gentleman (single cutaway)

YEAR

1961

PRODUCTION

1957 to 1961

GRETSCH

News that Gretsch was working on a double-coil humbucking pickup spurred Gibson to speed up their own development of a humbucker, and Gibson beat Gretsch to the market in 1957. However, Gretsch one-upped Gibson a year later when the Country Club appeared with not only new humbuckers, but with split coils for stereo capability.

Guitarist Jimmie Webster introduced the "Project-o-sonic" Country Club in a flyer that proclaimed "The biggest guitar news since electrification." The two Filter'Tron pickups had only three polepieces, with one set of polepieces under the bass strings and the other under the treble strings. With a click of the three-way "closing switch," the player got "Stereophonic Bi-Aural sound disbursement," with the treble strings going to one amplifier and the bass strings to another.

The system required a special cord and jack box, plus an extra amplifier, and it was only well-suited for players whose style effectively split the guitar into a three-stringed treble instrument and a three-stringed bass instrument. While basic Country Clubs continued to sell well, the stereo version did not last five years.

MODEL
Gretsch Country Club Stereo

YEAR
1958

PRODUCTION
1958 to 1960

In 1958, following Gretsch's introduction of the Country Gentlemen as the high-end Chet Atkisn model, the company balanced out the Atkins line expansion with a plainer model called the Tennessean.

With a body width of 16 inches, the Tennessean was the same size as the original Atkins Hollow Body (Model 6120), but it only had one pickup – a Filter'Tron humbucker mounted in the bridge position. It had open f-holes until 1961, after which they became simulated with paint or binding, just like those on the Country Gentleman. Like all Atkins models of the era, the Tennessean had a metal nut and a Bigsby vibrato tailpiece. Most examples had a cherry or walnut stain finish, but a few sported the eye-catching orange more often identified with the 6120.

Curiously, the Tennessean did not change to a double-cutaway body when the higher Atkins models did in 1961, but it nevertheless remained a solid sales performer in the Gretsch Hollow Body line until Atkins ended his endorsement in 1980.

YEAR
Gretsch Tennessean
6119

YEAR
1958

PRODUCTION
1958 to 1979

GRETSCH

Gretsch celebrated its 75th anniversary in 1958 with an Anniversary model, available with one or two pickups. The 16-inch single-cutaway model was basically a renamed and renumbered Streamliner (which had been introduced in 1951) or, from another perspective, it was simply a Chet Atkins Hollow Body (6120) with a different finish.

Colorful finishes were Gretsch's calling card in the second half of the 1950s, and the Anniversary introduced a new color scheme – a two-tone Smoke Green that was lighter on the top and darker on the back (traditional sunburst was also available). With an unbound fingerboard and peghead it was less expensive than the fancier models, but its pickup was the same Filter'Tron humbucker (until 1960, at least) that Gretsch put on the more expensive models.

The Anniversary of 1958 was successful enough that Gretsch continued the "celebration party" indefinitely, making the Anniversary a permanent member of the Gretsch electric archtop line. The single-pickup version remained in production through 1971, and the double-pickup model lasted even longer.

MODEL
Gretsch Anniversary

YEAR
1958

PRODUCTION
1958 to 1971

The two pickups – not the anniversary –
were the "double" element of Gretsch's
Double Anniversary model of 1958. Along with
a single-pickup version, it marked the
company's 75th anniversary and then
continued as a regular production model.

Initially fitted with Gretsch's Filter'Tron
humbucking pickups, the Anniversary was
curiously downgraded in 1960 to the weaker Hi-
Lo'Trons. Further evidence that someone at
Gretsch had lost the celebratory spirit came in
1961, when the Chet Atkins Hollow Body (Model
6120) – essentially the same guitar as the
Anniversary but with a different finish – went to
a double-cutaway body, along with other high-
end models, while the Anniversary models
stayed with the single-cutaway body.

At the same time, in a dubious gesture to
offset the Anniversary's second-class status,
Gretsch offered the Double Anniversary with
stereo for several years (1961–63) and
gave it a bound fingerboard. In the
1970s, Gretsch took away the
model's identity by
discontinuing the Smoke
Green finish and eliminating
the nameplate on the peghead,
and in 1974, the 16-year-long
Anniversary celebration finally
came to an end.

MODEL
**Gretsch Double
Anniversary**

YEAR
1961

PRODUCTION
1958 to 1974

GRETSCH

I n 1958, Gretsch backed off a bit on the White Falcon's ornamentation but maintained its place at the top of the hollowbody electric line by offering it with stereo electronics.

The split-coil pickup, with apparent missing polepieces, was the telltale sign of stereo capability on the first stereo Falcons. Despite the more complicated choices offered by stereo, the controls were initially no more elaborate than on the non-stereo version. Instead of three knobs and two switches, the first stereo Falcon had two knobs and three switches.

In ormanenattion, a straight-across peghead logo replaced the Falcon's original vertical logo with gold wings, and engraved "humptop block" fingerboard inlays gave way to the "neo classic" (as Gretsch called them) or "thumbprint" (as everybody else called them) markers. It could be argued that the smaller inlays were more tasteful and that they allowed the ebony fingerboard to elegantly contrast with the white and gold, but the Falcon had always been about opulence, not elegance. The 1958 Falcon was still an eye-catcher, but it was a step down from the original.

MODEL
Gretsch White Falcon Stereo (first version)

YEAR
1958

PRODUCTION
1958 to 1959

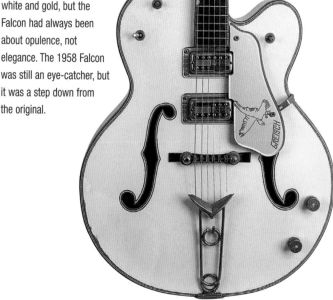

Gibson introduced double-cutaway thinline electrics in 1958 with the ES-335 semi-hollow model, and Gretsch was not far behind. But rather than going through the expense of introducing and marketing an all-new model, in 1961 Gretsch simply began "upgrading" its top models from single-cutaway to double-cutaway.

By the time the Chet Atkins 6120 went to the double-cut body, it had lost most of its Western ornamentation. Even the rural signpost on the pickguard was gone, although the signature remained. The horseshoe on the peghead would last only until 1964 when the generic Hollow Body name was replaced with Nashville and a metal plate with the model name replaced the horseshoe.

In the meantime, the model acquired several new features, including Filter'Tron humbucking pickups (1958), a distinctive Gretsch version of the Bigsby vibrola, a foam-rubber string mute (just above the bridge), and a large, snap-on back pad. Discontinued when Atkins left Gretsch in 1980, the Nashville would be revived in both single- and double-cutaway versions in the 1990s.

281

MODEL
Gretsch Chet Atkins Hollow Body (double cutaway)

YEAR
1962

PRODUCTION
1961 to 1980

GRETSCH

In the first ten years of Chet Atkins's association with Gretsch, Atkins had gone from an up-and-coming country musician to one of the most influential figures in the music business. As a guitarist, his records were played by pop radio stations, and his distinctive finger-picking style was being copied by guitarists around the world. Moreover, he had begun producing records for RCA and was one of the architects of the Nashville Sound, the smooth, echo-laden productions that revived country music record sales in the early 1960s.

The growing notoriety of Gretsch's Chet Atkins line was pushed into overdrive in 1964, when The Beatles appeared on American TV, featuring George Harrison playing a double-cutaway Country Gentleman. His choice of an Atkins model was no coincidence, as evidenced by his Atkins-style solo in the middle of the Beatles hit "All My Loving."

Among vintage guitar collectors, the earlier single-cutaway of the Atkins Hollow Body (6120) is more popular than the double-cut, but thanks to The Beatles, the double-cutaway Country Gentleman is the most highly coveted version of that model.

MODEL

Gretsch Country Gentleman (double cutaway)

YEAR

1963

PRODUCTION

1961 to 1980

Gretsch changed its two top 17-inch models, the White Falcon and the Country Gentleman, from single-cutaway to double-cutaway bodies in 1961, but curiously, the Country Club was left with a single cutaway. That left a hole in the line that Gretsch filled with the double-cut Viking model in 1964.

The Viking had the standard appointments of a high-end guitar, including Gretsch's new Super'Tron humbucking pickups, a string mute, gold-plated hardware, and a nameplate on the peghead. But that was just a starting point. The new "T-Zone" fingerboard featured slightly slanted frets in the area of the dot inlays, which were designed to provide better intonation.

Perhaps the most bizarre Gretsch innovation was the "tuning fork" bridge – a floating piece of metal that extended into the body, where it was shaped like an actual tuning fork. The idea was presumably to create a resonance, but it would only be effective in keys related to the pitch of the tuning fork. Players who wanted better functionality from the Viking removed the tuning fork and repositioned the roller bridge.

MODEL
Gretsch Viking

YEAR
1967

PRODUCTION
1964 to 1974

GRETSCH

The phenomenal success of the Beatles film *A Hard Day's Night* prompted Hollywood to create a similar product that could be fed on a weekly basis to American TV audiences. They auditioned musicians for a group called The Monkees and hired pop music publishing impresario Don Kirshner to ensure that the songs were good. *The Monkees* debuted in 1965, and the show was an instant success, helped in no small part by a series of bona fide hit records.

Gretsch was already enjoying considerable notoriety from George Harrison's use of a Chet Atkins Country Gentleman model with The Beatles, and The Monkees presented a golden opportunity for even greater success. The Monkees model featured a double-cutaway body and a fingerboard with "thumbprint" inlays on both sides. The pickguard sported the group's logo, and just in case the picture wasn't clear, the metal plate on the peghead identified this guitar as "Rock 'n' Roll Model."

The TV show ran through 1968, and when it was canceled, the Gretsch Monkees model met the same fate.

284

MODEL
Gretsch Monkees

YEAR
1967

PRODUCTION
1966 to 1968

Lagging a bit behind Rickenbacker, Gibson, and Fender, who all introduced 12-string electrics in 1965, Gretsch jumped on the 12-string bandwagon in 1967.

The Gretsch was a hollowbody, different from the semi-hollow or solidbodies of its main competitors, but the Rickenbacker influence was evident in Gretsch's abbreviated triangular fingerboard inlays, which never appeared on another Gretsch, before or after the 12-string. Introduced just as Gretsch was being sold to the Baldwin company, the 12-string lacked the flair of a colorful finish (it was offered only in sunburst or natural). Moreover, the company seemed a little confused about its specifications, offering it with a 16-inch or 17-inch body, but under only one model number per finish color.

The model got an unexpected boost when, despite the existence of a Gretsch Monkees model, Monkees guitarist Mike Nesmith appeared on their TV show playing a natural-finish, 17-inch 12-string. Like The Monkees, whose show ended after the 1968 season, the electric 12-string proved to be only a passing attraction, and after 1972, Gretsch only offered the 12-string by special order.

MODEL
Gretsch 12-String

YEAR
1967

PRODUCTION
1967 to 1972

GRETSCH

The Rally was the lowest of the Gretsch's three new 16-inch double-cutaway hollowbodies of 1967, by virtue of its single-coil Hi-Lo'Tron pickups.

Except for the pickups, the Rally's electronics were the same as the higher two models, the Black Hawk and Streamliner, and what the Rally may have lost in sound, it made up for in aesthetics. In a throwback to Gretsch's color splashes of the 1950s, the model sported a dark Rally Green stain finish that let the wood grain show through or a two-tone finish scheme that featured a Bamboo Yellow top and Copper Mist back, sides and neck. To drive home the connection to fast cars, the Rally's pickguard and truss-rod cover featured sports car style racing stripes.

The Rally failed to capture the interest of anyone in the guitar market except, surprisingly, Fender. In 1969, as the Rally was about to be discontinued, someone at Fender thought the automotive tie-in was a good idea and put racing stripes on a Fender Mustang to create the Competition Mustang.

MODEL
Gretsch Rally

YEAR
1967

PRODUCTION
1967 to 1969

Georgе Van Eps was the father of the seven-string guitar, and Gretsch was the only company to offer a seven-string jazz guitar as a regular catalog model.

Van Eps was the son of classical/ragtime five-string banjo player Fred Van Eps. He started his career as a swing guitarist, joining Benny Goodman's band in 1934. In 1938, he had Epiphone make a seven-string for him, and with the extra bass string he developed a unique style that featured a bass line, chordal support, and melody – all at the same time. He made a series of definitive recordings with the seven-string, beginning with *Mellow Guitar* in 1956.

Van Eps's seven-string style had a sizeable enough following for Gretsch to give him a signature model in 1968. The 17-inch cutaway archtop had a pair of Gretsch's Filter'Tron humbucking pickups with extra-heavy metal covers. It was also offered in a six-string version (Van Eps wrote instructionals and arrangements for six-string guitar as well). Gretsch continued to catalog the Van Eps model through 1979, and jazz players continue to play seven-strings today.

MODEL
Gretsch Van Eps

YEAR
1977

PRODUCTION
1968 to 1979

GRETSCH

Beginning in the mid 1950s, Gretsch's Chet Atkins models were the foundation of the company's success. Atkins never cared for the flashy ornamentation – the "cows and cactus" inlay engraving, the large G-brand on the body, etc. – of his early models. He finally took design matters into his own hands in 1972 with the Super Chet model.

His goal was simply to design the most beautiful guitar, period. To that end, he put floral-pattern, abalone pearl inlays on the peghead and fingerboard, and he even created a tailpiece with a wooden insert where more abalone could be inlaid. Gold-plated hardware and an Autumn Red finish (or Rich Walnut) enhanced the elegant look. If advertising was to be believed, Atkins achieved his goal. In ads for the Super Chet, above his signature he was quoted: "It's the best there is."

Atkins made this Super Chet – one of his personal instruments – even better. In place of the pickup selector switch on the upper bass bout, he added four mini-toggle switches for extra electronic effects.

MODEL
Gretsch Super Chet

YEAR
1972

PRODUCTION
1972 to 1980

Gretsch's Project-o-sonic stereo, which was available on the White Falcon in 1958, had initially been controlled with a simple two-knob, three-switch system, but within a year of Project-o-sonic's introduction, Gretsch's head designer Jimmie Webster couldn't resist making it better – or at least more complicated.

The Filter'Tron pickups with three missing polepieces were no longer a visual indication of stereo, having been replaced by standard-looking units, but a stereo guitar was now even more easily identifiable by the extra switches – five switches in all, along with two knobs. The 1959 version featured four switches on the upper bass bout; by 1965, they were moved to the lower treble bout.

Like the higher Chet Atkins Hollow Body and Country Gentleman, the White Falcon was "modernized" with a double cutaway body in the early 1960s. By the early 1970s, however, there was enough demand for the original single-cutaway that Gretsch reintroduced it, and the White Falcon became the only Gretsch model offered in single- and double-cutaway versions at the same time.

289

MODEL

Gretsch White Falcon Stereo (double cutaway)

YEAR
1980

PRODUCTION
1972 to 1980

GRETSCH

By the 1970s, Gretsch was losing the attention of rock'n'roll players, and in an attempt to recapture some of its earlier glory, the company "undid" a design mistake of the early 1960s and brought back the single-cutaway version of its Duo-Jet series. Although usually grouped with solidbodies because of their small body and lack of soundholes, the backs of these guitars were heavily routed.

The Country Roc of 1974 was modeled after two similar 1950s models: the Round-Up and the Chet Atkins 6121. The horseshoe, the "cows and cactus" inlay, the G-brand, the belt-buckle tailpiece, the tooled leather on the rims – every element of ornamentation was purely Western, but in the music world, country and Western music had separated. Western swing was all but forgotten, while country music – particularly the rock-tinged country played by bands such as The Eagles – was on the rise.

Gretsch tried to cash in on the new trend by naming this model Country Roc, but as guitar buyers quickly noticed, it was not really a country or a rock guitar, and it lasted less than five years.

MODEL
Gretsch Country Roc

YEAR
1975

PRODUCTION
1974 to 1978

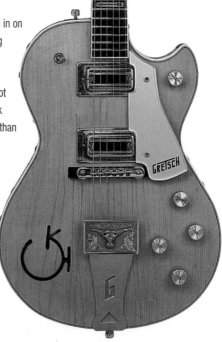

Although Chet Atkins's influence continued to be as strong through the 1970s as it was in earlier periods, Gretsch's quality was falling, and one of the most successful endorsement relationships in guitar history (second only to Gibson and Les Paul) ended in 1980.

Ownership of Gretsch had left the Gretsch family in 1967, when the company was sold to the Baldwin piano company, and Gretsch changed hands again in 1980, after which production slowed to a trickle. Fred Gretsch, great-grandson of the founder, reacquired his family's company in 1985 and began offering new, Japanese-made models in 1990.

Gretsch revived the Atkins models – the foundation of Gretsch's success a generation earlier – without the Atkins signature or model name, and the Country Gentleman (Model 6122) became the Country Classic. The Country Classic II was the double-cutaway with 1962 styling, eventually becoming model G6122–1962, while the single-cut 1958 version was dubbed the Country Classic I. After Atkins's death in 2001, his estate returned his endorsement to Gretsch, and this model is once again called the Chet Atkins Country Gentleman.

291

MODEL

Gretsch Country Classic G6122-1962

YEAR

1993

PRODUCTION

1990 to current

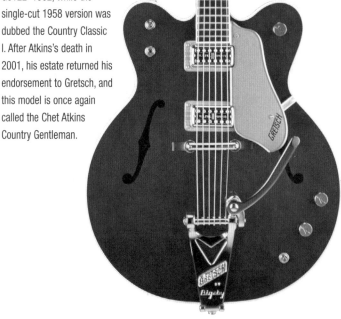

GRETSCH

classic electrics

Gretsch refrained from jumping into the doubleneck arena with Gibson in the 1960s or with Rickenbacker in the 1970s, but if Gretsch had made a doubleneck electric back then, it might have looked like the Nashville G6120-6/12.

Introduced in 1997, the six-string and 12-string model took its inspiration – like most of the guitars in the modern Gretsch line – from a tried-and-true model dating back to Gretsch's glory years of the late 1950s and early 1960s. The horseshoe on the pegheads, the orange-stain finish, and the Gretsch/Bigsby vibrola were all lifted directly from the Chet Atkins Hollow Body, aka Model 6120. The attempt to incorporate the single-cutaway body shape the early 6120s, however, left the doubleneck with an awkward bulge on the upper bass bout.

Chet Atkins's endorsement was not available at the time the 6120-6/12 was introduced, so the doubleneck, like other 6120-styled models in the new Gretsch line, was named Nashville – which has been Gretsch's name for the 6120 from 1964 to current times.

292

MODEL

Gretsch Nashville Double Neck G6120-6/12

YEAR

1997

PRODUCTION

1997 to current

Brian Setzer's signature Gretsch models played a vital role in the 1990s in reviving Gretsch's reputation and promoting the company's new line of high-quality, Japanese-made guitars.

As front man for the Stray Cats, Setzer had led a rockabilly revival in the early 1980s, playing hot guitar licks on his 1959 Gretsch Chet Atkins 6120. In the 1990s, he reinvented himself in a swing band setting, and the Brian Setzer Orchestra led a new wave of interest in big band music with their remake of "Jump, Jive an' Wail."

Gretsch took advantage of Setzer's second round of fame by giving him a signature model in 1994 that was based on his vintage 6120. The Brian Setzer Hot Rod followed in 1999, featuring vintage-style "trestle" top bracing along with such Setzer specs as oversized soundholes, locking tuners, and custom-wound humbucking pickups (or, as an option, pickups made by TV Jones). In the best Gretsch tradition, the Hot Rod was offered in an array of flashy finish colors ranging from Lime Gold to Purple to Tangerine.

MODEL

Gretsch Setzer Hot Rod G6120SH

YEAR

2003

PRODUCTION

1999 to current

GRETSCH

The neck-position pickup looks out of place among the vintage style appointments of this reissue of the 1957 Chet Atkins Hollow Body (Model 6120). It's actually a Gibson-style P-90, and it's on this Gretsch because rockabilly star Eddie Cochran put one on his Gretsch 6120 in the 1950s.

Cochran hit the Top Ten in 1958 with "Summertime Blues" and appeared in three rock'n'roll movies before he died in a London traffic accident in 1960. Along with instrumental star Duane Eddy (whose "twangy guitar" was a Gretsch 6120 before it was a Guild), Cochran helped build Gretsch's reputation as the home of the rockabilly guitar – a reputation that continues today with Brian Setzer's endorsement.

Gretsch's press announcement for the model in 2001 was headlined "Rockabilly Legend Eddie Cochran Remembered with G6120W-1957 Model," but before long, Gretsch seemed to forget. The current promotional pitch for the model known as the 1957 Chet Atkins Hollow Body begins with "C'mon Everybody," the title of one of Cochran's singles, but Cochran's name is no longer mentioned.

MODEL
Gretsch Nashville 1957 Western G6120W-1957

YEAR
2003

PRODUCTION
2001 to current

Despite having 1959 in its model name, this Country Classic was not a reissue of a 1959 Chet Atkins Country Gentleman (Model 6122). It was actually a custom-design model from guitarist Paul Yandell, who performed with Atkins for decades and was instrumental in convincing Atkins's estate to bring the Atkins endorsement back to Gretsch after Atkins's death in 2001.

When Chet Atkins left Gretsch in 1980, after a quarter-century of endorsement support, Gretsch tried to continue the Country Gentleman under the new name of Southern Belle, but the company was in such deep financial trouble that only a few were assembled in Mexico from leftover parts. In the 1990s, with Atkins firmly established as a Gibson endorser, new owner Fred Gretsch (great-grandson of the founder) introduced Japanese-made reissues of the 1958 single-cutaway Country Gent and the 1962 double-cutaway version under the model name Country Classic.

When Fender took over development and distribution of Gretsch in 2003, the Yandell-designed Country Classic 1959 appeared, featuring a slightly wider neck, custom TV Jones pickups, and a tubular-arm Bigsby vibrato.

295

MODEL
Gretsch Country Classic 1959 G6122-1959

YEAR
2003

PRODUCTION
2003 to current

GRETSCH

Although Gretsch's standard 1990s line of Japanese-made guitars already capitalized on the vintage appeal of the company's classic 1950s models, when Gretsch came under Fender's management control in 2003, Fender created a higher echelon of historic reissues, made in the Gretsch (Fender) Custom Shop in Corona, California.

The White Falcon G6136CST (CST for Custom Shop) featured all the trimmings of the original Falcon, including the "Cadillac" tailpiece, red rhinestones in the control knobs, pickups recreated by renowned vintage pickup maker Seymour Duncan, engraved pearl inlays, Melita bridge, gold sparkle binding, vintage-style body and neck construction, and even a nitrocellulose lacquer finish.

The original White Falcon of 1955 was the highest-priced model in the Gretsch line and, in the 21st century, the Custom Shop version maintained that position. Its list price of $11,000 was more than twice that of Gretsch's most expensive regular-production model, and it paved the way for a Custom Shop Chet Atkins Hollow Body and other limited-run models to follow.

MODEL

Gretsch White Falcon G6136CST

YEAR

2004

PRODUCTION

2004 to current

In the late 1950s, before restrictions on imports were lifted, London-based Emile Grimshaw made some of the highest-quality guitars available to British players. Grimshaw and his father, Emile Sr. (who died in 1943), had been making banjos and guitars since 1934, and his electrics combined quality with unique designs.

The deep cutaway of this Electric Deluxe model stood out like a sore thumb, but its most unusual feature was its electronic configuration. The controls were housed in the pickguard (which had its own unusual, meandering shape), but the pickups were not the "floating" type that were typically found with pickguard-mounted controls. The humbucking pickup in the bridge position was clearly mounted in the top, and there was a second pickup concealed in the fingerboard extension – a concept borrowed from Gibson's J-160E electric flat-top model.

Grimshaw found some success in the 1960s making copies of Gibson Les Pauls at a time when Gibson did not offer the model, but ultimately, Japanese makers did it at a lower cost and drove Grimshaw out of business by the end of the decade.

MODEL
Grimshaw Electric Deluxe

YEAR
Late 1950s

PRODUCTION
Late 1950s to early 1960s

GUILD

The six pushbuttons on Guild's Stratford X-350 of 1953 looked remarkably like the pickup selector system on Epiphone's Zephyr Emperor Regent model, and the similarity was no coincidence. Guild was formed with key employees from Epiphone who had stayed in New York when Epi production was moved to Philadelphia.

Guild made a huge splash with its debut line in 1953, which included seven large-bodied (17 inches wide) electric archtops – five with cutaways and two non-cutaways. Despite the X-350's upscale appointments – including block inlays, gold-plated hardware, three pickups, and the pushbutton system – it was only a midline model.

It went through a number of changes, among them a laminated maple top (the original was laminated spruce), a shorter scale length (from 25.5 to 24.75 inches), and humbucking pickups, but like Gibson's three-pickup ES-5, it succumbed in the 1960s, as the Folk Boom switched Guild's focus to acoustics and electric players began to realize that, for most performance situations, two pickups were enough.

MODEL
Guild Stratford X-350

YEAR
1954

PRODUCTION
1953 to 1964

In carrying on the Epiphone tradition with ex-Epiphone employees, Guild borrowed the signature inlay of high-end Epi models – a mother-of-pearl block with abalone V-wedge – for the top model in the Guild line, the Stuart X-550.

Guild initially gave natural-finish guitars a higher model number than the sunburst equivalent, so the sunburst version was the X-500. Around 1960 that disparity was eliminated when the X-550 became the X-500B (B for Blond finish). Beyond the name adjustment, the model went through few changes, receiving humbucking pickups in 1963 and a master volume control around 1961.

Although most high-end guitars did not sell as well as lower-priced models, the Stuart remained the flagship of Guild's archtop electric line through folk, rock, disco, metal and every other kind of music in the second half of the 20th century, while its fellow 1950s models fell by the wayside (most of them in the 1960s). The Stuart X-500 finally met its end in 1994 when it was upgraded, ironically, to a version with a solid spruce top called the X-700.

MODEL
Guild Stuart X-550

YEAR
1958

PRODUCTION
1953 to 1994

GUILD

The Artist Award was Guild's Johnny Smith Award model, but only for a brief period.

Guild was founded in 1952, the same year Smith released "Moonlight in Vermont," the record that brought him fame for his lush "chord melody" jazz style. In 1955, Guild tapped him for a signature model, and the Johnny Smith Award debuted in 1956, by which time Smith was one of the most influential and respected guitarists in jazz (although he never considered himself a true jazz musician). Though not as flamboyant as Gibson's Les Paul, Smith brought an impeccable reputation to the Guild line.

Unfortunately, the Johnny Smith Award was not the guitar Smith had specified. Guild had altered it in order to make it easier to produce, and Guild's production head refused to change it back to Smith's specs. Smith ended the relationship, and Guild simply renamed the model the Artist Award. It remained the most prestigious model in Guild's archtop line through several Guild ownership changes but was finally discontinued – along with all other Guild electrics – in 2007.

MODEL
Guild Artist Award

YEAR
1976

PRODUCTION
1956 to 2007

Guild introduced a pair of thin-bodied archtops with a pointed cutaway in 1958, so the Starfire models of 1960 were not really new – they were just better looking. Their cherry-stained "Starfire red" finishes set them apart from the traditional sunburst and natural finishes on every Guild that preceded them.

The Starfire I had a single pickup, the II had a pair of pickups, and the III featured two pickups plus a vibrato made by Bigsby. In 1963 the Starfires were further distanced from the more traditional thinline models when their single-coil pickups were replaced with humbuckers. By that time, all three Starfires were offered in such eye-catching finish colors as Emerald Green, Honey Amber and Ebony Grain.

The Starfire name worked well enough that Guild used it on a series of double-cutaway semi-hollow models – The Starfire IV, V, VI and XII – beginning in 1963. The single-cut Starfire III was discontinued in 1974 but Guild brought it back as a reissue from 1995–2005.

MODEL
Guild Starfire III

YEAR
1961

PRODUCTION
1960 to 1973

GUILD

There were rock'n'roll guitarists before Duane Eddy, but his 1958 instrumental hit "Rebel Rouser" made him the first genuine guitar god.

"Mr. Twangy Guitar," as Eddy was nicknamed, initially got his low, cutting tone from a Gretsch Chet Atkins Hollow Body (6120), but as early as 1960 he was playing a Guild Manhattan X-175, the plainest of Guild's 17-inch, double-pickup archtops. Guild had just lost the endorsement of Johnny Smith, one of the most prominent jazz players of the 1950s, and Eddy more than filled the void.

For Eddy's signature model, Guild started with the top-of-the-line Stuart X-500 but with the thinner, 2-inch body depth of the newly introduced T-500. With the addition of a Bigsby and a master volume control, the DE-500 was complete. The original version featured white DeArmond single-coil pickups, which were replaced by Guild humbuckers in 1963. Although Eddy would not have another Top 20 single, his name gave Guild needed credibility in the world of rock'n'roll, and his model became one of Guild's few vintage classics.

MODEL

Guild Duane Eddy Deluxe DE-500

YEAR

1962

PRODUCTION

1962 to 1986

Bert Weedon was the first British guitarist to score an instrumental hit. His 1959 recording of "Guitar Boogie Shuffle" and his instructional book *Play in a Day*, made him one of the earliest influences on a generation of British rockers.

In the early 1960s, Weedon's guitar of choice was Guild's new thinline, single-cutaway Starfire III, and he got together with Guild's British distributor, Boosey & Hawkes, to put his signature on a Guild model. They came up with what was essentially a Duane Eddy model except for the body, which was a double-cutaway semi-hollow style that was new to Guild. Weedon received his guitar in early 1963, and later that year Guild introduced its first double-cutaway Starfire models, using the same body.

While Weedon had quite a successful career as a session player, he didn't look or act like a rock star. He was unknown in the U.S., so Guild only offered the model in the U.K. Even in his home country it did not sell well, and it was last made in 1966.

MODEL
Guild Bert Weedon

YEAR
1966

PRODUCTION
1963 to 1966

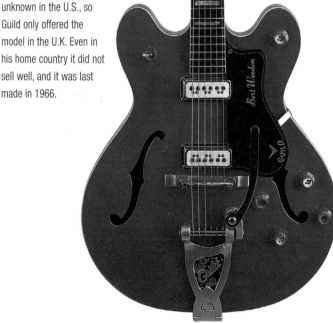

Beginning in 1954, when Guild first put names with its original model numbers, the Stuart name signified the company's best electric archtop. The Stuart X-500 was one of the few consistencies in the model line as Guild underwent three ownership changes: to Avnet, an electronics company, in 1966; to an investment group, doing business as Guild Music Coproration, in 1986; and then in 1989, in the midst of a court-ordered financial restructuring, to FAAS Corporation, which became U.S. Music.

In 1994, Guild upgraded the Stuart model, as indicated by the change in model number from 500 to 700. The only significant change was the top – from laminated maple to solid, carved spruce.

The Stuart X-700 made it through yet another ownership change, when Fender bought Guild in 1995, and then received another upgrade in 1999 when famed archtop maker Bob Benedetto joined Fender and gave it a makeover. It continued simply as the Stuart model in the Benedetto series, and its long run ended when Benedetto left Fender/Guild in 2006.

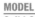

MODEL
Guild Stuart X-700

YEAR
1995

PRODUCTION
1994 to 2000

L ike virtually all Harmony guitars since the company's founding in the 1890s, the Meteor of the early 1960s was an "entry-level" instrument, a guitar designed for beginning players or musicians on a budget. As this rare left-handed Meteor shows, it had the same essential elements as a Gibson – two pickups, each with a tone and volume control. It wasn't until the guitar was played that the difference in quality – particularly the weak pickups – became apparent.

Not all guitarists viewed the low-level performance of the Meteor as a hindrance, however. Dave Davies of The Kinks put it to good use, pushing the Meteor's thick, distorted pickup sound through a small Elpico amplifier (with a cut speaker cone) to create the classic "hook" guitar lick that drove The Kinks' 1964 hit "You Really Got Me."

Another influential British guitarist, Peter Green, started out on a Meteor, but he didn't find it as useful as Davies did; it was the Meteor that Green traded in for the Les Paul that he played when he replaced Eric Clapton in John Mayall's Bluesbreakers.

MODEL
Harmony Meteor H70

YEAR
1965

PRODUCTION
Early 1960s 1967

HARMONY

Harmony capitalized on the dawn of the Space Age with such "buzz-word" model names as Meteor, Mars, Mercury, Jupiter and – the most popular of all – the Rocket.

Initially offered in sunburst finish only, the Rocket gained its more familiar red finish in 1963. Available as the Rocket I (single pickup), Rocket II (two pickups) and Rocket III (three pickups), it provided not just a cheaper alternative to Gibson's ES-125T, but an alternative with more features. The pickups, for example, were "GoldenTone Indox" units made by DeArmond. The "Ultra-Slim" neck featured a "Torque-Lok" adjustment feature. While these were high-class names for a low-end product, the H59 nevertheless sported three pickups, a feature that was only available in the Gibson archtop electric line on the ES-5, at several times the cost of the Harmony.

The Rocket was upgraded to a double-cutaway in 1968, and it eventually gained the dubious status of being offered in a build-it-yourself version marketed by the Heathkit eletronics company. It lasted in the line until 1970.

MODEL
**Harmony Rocket III
H59 (single cutaway)**

YEAR
Circa 1964

PRODUCTION
1960 to 1967

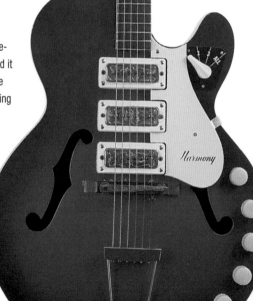

The H77 was about as fancy a guitar as could be expected from a budget brand. Harmony catalogs touted it as having "maximum electronics," and each of the three DeArmond pickups had its own tone and volume controls plus its own on/off switch – giving it more versatility than any Gibson three-pickup guitar ever had.

The H77 represented the last shining moment in Harmony's long history as one of America's leading makers of budget-priced instruments. The company has typically been grouped with Kay as a victim of cheap Japanese imports in the 1960s, but the turning point for Harmony was actually the death in 1968 of longtime owner Jay Kraus, who had bought Harmony from the giant Sears Roebuck catalog company in 1940.

After Kraus's death, the company bought several distributors in an attempt to secure its market base. Although sales of guitars remained respectable – even in the face of Japanese imports – the expansion attempt stretched the company's finances to breaking point. That point came in 1974, and Harmony's assets were sold at auction.

MODEL
Harmony H77

YEAR
1964

PRODUCTION
1963 to 1972

HARVEY THOMAS

This unusual hollowbody guitar was actually one of the *least* radical and flamboyant guitars made by Harvey Thomas of Midway, Washington.

Descriptions of Thomas, who made guitars from the late 1950s into the 1980s, range from "eccentric" to "maniac." He gained some notoriety – or infamy – for solidbody guitars shaped like axes and Maltese crosses. He was a country music performer whose stage guitar was a triple-neck that was part of a rig he billed as the Infernal Music Machine.

Thomas's La Paz model featured one-piece front and back components that were hollowed and seamed together. The "C bouts" (C-shaped waists) were borrowed from violin design, though they were not in the symmetrical arrangement of conventional instruments. The fingerboard markers were "drum pearl" – celluloid material, possibly taken off of a drum – which were inlaid and then filled with fiberglass. Aside from the pickups and bridge, which came from the German maker Framus, the La Paz showed that Thomas gave no quarter to traditional guitar design, even when he built a model in the archtop genre.

MODEL
La Paz Classic Special Custom

YEAR
Late 1960s

PRODUCTION
Late 1960s

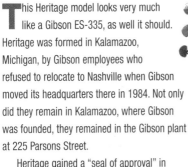

This Heritage model looks very much like a Gibson ES-335, as well it should. Heritage was formed in Kalamazoo, Michigan, by Gibson employees who refused to relocate to Nashville when Gibson moved its headquarters there in 1984. Not only did they remain in Kalamazoo, where Gibson was founded, they remained in the Gibson plant at 225 Parsons Street.

Heritage gained a "seal of approval" in 1989 when longtime Gibson signature artist Johnny Smith showed his loyalty to those who had made his guitars by endorsing a Heritage model. Country star Roy Clark gave Heritage its greatest TV and concert exposure. Two British rockers who had been closely identified with Gibsons – Alvin Lee and Gary Moore – also came over to Heritage for signature models.

The Heritage headstock was inspired by the narrow "snakehead" design featured on Gibson mandolins in the mid 1920s. The wood pickguard, with grain lines matching those of the top of the guitar, provided the extra touch of craftsmanship that guitar buyers expected from a company that, more so than Gibson itself, carried forth Gibson's tradition of excellence.

309

MODEL
Heritage H-535

YEAR
1990

PRODUCTION
1987 to current

HOFNER

During the 1950s, when U.S. imports were banned in Britain, the German-based Hofner company offered some of the better-quality electric hollow-body models available to British guitarists. With the Hofner Club 50, guitarists had the appearance, at least, of a guitar comparable to Gibson's Les Paul.

Where the Gibson was a true solidbody, however, the Hofner's lack of soundholes belied a hollowbody underneath its solid spruce top. As with Hofner's more famous violin-body "Beatle bass," the small, hollowbody not only made it lighter in weight, it provided a unique sound.

The single-pickup Club 40, double-pickup Club 50 and fancy, maple-bodied Club 60 played a role in the early careers of some of Britain's best-known rock guitarists. John Lennon's first electric guitar was a Club 40. Ritchie Blackmore of Deep Purple started his career on a Club 50, but the boomy sound prompted him to trade it in towards a Gibson semi-hollowbody. The fancier, maple-bodied Club 60 helped along Moody Blues guitarist Justin Hayward and Pink Floyd's Dave Gilmour.

MODEL
Hofner Club 50

YEAR
Circa 1958

PRODUCTION
1954 to 1962

Hofner may have been an old-school German company with roots in the 1880s, but in the years after World War II, Hofner family members were well aware that the strongest market for their electric guitars was in the U.K. If British guitarists had felt any resistance to a German-made product, Hofner ingeniously dispelled it by creating a guitar that Brits could legitimately call their own.

Hofner called it the Committee because it was designed by a committee of British guitarists, including Frank Deniz, Ike Isaacs, Jack Llewellyn, Freddie Phillips, Roy Plummer and Bert Weedon.

Easily identifiable in its early years by its fancy peghead, the Committee got one of its biggest boosts from Denny Wright, a jazz guitarist who "moonlighted" in the recording studio with popular skiffle artists Lonnie Donegan and Johnny Duncan. The Committee was so important to Duncan's sound that, in later years, when session guitarist "Big Jim" Sullivan joined him in the studio, he made Sullivan put down his Les Paul and play a Committee.

311

MODEL
Hofner Committee

YEAR
1959

PRODUCTION
1956 to 1972

HOFNER

The President was the least expensive of Hofner's single-cutaway full-depth electrics, although the theme of American government continued down the line to the non-cutaway Senator and Congress models.

With a 16.25-inch body, the President was a bit smaller than the Committee, which varied between 17.5 and 18 inches. And the President had less binding, plainer inlay and a less ornate peghead. But when it came to performance the President started out with the same rosewood covered pickups as the Committee, and it moved right along with the more expensive model to the "toaster" style units and on up to double-coil humbuckers in the early 1960s.

The President, like most traditional archtop electrics, fell by the wayside in the 1970s, but Hofner revived the name in the 1990s for an updated version called the New President and an offshoot called the Vice President. In 2004, the political names took a curious turn toward the company's homeland when Hofner introduced a more expensive model called the Chancellor.

MODEL
Hofner President

YEAR
1959

PRODUCTION
1957 to 1973

In 1960, with the Committee well-established as one of the best electric guitars available in Britain, the German-based Hofner company topped it with an even bigger and fancier model called the Golden Hofner.

At 18 inches wide, the Golden model was larger than the Committee. It featured the same intricate peghead design and fingerboard inlay, but the neck was an 11-piece laminate. The body featured more binding, typically with an outer layer of pearloid. The most obvious identifying feature was the Golden Hofner's elaborately engraved, gold-plated "Escutcheon" tailpiece.

Hofner immodestly proclaimed the Golden to be "a masterpiece of guitar perfection." At a list price of 95 guineas (a guinea was a little over a pound), the Golden cost 50 per cent more than the Committee. It was either beyond the means of most guitarists, or else they realized they could get the same pickups and electronics on the Committee. After two years, Hofner had sold no more than 100 Goldens, and the last was made in 1962.

MODEL
Golden Hofner

YEAR
1961

PRODUCTION
1960 to 1962

HOFNER

Bert Weedon, one of Britain's earliest guitar stars and the author of the popular *Play in a Day* instructional, had been one of the select guitarists on the committee that Hofner had enlisted to design the Committee model, but he couldn't resist the allure of the Hofner Golden when it was introduced in 1960.

This 1961 Golden Thin was Weedon's personal guitar. Like the Committee and other Hofner archtops, the Golden was also offered with a thinner body, and Weedon chose that option along with a Bigsby vibrola instead of the standard "Escutcheon" tailpiece.

The earliest Goldens (as pictured in the catalog) were fitted with Hofner's "black bar" single-coil pickups. Almost immediately, Hofner upgraded the pickups to the units on Weedon's guitar – the slotted metal-covered style that was nicknamed "toaster." Within a year or so, Hofner developed a double-coil humbucking pickup and upgraded the Golden again. The Hofner Golden is rare enough – no more than 100 total (electric and acoustic) – and the Golden Thin is even rarer, with an estimated production of less than 25 guitars.

314

MODEL
Golden Hofner Thin

YEAR
1961

PRODUCTION
1960 to 1962

H ofner's established models came in full-depth (3 inches or more) and thin (around 2 inches), but in 1960 the Hofner Verithin took it all the way down to 1.25 inches. The anorexic body was complemented by a thin "Slendaneck."

The influence of Gibson's ES-335 model, which had been introduced in 1958, was obvious in Verithin's double-cutaway shape – albeit with squashed-down horns. Unlike the semi-hollow 335, however, which had a laminated maple top and a solid block down the center of the body, the Verithin maintained elements of traditional archtop design with a fully hollow body and a braced spruce top.

The Verithin introduced a new look to the Hofner line with its full-width fingerboard markers of pearloid and tortoise, and the constrasting bars would become a Hofner signature look as they appeared on one new model after another in the 1960s. Hofner changed the Verithin's cutaways to a pointed shape in 1966, but it languished in the shadows of the more traditional archtops and disappeared in the early 1970s.

MODEL
Hofner Verithin

YEAR
1961

PRODUCTION
1960 to 1972

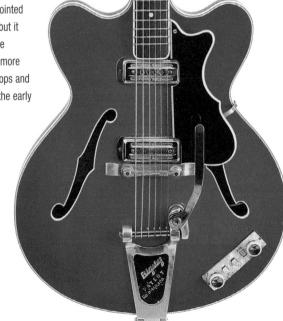

HOFNER

This guitar with a violin-shaped body was clearly modeled after Hofner's 500/1 bass guitar and intended to exploit the notoriety that the bass had gained in the hands of The Beatles' Paul McCartney. Although the violin-body guitar had a bolt-on neck rather than the set neck of the bass, the guitar had the upscale full-width fingerboard inlays while the bass only had pearl dots.

Hofner had previously used the model number on an unrelated, traditional archtop model. The new 459, introduced around 1965, was available in several variations. The VTZ version featured active electronics with treble boost and distortion control. The very rare 459/VTZ Super sported more elaborate ornamentation, gold-plated hardware and a natural finish (similar to Hofner's 500/5 violin bass).

McCartney had moved on from his Hofner bass to a Rickenbacker by the time the 459 guitar appeared, so the guitar never had much of a chance and was discontinued in 1970. Hofner's violin-body basses have become vintage classics, but the guitar version remains little more than an interesting footnote in Hofner history.

MODEL
Hofner 459/VTZ

YEAR
Circa 1965

PRODUCTION
1965 to 1970

The A2L's tailpiece and peghead shape are easily distinguishable from some of Hofner's fancier designs of earlier decades, but for all practical purposes, this 1983 Hofner with its floating pickup is a timeless, classic jazz guitar or – depending on the point of view – a nostalgic look back to 1950s guitar design.

Hofner's heyday was decades in the past when this guitar was made. Rock'n'roll music, solidbody electric guitars, the widespread importation of American guitars into the U.K., and the growth of the British guitarmaking industry – every element of 1960s musical culture – had a devastating effect on the German-based company.

Yet in the electric guitar market, Hofner seemed to resist changing times and remained committed to traditional hollowbody archtop guitars, to the point that through the 1970s and '80s, its instruments were better-made than those of its "classic" years. Its commitment may not have paid off in sales, but the company is still making guitars in Germany and is still respected for its archtop jazz guitars.

MODEL
Hofner A2L

YEAR
1983

PRODUCTION
1978 to 1986

HOPF

Caspar Hopf began putting his name on musical instruments in 1669, and the family business was passed down through a dozen generations before arriving at Dieter Hopf, who led the Hopf company into the electric guitar era in the 1950s. Working with designer Gustav Glassl, Hopf created some of the most modernistic guitars of the 1960s.

One of Hopf's signature features was cat's eye soundholes. Gretsch had introduced the smooth, tapered design on its high-end Synchromatic acoustic guitars in the late 1930s, but when Grestch dropped the cat's eye holes in the 1950s, Hopf picked them up and put them to good use.

The Saturn 63's body shape was inspired by Fender's solidbody Jazzmaster, but the double soundholes on the bass side – accentuated by metal binding – gave it a memorable look that was distinctive from a Jazzmaster or any other guitar, for that matter. Thanks in part to being featured in an ad for Star Club in Hamburg, the Saturn 63 was the most successful Hopf of the 1960s.

MODEL
Hopf Saturn 63

YEAR
Circa 1965

PRODUCTION
Mid 1960s

George Benson's Ibanez signature model of 1976 served as a wake-up call for American guitarmakers who had assumed that Japanese companies could never win over top American musicians.

Benson had been well-known as a versatile jazz guitarist since the 1960s, and his albums occasionally included a vocal track. In 1976, "This Masquerade" changed him from a great guitarist who could also sing to a great singer who could also play guitar, and the record went to No. 1 on the pop, jazz and R&B charts.

By the mid 1970s, Ibanez had gained a reputation for making better-quality copies of American guitars than the American makers were making, but Benson's model helped establish Ibanez as a maker with its own designs. The GB-10 body was smaller than the typical Gibson archtop – 14.75 inches rather than 16 – and the cutaway split the difference between a traditional rounded shape and the pointed horn of Gibson's ES-175. Through the years, Ibanez has offered seven different Benson guitars, and the GB-10 is its longest-running signature model.

MODEL
Ibanez George Benson GB-10

YEAR
1978

PRODUCTION
1977 to current

JACKSON

Although the Jackson name will forever be linked with the first hot-rodded "Super Strats" of the 1980s, the Charvel Surfcaster of the early 1990s was also memorable enough to be worthy of a revival at the end of the decade.

By this time both of the company's founders, Wayne Charvel and Grover Jackson were long gone. Charvel sold his parts business to Jackson in 1978, and Jackson left the company in the hands of a Texas-based distributor in 1989. The Japanese electronic instrument company Akai bought the brands in 1997 and brought back the Surfcaster a year later under the Jackson brand.

Where the basic Charvel Surfcaster of the early 1990s had a basswood body, or else a mahogany back with figured maple top, the later Jackson version had a mahogany top and back. Also, a more powerful, more appealing humbucker replaced the Charvel's cooler-looking "lipstick" single-coil bridge pickup. Like the original, the revived Surfcaster had a hip nostalgic appeal that wore off quickly, and it only lasted in production for three years.

MODEL
Jackson Surfcaster

YEAR
1998

PRODUCTION
1998 to 2001

Blues artist Jimmy Reed, a major influence on The Rolling Stones, played an unusual Kay electric guitar with a flat top and no soundholes. He became so closely identified with it – Kay even pictured him in catalogs with the guitar – that it is widely known today as the Jimmy Reed model. Its official name, however, was the Kay Thin Twin.

The Kay company, based in Chicago, was named for its president Henry Kay Kuhrmeyer. It began as Groeschel (founded in 1890), which became Stromberg-Voisinet, the first company to market an electric guitar and also one of the first to make guitars with laminated wood bodies. Kuhrmeyer changed the company name to Kay in 1931, and made it an industry leader in budget-priced guitars.

The Thin Twin took its name from its body depth, which was only slightly thinner than a conventional acoustic guitar, and from its two pickups. The lack of soundholes gave the top enough stability to make the Thin Twin, along with a companion bass, one of the better performing Kay electrics of any era.

MODEL
Kay Thin Twin

YEAR
1954

PRODUCTION
1952 to 1959

Sidney Katz succeeded Hank Kuhrmeyer as president of Kay in 1955, and his first order of business was to elevate Kay's budget-brand reputation. To that end, he enlisted jazz guitarist Barney Kessel to endorse not just one but three Kay models. A Charlie Christian disciple, Kessell had made a name for himself in the Oscar Peterson trio and had just been featured prominently on Julie London's torchy 1955 pop hit "Cry Me a River."

The Artist was the middle model of Kessel's three Kay signature guitars, between the small, soundhole-less Pro and the fancier Special. All three featured what vintage guitar buffs today refer to as the "Kelvinator" peghead, nicknamed because it brings to mind 1950s-style appliances.

The Kessel models were a high-water mark for Kay, and the company reverted to budget-brand status in 1960 when Kessell moved his endorsement to Gibson. Kessell's career continued to rise, as he became a first-call studio musician, but Kay did not make it through the 1960s.

322

MODEL
Kay Barney Kessel Artist

YEAR
Circa 1958

PRODUCTION
1956 to 1960

Shortly after the arrival of Barney Kessel as a Kay endorser in 1956, Kay expressed its enthusiasm in the model name of a new series of cutaway electric archtops – the Up-Beat. The model name also played off the popular jazz magazine *downbeat*.

The Up-Beat was originally available with one or two pickups. The three-pickup Up-Beat K8995 was added late in 1959, and it is was an eye-catching instrument, with contrasting black finish and white plastic parts, along with the massive "Kelvinator" headstock. With a full complement of controls knobs – separate tone and volume for each pickup – it appeared to be a high-quality guitar, although the pickups were single-coils rather than the double-coil humbuckers that high-end guitars from Gibson and Gretsch featured by the late 1950s.

When Kessel left Kay for Gibson in 1960, he took Kay's cloak of respectability with him. In the meantime, three-pickup jazz guitars were fast becoming passé (Gibson's ES-5, the model that started it all in 1949, would only last only into 1961), and Kay's Up-Beat played its last beat in 1960.

MODEL
Kay Up-Beat K8995J

YEAR
Circa 1960

PRODUCTION
1959 to 1961

323

KAY

Following the lead of Gibson's double-cutaway, thin-bodied ES-335 of 1958, Kay came with its own version in 1960 called the Jazz II.

Like many lower-quality guitars, this Kay was more style than substance. Its humbucker-sized pickups were actually single-coils, nicknamed "Kleenex box" style by vintage collectors. The fingerboard inlays took their quarter-circle design from the guitars of National, another Chicago-based maker of budget-priced instruments. And the "Slim-Lite" neck was bolted-on, a feature it shared with no high-quality jazz guitars.

Despite the model name, Kay's target for this guitar was questionable. It had a long, 26-inch scale at a time when the trend among some jazz players was toward the shorter scales lengths of Gibson's Byrdland and ES-350T models. The Jazz II became most famous, ironically, in blues-rock circles. Eric Clapton's grandmother bought him a Jazz II (or a similar model) for his birthday, and that was the instrument wielded by the future guitar god in 1963 when he joined his first band, The Roosters.

MODEL
Kay Jazz II K776

YEAR
1961

PRODUCTION
1960 to 1963

324

The K592 "Red Devil" brought the bold look of pointed horns to Kay's archtop line in the early 1960s, but it nevertheless represented the toning down of Kay models after the gaudy "Kelvinator" headstocks and "Kleenex box" pickups of the late 1950s. The earliest version of the model had a very simplified "Kelvinator" headstock, but by the time of this example, the peghead logo had been reduced to a stenciled letter K.

Kay had moved into a larger factory in suburban Chicago in 1964, which would suggest that the company was doing well, but model K592 proved to be a more accurate indicator – an early sign of troubled times, as the company consistently lost market share in competition with cheap Japanese imports.

The Seeburg jukebox company bought Kay in 1966 and then sold it a year later to the Chicago-based Valco company, which was struggling with its National and Supro brands. In 1968, Valco went bankrupt. The Kay name was bought at auction in 1969 and was used on cheap, Asian made guitars after that.

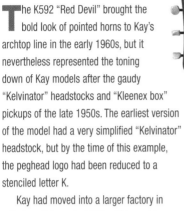

MODEL
Kay K592

YEAR
Circa 1964

PRODUCTION
Circa 1962 to circa 1964

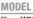

KENT

Buegeleisen and Jacobson, a New York-based full-line instrument distributor, began importing Japanese guitars in the 1960s, appropriating the names of two of America's most popular cigarette brands – Winston and Kent. Among the companies contracted to build these guitars were Guyatone, Teisco and, in the case of the Kent 742, probably Kawai.

This Kent 742 from the late 1960s took its inspiration from the pointed horns of Gibson's SG solidbody models. Cosmetically it had all the trimmings – eight-ply binding (one layer more than Gibson's fanciest) around the body, bound fingerboard and peghead, and figured maple top contrasting with a tortoiseshell pickguard. Functionally, it was typical Japanese overkill, with four pickups – each with its own on/off control and its own tone and volume control. A Gibson-style tune-o-matic bridge provided good intonation, and a vibrato unit (this one may have been lifted from a Gibson) completed the appearance, at least, of a high-performance package.

Buegeleisen and Jacobson abandoned the Kent line by the end of the 1960s, and the company eventually became a part of Kaman Music (Ovation's parent company).

MODEL
Kent 742

YEAR
Circa 1968

PRODUCTION
Late 1960s

Dick Knight started as a banjo and clarinet player but a hand injury turned him to making instruments. After World War II he worked for Selmers music store in London, repairing and building instruments, and also with Selmers shop manager, Joe Van Stratten, building Stratten-brand guitars. When his wife became ill, he worked as a mill foreman until her death in 1963, when he began making guitars full-time.

Based in Surrey, England, Knight made all types of guitars but specialized in archtops such as the Imperial. Although it appeared to be a standard archtop jazz guitar with a floating pickup, the top bracing was actually carved and integral with the top. The neck construction was also a special Knight feature that he called the "billiard cue" design.

Knight suffered a heart attack in 1986 – about the same time this Imperial was made – and quit making guitars. He died in 1996, but his son-in-law Gordon Wells (who had been working with Knight since 1967) and Wells's son Rob carried on the business.

MODEL
Knight Imperial

YEAR
Circa 1986

PRODUCTION
Circa 1986

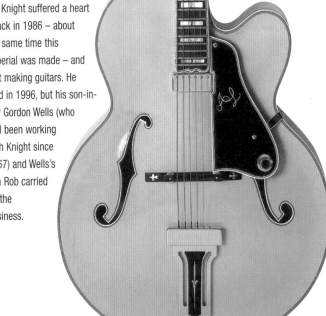

KRUNDAAL

The Krundaal Bikini appears to be the perfect instrument for buskers – a guitar that carries its own transistor amplifier. The creator of this instrument is referenced by the stylized letter W in the tailpiece, Antonio "Wandre" Pioli. He began making instruments in his hometown of Cavriago, Italy, around 1956, then had them produced by Framez in Milan from 1960–63, then by Davoli in Parma from 1963–65.

Hofner had tried a similar model, called the Bat, but had only made it in limited numbers. Pioli put it into production, calling it the Bikini, presumably to draw a connection between its two components and the two-piece Bikini bathing suits that had become the rage in the early 1960s. Australians, however, saw a different connection and nicknamed it the Buggerlugg for its resemblance to the human ear.

Many of Wandre's instruments were branded with his own name, but they also appeared under such brands as Noble (in the U.S.), JMI (in Britain), Avalon, Avanti I, Davoli, and Krundaal (one of Davoli's brands).

MODEL
Krundaal Bikini

YEAR
Circa 1963

PRODUCTION
Early 1960s

Magna Electronics of Inglewood, California, (an area of Los Angeles) made some of the most famous amplifiers, memorable lap steels, and obscure guitars of the 1950s.

Paul Bigsby, a pioneer of solidbody electric guitars and pedal steels, designed the Mark IV (with trapeze tailpiece) and Mark V (with Bigsby vibrola) for Magnatone in 1956, at a time when the company seemed to have everything going for it. Magnatone lap steels were eye-catching creations covered in flashy pearloid or made from colorful transparent acrylic. Rock'n'roll legend Buddy Holly played a Magnatone amp. And Bigsby's guitar design was certainly on track – the Mark V's double-cutaway body with pointed horns may well have inspired Gibson's SG body style five years later. But despite Bigsby's contributions, the guitars went nowhere.

Magnatone continued introducing new models – but selling very few guitars – as it relocated to Harmony, Pennsylvania, in 1966 and then met its demise when it was bought by a toy company in 1971.

MODEL
Magnatone Mark V

YEAR
1959

PRODUCTION
1956 to early 1960s

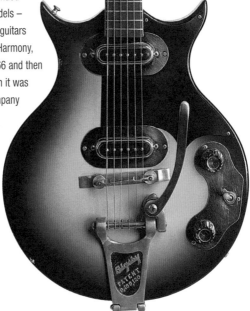

MARTIN

Since the 1830s, the C.F. Martin of Nazareth, Pennsylvania, has been renowned for its acoustic flat-top guitars, and the company has seldom fared well when it has tried to expand into other guitar styles. The GT-75 was a case in point.

Martin's electric dreams began in the late 1950s, when several acoustic models were fitted with DeArmond pickups (the same pickups that Gretsch and Guild were using). In 1961, Martin introduced the F-series of thinline hollowbody electrics, but while the body design was contemporary enough, the headstock had the squared-off shape that had identified a Martin acoustic guitar since the 1930s. Surmising that perhaps the headstock was hampering sales, Martin put a flared headstock on a new electric series in 1965, consisting of the single-cutaway GT-70 and the double-cut GT-75.

Neither the headstock of the GT guitars nor the finish selection of black or burgundy – and the occasional red – created a sensation, and electrics were quickly abandoned. Martin would venture again into the electric market with solidbodies in the late 1970s and early 1980s with similar results.

MODEL
Martin GT-75

YEAR
1967

PRODUCTION
1965 to 1967

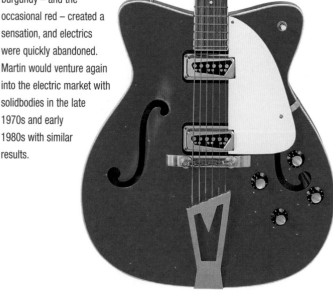

The Micro-Frets Orbiter of 1967 was a showcase of innovative and unconventional designs, from the adjustable nut to the calibrated vibrato, not to mention the out-of-control body shape and – perhaps most important – the wireless transmitter.

Micro-Frets was founded in 1967 by Ralph Jones of Frederick, Maryland, with financial backer Marion Huggins. The company's name came not from a special sort of fret but from Jones's segmented nut (technically the zero fret), which allowed players to adjust string height as well as string length. Jones also focused on fine-tuning the other end of the strings, and his Calibrato vibrato was designed to keep chords in tune through as much as an octave of pitch change.

The most forward-looking Micro-Frets innovation was an FM transmitter (tuned to 102.3), available by special order, that freed musicians from the restraints of a guitar cord. On this Orbiter, the antenna was built into the bass-side horn. It would be more than a decade before wireless technology became commonplace on concert stages, but the foundation was laid by Micro-Frets in the late 1960s.

331

MODEL
Micro-Frets Orbiter

YEAR
Circa 1968

PRODUCTION
1967 to circa 1969

MICRO-FRETS

As if Micro-Frets' nuts, vibratos and body shapes were not innovative enough to grab the attention of electric guitarists, the company gave this Golden Melody model a glowing green sunburst finish called Moonscape. (A later version with darker green finish was called Martian Sunburst.)

Practically every feature of a Micro-Frets was a departure from conventional guitar deisgn. The front and back of early models were joined together by a plastic gasket (much like the molded fiberglass bodies of National's early-1960s models). The control knobs were tastefully incorporated into the edge of the pickguard. The soundhole had a shape that repeated the lines of the company's logo. The pickups, supplied by Gretsch, had actually been designed for Martin's short-lived electric model line.

The Golden Melody only lasted a few years before it evolved into the Spacetone and Stage II models, which featured more conventional, symmetrical body shapes, but it made a lasting impression. It was one of the five models revived by a new Micro-Frets company, founded by Will Meadors and Paul Rose in 2003.

MODEL
Micro-Frets Golden Melody

YEAR
Circa 1970

PRODUCTION
1967 to circa 1969

The Huntington model was the standard-bearer of Micro-Frets' unorthodox body shapes throughout the company's brief existence in the late 1960s and early 1970s.

The Micro-Frets facility in Frederick, Maryland, was a hotbed of design ideas, but in 1973, founder Ralph Jones died. His partner and financial backer wanted to keep the company going, but Jones's widow did not, so after six years in business and a total output of no more than 3,000 guitars, Micro-Frets closed its doors in 1974. Some leftover parts appeared in the next few years on Diamond S guitars.

Although models such as the Huntington and Orbiter were attention grabbers, with their four body points and slightly bloated look, the more conventional, symmetrically shaped Micro-Frets designs were more widely seen. Mark Farner of Grand Funk Railroad played a Signature model, and Carl Perkins played a Calibra during the company's heyday. In the 1980s, long after the company's demise, Martin Gore of Depeche Mode kept the brand name in front of audiences, playing a Micro-Frets Spacetone.

333

MODEL
**Micro-Frets
Huntington**

YEAR
Circa 1971

PRODUCTION
1967 to 1973

MOSRITE

The double logo, like the pickups on this resonator guitar, represent the incongruous union the resulted when Semie Moseley, founder of Mosrite, acquired the Dobro brand in 1965.

Mosrite was riding a wave of success in the mid 1960s, thanks to a solidbody electric model endorsed by the popular rock instrumental group, The Ventures. The Dobro brand, named after the *Do*pyera *bro*thers, who founded the National company and invented the resonator guitar in the 1920s, had been virtually dormant since World War II.

Dobros were played almost exclusively in bluegrass by the 1960s and Mosrite models, such as the California, with its thin, double-cutaway body, sieve-like soundholes (the prewar Dobros had smaller soundholes covered by window screen), and electronics, were so far afield from traditional, bluegrass instruments that any advantage of brand recognition was also removed. In the meantime, Dopyera family members began producing instruments again, and when Mosrite's fortunes fell in the late 1960s, the Dopyeras reacquired the Dobro name and returned it to the headstocks of traditional-style resonator guitars.

MODEL
Mosrite California D-100

YEAR
Late 1960s

PRODUCTION
1965 to 1969

The fiberglass body of the Studio 66, along with its oyster-shell pickup shape and curvy pickguard, exemplified the modern, innovative flair of National's guitars in the early 1960s.

National had a reputation for innovation, going back to its origins in the late 1920s as the company that invented the resonator guitar. Founded in California, the company moved headquarters to Chicago in the mid 1930s and changed its name to Valco. One of the early players in the electric guitar arena, Valco had foreseen the rise of the electric guitar in the 1930s and in the postwar years focused almost exclusively on electrics.

By the end of the 1950s, National had a reputation for flashy but, for the most part, cheaply made instruments. In the early 1960s, buyers' concerns about quality were diverted by a series of new models with bodies of molded fiberglass. While the Studio 66 stood out visually from the guitar of any other maker, the company's financial troubles, along with the inferior performance quality of its instruments, doomed National's fiberglass models to a five-year lifespan.

MODEL
National Studio 66

YEAR
1961

PRODUCTION
1961 to 1964

NATIONAL

The transition of National's Studio 66 to the Varsity 66 accurately represented the falling fortunes of National's parent company, Valco, in the mid 1960s.

The Studio had introduced modern materials – such as the fiberglass body – and unconventional pickguard and pickup designs, but the Varsity seemed to remove all the flair. The single pickup looked as if it had been lifted off some budget-brand model from the 1950s, and the screwed-down pickguard had more in common with the ultra-cheap Danelectro/Silvertone models that Sears sold than with the stylish creations National was known for.

The offset cutaways gave the Varsity 66 the appearance of modern playability, and the black plastic headstock overlay had a beveled edge that simulated the binding on more expensive guitars, but with a plain, dot-inlaid fingerboard, a single pickup, and an almost homemade-looking pickguard, the Varsity 66 would have been more at home in Valco's budget-priced Supro line. Its performance was no better than its design, and it barely lasted a year before National discontinued it.

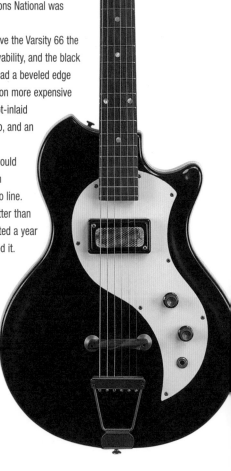

MODEL
National Varsity 66

YEAR
1964

PRODUCTION
1964 to 1965

National coined the term Res-o-glas for the fiberglass bodies of its early 1960s guitars and described the material as "polyester resins with threads of pure glass." National also claimed that its Res-o-glas was "more adaptable and workable than conventional wood," and the company seemed to prove that point in 1962 with the introduction of guitars with bodies resembling a map of the United States.

Res-o-glas was, in fact, easier to work with when it came to finishes. National sprayed the finish color into the mold for the body, then filled it with the fiberglas material, and the two body pieces came out of the mold already finished.

The map-shapes came in three groups of three models each. At the top were the Glenwoods, with model numbers in the 90s. Next came the Newports, with numbers in the 80s, followed by the wood-bodied Westwoods, with model numbers in the 70s. Within each series, models featured a variety of finish colors, electronic configurations and ornamentation. The Glenwood 95 had a pair of pickups, a "vermillion" finish, and flashy diamond-in-square fingerboard inlays.

337

MODEL
National Glenwood 95

YEAR
1964

PRODUCTION
1962 to 1964

NATIONAL

National's Newport 84 debuted in 1962 as the Val-Pro 84, sporting an Arctic White finish. A year later, with the name change to Newport, the finish also changed to Sea Foam Green.

Like all the higher models in the map-shaped series, the Newport 84 featured, in addition to one or two standard magnetic pickups, a unit that picked up vibrations from the bridge rather than directly from the strings. Although it seemed to be a preview of the piezo pickups that would be developed for acoustic guitars later in the 1960s, it was actually a throwback to late-1920s pickup designs. It produced a weak signal, as did National's conventional pickups.

Weak pickups were not the only problem with the Glenwood and Newport map-shaped models. Their bodies were hollow, with two pieces of molded fiberglass held together by a vinyl gasket. Res-o-glas, as National called it, was anything but resonant, and that, coupled with the weak pickups, made these guitars more enjoyable to look at than to play.

MODEL
National Newport 84

YEAR
1964

PRODUCTION
1963 to 1964

The Newport 82 was the lowest of the three models in the Newport model family of map-shaped guitars. It was initially called the Val-Pro 82 (a play on the name of National's parent company, Valco), but a year after its introduction, National decided that Newport – a beach town in California as well as a seaport in Rhode Island – would have more appeal. The finish changed, too, but only nominally, from Scarlet to Pepper Red.

National claimed that Res-o-glas (its term for fiberglass) was easier to work with than wood, and that was probably true. Bodies were produced in a mold, and the finish color could be sprayed into the mold, so skilled work – shaping, sanding, finishing – was minimized. Unfortunately, though, fiberglass guitars were still not any cheaper to make than wood-bodied instruments.

The rise of cheap Japanese imports pushed National's parent company, Valco, into financial trouble by the mid 1960s. In 1967, Valco somehow managed to buy Kay – a long-established budget brand that was in even worse shape – and the whole ship went down a year later.

MODEL
National Newport 82

YEAR
1964

PRODUCTION
1963 to 1965

Ted McCarty's name was legendary by the 1980s as the man who led Gibson through a golden age of electric guitar innovation in the 1950s. As president of the company from 1948–66, he brought Les Paul to Gibson and was personally responsible for the invention of the semi-hollowbody guitar (Gibson's ES-335).

Paul Reed Smith's guitars, introduced in 1985, were inspired in part by the solidbody Gibsons of the McCarty era, and in 1986 Smith contacted McCarty for advice on production issues. McCarty became a friend and mentor, as well as a PRS consultant, and Smith thanked him by creating a PRS McCarty line in 1994.

The first McCarty models were solid, but appropriate to McCarty's history with the company that invented the archtop guitar, Smith introduced PRS's first hollow models under the McCarty name. The McCarty Hollowbody of 1998 wasn't fully hollow; the routed mahogany back came up to meet the top under the bridge – an important feature that negated the need for a trapeze tailpiece as well as any tendency for the guitar to feed back.

MODEL
Paul Reed Smith McCarty Hollowbody I (Private Stock #62)

YEAR
1998

PRODUCTION
1998 to 2003 (continues as Hollowbody I)

A long with the McCarty Hollowbody of 1998, PRS introduced a deeper-bodied model called the PRS McCarty Archtop. And topping the Archtop was the super high-end, special-order Archtop Artist, with Brazilian rosewood fingerboard, bird inlays with gold-inlaid outlines, gold-plated hardware, and an abalone peghead signature.

The Archtop design come from PRS master luthier Joe Knaggs, who created PRS's first archtops for their Guitar of the Month and Private Stock programs. As a self-described ex-jazz guitarist, Knaggs felt that the wide bodies of traditional jazz guitars – a carryover from the pre-electric era, when a guitar had to be big to be heard – were simply uncomfortable to play, and he wanted to capture the performance of a Gibson L-5CES, for example, in a smaller-bodied instrument.

With a depth of 2.75 inches at the rim and a full 4 inches in the center of the body, the PRS McCarty Archtop was substantially deeper than the standard PRS or a typical "thinline" guitar, but it still had the compact, easy-to-play body of a solid model.

341

MODEL
Paul Reed Smith McCarty Archtop Artist

YEAR
1998

PRODUCTION
1998 to 2001

PRS

As with all PRS models, the McCarty Hollowbody was designed with one eye on performance and one on aesthetics, and for those buyers who couldn't get enough of the look of highly flamed maple, there was the McCarty Hollowbody II. Introduced in 1998 along with the Hollowbody I and Archtop, the II featured an enticing carved maple back instead of the mahogany back of the Hollowbody I.

After a year in production, both the McCarty Hollowbody I and II received an upgrade in the form of a piezo pickup (made by the L.R. Baggs company) that, appropriate to the tradition of archtop guitars, added an acoustic dimension to the PRS sound.

Ted McCarty, the former Gibson president and mentor to Paul Reed Smith, passed away in 2001, and three years later the PRS McCarty line was scaled back to its original solidbody models. The distinctive f-hole archtop look of the McCarty hollow models continues today in the PRS line without McCarty's name as the Hollowbody I and Hollowbody II.

MODEL
Paul Reed Smith McCarty Hollowbody II

YEAR
1998

PRODUCTION
1998 to 2003 (continues as Hollowbody II)

Rickenbacker introduced an electric "Spanish" or conventional-style guitar concurrent with its famous "Frying Pan" electric Hawaiian model in 1932, but even though they both had the same "horseshoe" pickup, the Hawaiian models were immediately embraced by musicians, while the Spanish models – the first viable, modern electric guitars – remain a footnote in electric guitar history.

The reason for their obscurity is the scant design effort that went into them. While the company invented radical new styles of Hawaiian guitars, first with a cast-aluminum body and neck, then with a body of Bakelite, when it came to Spanish models, Rickenbacker simply bought a cheap archtop guitar from the Harmony company (or occasionally Kay) and installed a pickup.

At a time when Epiphone offered a Zephyr Deluxe Regent and Gibson had an ES-350, Rickenbacker's model name was anything but inspiring. This guitar from the late 1940s was still just the Rickenbacker Spanish model. Not until the mid 1950s would Rickenbacker, under new ownership, become a contender in the electric Spanish-style guitar market.

MODEL
Rickenbacker Spanish

YEAR
Late 1940s

PRODUCTION
1946 to 1949

RICKENBACKER

In contrast to Gibson's haphazard model naming scheme (which would appear to place the L-5 below the ES-175) and Gretsch's confusing array of models and finish colors, Rickenbacker's Capri line was refreshingly easy to understand.

The Capris were organized into three basic model groups: a short-scale model with plain ornamentation, a standard-scale with plain trim, and a fance standard-scale model. Model groupings started with numbers 310, 330, and 360, and model numbers increased by 5 with each upgrade, starting with two-pickups (the 310, 330, and 360), then two pickups with vibrato (315, 335, and 365), then three pickups, finally three pickups with vibrato.

The 330 was the basic two-pickup model and the least expensive full-scale Capri model, and consequently, it became the most popular and the most enduring of all Rickenbacker models. Although it had no frills – no binding on the body or neck, simple dot inlays on the fingerboard – it still had an elegant look that distinguished it from the designs of any other maker.

MODEL
Rickenbacker 330

YEAR
1958

PRODUCTION
1958 to current

RICKENBACKER

Rickenbacker's Roger Rossmeisl was the most successful of any guitar designer at bringing together elegance, modernism, and functionality. The proof was in the Capri series that Rickenbacker introduced in 1958.

The 360 was the basic two-pickup, no-vibrato model of the Capri series' high-end model grouping. Its "sweeping crescent" double-cutaway style was not only highly modernistic – Gibson introduced its first double-cutaway archtop, the ES-335, the same year, but it had more traditional rounded horns – it also provided more accessibility to the upper-register (all 21 frets were clear of the body) than any other guitar on the market. The rout for the tailpiece made the guitar aesthetically less bottom-heavy, and it also increased the angle of the "string break" across the bridge for better performance.

The elongated gold logo plate on the peghead (which doubled as a truss-rod cover), the gold split-level pickguard, the triangular fingerboard inlays, the slash soundhole, the large diamond-pattern knobs – every element of the 360 was new and elegantly designed, setting the Capris apart from the era's traditional Gibsons and gaudy Gretsches.

MODEL
Rickenbacker 360
(Old Style)

YEAR
1959

PRODUCTION
1958 to 1968

RICKENBACKER

classic electrics

F or Rickenbacker's F-series models of 1959, designer Roger Rossmeisl seemed to take a step back from the sweeping cutaway shapes and "German carve" body contours of his earlier Rickenbackers. The new semi-hollow models, known by the seemingly contradictory term "Thin Full-body" because of their thin depth and full-size width, featured a traditional rounded cutaway and were the most conventional-looking electric models of Rickenbacker's modern era (which began with F.C. Hall's acquisition of the company in 1953).

Rickenbacker appropriated the orderly model numbering system of the Capri-series for the F-series. Like the 360, the 360F was the basic two-pickup model with fancy trim – triangular fingerboard inlays and body binding. Model numbers increased when a vibrato and/or a third pickup were added. The 330F was the plainer model, with dot inlays and no body binding. The short-scale Capris (models 310-325), were not offered in the "full-thin" F-series.

Although the Capris had only been introduced a year earlier, their modern styling set an aesthetic standard for Rickenbackers that the Thin-Full models couldn't live up to. The F-series lingered into the 1970s but never really found a market.

MODEL
Rickenbacker 360F

YEAR
1959

PRODUCTION
1959 to 1972

In Rickenbacker's "Thin Full-Body" (thin depth, full width) F-series, as in the Capri series, number 375 signified the top model. The 375F came with all the trimmings, including three pickups, a vibrato, triangular fingerboard inlays, and body binding.

The F-series models featured Rickenbacker's most traditional design, but on the vibrato-equipped models, the side-pull Kauffman unit went beyond tradition, and not in a good way. Invented by Clayton Orr "Doc" Kaufmann, Leo Fender's original partner (they made electric Hawaiians and amps under the K&F brand in 1946), the Kauffman vibrato had appeared on Rickenbackers as early as 1935. Compared to the Bigsby units that Gibsons and Gretsches sported in the early 1950s, or the Fender unit that debuted on Stratocasters in 1954, the Kauffman was an ancient relic.

Even with more modern vibratos, the F-series guitars, with their single-cutaway design, failed to inspire guitar buyers. Production totals show less than 40 of the plainer 330F family, the last of which were made in 1963. The fancier models lasted a decade longer but never sold in respectable numbers.

MODEL
Rickenbacker 375F

YEAR
1964

PRODUCTION
1959 to 1972

RICKENBACKER

When The Beatles arrived in New York in February 1964 to make their American debut on the Ed Sullivan TV show, Rickenbacker president F.C. Hall was waiting for them, with a special room set up to demonstrate guitars at the Savoy Hilton hotel.

Among the guitars Hall brought with him was a prototype for a 12-string based on Rickenbacker's two-pickup, fancy-trimmed Capri 360 model. Harrison was sick with the flu in his hotel room, but Lennon played the 360/12 and suggested that they take it to Harrison to try out.

Harrison used the Rick 12-string for the broad opening chord of "A Hard Day's Night," and its octave effect enhanced his solo in the middle of that record. When he appeared with the 360/12 in the Beatles movie *A Hard Day's Night*, California folkie Roger McGuinn saw it and was so moved that he traded in his acoustic 12-string for a guitar like Harrison's. McGuinn went on to make the Rick 12-string a vital part of The Byrds' sound as they brought folk and rock music together.

MODEL
**Rickenbacker –
360/12**

YEAR
1964

PRODUCTION
1964 to 1989

RICKENBACKER

hollowbody guitars

Rickenbacker started the electric guitar era in 1932, but under the ownership of Adolph Rickenbacker (a machinist – not a musician, instrument designer or salesman) the company fell well behind Gibson, Fender, and Epiphone by the early 1950s. Rickenbacker sold his company in 1953 and new owner F.C. Hall hired German-born designer Roger Rossmeisl. New solidbodies appeared immediately, and in 1958 Rossemeisl hit his stride with the elegant new Capri series, identifiable by the sweeping curve of their cutaway bouts.

In Britain, Rick distributor Rose, Morris & Co., Ltd., offered a limited selection of Capris, all with a traditional f-hole rather than the "slash" hole (or, in the case of the short-scale models, no soundhole at all), and Rose, Morris's Model 1996 corresponded to the short-scale 325 model.

John Lennon's 1958 Rickenbacker 325 had no soundhole because he bought it when The Beatles were playing in Hamburg, Germany, in 1960. Rickenbacker later offered a Lennon signature model, but the more accurate reissue of Lennon's first Rick was the 325V59 Hamburg, introduced in 1984 and still in production.

349

MODEL
Rickenbacker 1996

YEAR
1964

PRODUCTION
1964 to 1969

RICKENBACKER

When Rickenbacker owner F.C. Hall gave George Harrison a 12-string in February 1964, Beatles manager Brian Epstein shrewdly snagged a second one for one of his other artists, Gerry Marsden, front man for Gerry and the Pacemakers.

In the hands of those two gutiarists, the Rickenbacker 12-string was assured a warm welcome in Britain, and distributor Rose, Morris promptly began importing a model. Like all of the models Rickenbacker made for export to Britain, Model 1993 featured a conventional f-hole rather than Rickenbacker's trademark "slash" soundhole. It had a bound top, which the standard Rickenbacker 330 did not have, but for all practical purposes it was a 330/12.

Instead of the typical, crowded, six-in-a-row tuner configuration of typical 12-strings, Rickenbacker came up with an innovative design that combined slot-head and solid-peghead configurations so that half the tuner posts pointed to the back of guitar (as they do on a slot-head) and half were at a right-angle to the peghead. Consequently the tuners were not only in their familiar places, they were also easily paired with their proper counterparts.

MODEL
Rickenbacker 1993

YEAR
1964

PRODUCTION
1964 to 1969

Today, Rickenbacker's Capri Series has a timeless, classic appeal, but the company apparently didn't see it that way in the early 1960s. No sooner had designer Roger Rossmeisl left (he went to Fender in 1962) than Rickenbacker began "improving" the high-end 360 model group.

The original 360 had featured a bound top but, in 1964, the top borders were rounded off and relieved of binding. Binding was added to the soundhole, and curiously, the back binding – which was rarely seen by an audience – was upgraded to a checkered pattern.

While the official model 360 had the new features, the original top-bound version was still available, and the Old Style and New Style vied against each other for the next 40-plus years. They co-existed through 1969, when the O.S. was dropped, but it made a comeback (as model 360V64) in 1991 and knocked the New Style out of production. The tables turned again in recent years with a Carl Wilson (Beach Boys) signature model with New Style features, and today, Rickenbacker's model 360 is available in New Style only.

MODEL
Rickenbacker 360 (New Style)

YEAR
1975

PRODUCTION
1964 to 1990

RICKENBACKER

It was not an optical illusion or a special effect from a computer designer – the frets really were mounted at an angle on this Rickenbacker 360/SF (SF for Slanted Frets).

Gretsch was the first major company to introduce the concept of slanted frets; its T-Zone fingerboard had frets in the upper register mounted at a slight angle (the opposite angle of Rickenbacker's slant) to provide better intonation. However, Rickenbacker's goal for slanted frets was simply to match the natural angle of the fingers of the left hand, to make the guitar more comfortable to play. The pickups seem to have fallen under the influence of the frets, too, as they were mounted at an angle.

While the slanted frets may have helped playability, they hurt the aesthetic of this model. The triangular fingerboard inlays that distinguished the 360 from lower models would not have lined up with these frets, and the dot inlays showed that Rickenbacker didn't have enough confidence in the SF to redesign its high-end inlays. Players felt the same way.

MODEL
Rickenbacker 360/SF

YEAR
1968

PRODUCTION
1968 to 1970

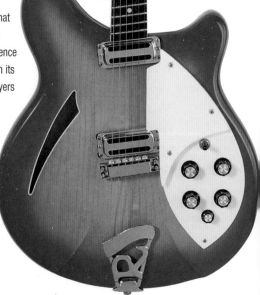

MODEL
Rickenbacker 362/12

YEAR
1975

PRODUCTION
1975 to 1992

The sweeping crescent shape of Rickenbacker's Capri models took an uncharacteristic aesthetic turn for the worse when the 360's body was stretched out to accommodate two necks.

The earliest Rickenbacker doublenecks, dating back to 1961, were six-string guitar and four-string bass combos, the best-known of which was played by Mike Rutherford of Genesis. In the meantime, Gibson's numerous (unlimited, really) combinations of doublenecks in the early 1960s settled down to only one model – a 6/12 solidbody model. Rickenbacker's answer was a 6/12 with a single neck, using a "converter comb" to pull half of the 12 strings out of the way for six-string use, but in 1975 the company gave up on the converter and came with its own 6/12 doubleneck.

The 362/12 was based on the Capri 360 model but with the "Old Style" body, with a bound top rather than the newer rounded-top design. Rickenbacker offered a solidbody doubleneck at the same time, but only with guitar/bass configuration. The semi-hollow model was the only 6/12 doubleneck Rick ever offered, and it remained in production until 1962

353

RICKENBACKER

Rickenbacker's 381 V69 (initially called V68) was a reissue of a 1969 model, which itself was a reissue of the original 381 made from 1958–63.

The 381 was part of a proposed series – few of which were ever produced – that featured what was a radical idea for Rickenbacker: a full-depth body. The deep body gave Rickenbacker designer Roger Rossmeisl plenty of room to exercise his "German carve" – the pronounced lip around the top edge that he brought to Rickenbacker from his native Germany.

The first version of the 381 attracted few converts, but the second, offered from 1969–73 found its way into the hands of John Kay, leader of the band Steppenwolf ("Magic Carpet Ride," "Born to Be Wild"). In 1988, Rickenbacker and Kay created a limited-edition signature model, the 381JK. At the same time, Rickenbacker offered the signature-less version as the 381 V69. It took ten years for Rickenbacker to sell out the run of 250 Kay models, and when the 381JK was retired, so was the 381 V69.

MODEL
Rickenbacker 381 V69

YEAR
1990

PRODUCTION
1987 to 1997

354

RIC
Rickenbacker

Hand-Crafted
QUALITY & EXCELLENCE

The Who's Pete Townshend bought his first Rickenbacker in 1964, after seeing John Lennon playing a Capri 325 with The Beatles, but unlike Lennon's guitar, Townshend's Model 1998 (the model number used by British importer Rose, Morris) didn't last out the year before he destroyed it in a club performance. He tried to take better care of future Rickenbackers, reserving his more easily repairable solidbodies for smashing, and he used a 1998 on the group's recording of "My Generation" in 1965

Townshend's guitar had an f-hole rather than a slash but was otherwise the equivalent of Rickenbacker's 345, with regular-scale, dot inlays, three pickup, and a vibrato. For his signature reissue, however, Towshend substituted the *R* tailpiece for the vibrato.

The pickguard on the 1998PT featured Townshend's name in block letters – ironic on a signature model – and an image of him with arm raised in the middle of his trademark windmill assault on the strings. Rickenbacker introduced the model in 1987, and the limited run of 250 sold out in a year.

MODEL
Rickenbacker 1998PT

YEAR
1998

PRODUCTION
1987 to 1988

RICKENBACKER

I n 1987, Rickenbacker dressed up the 360/12 with an eye-catching black-and-white color scheme known as the Tuxedo finish. The company produced, appropriately, only 12 of these "formal" 12-strings.

The body and neck – including the fingerboard – were white, while the plastic and metal parts were all black. The binding was black, too, but on this "New Style" body with curved top edges (introduced on the Capri 360 series late in 1964), only the back of the body was bound.

Rickenbacker 12-strings had a different sound than those of other makers, and the secret was in the stringing. From the days of the first acoustic 12-strings, the octave pairs had been strung so that the player's downstroke hit the high string first and then the low string. Conversely, the upstroke hit the low string first, emphasising the low octave, and the result was an accented off-beat when players alternated up- and downstrokes. Rickenbacker reversed the pairings, so that the low octave was struck first, giving greater power and depth on downstrokes and relieving the "wrong foot" sound of conventionally strung 12-strings.

MODEL
Rickenbacker 360/12 Tuxedo

YEAR
1987

PRODUCTION
1987

Roger McGuinn of The Byrds wasn't the first rock guitarist to play an electric 12-string, but his opening lick on the group's 1965 hit "Mr. Tambourine Man" immediately established the 12-string as a rock'n'roll instrument.

McGuinn's guitar was a Rickenbacker 360/12, with two pickups and the rounded-top "new style" construction (one of only six made in 1964). He had seen George Harrison playing one in the Beatles film *A Hard Day's Night*, and he immediately traded in a banjo and an acoustic 12-string to one for himself. Early in 1966, he sent it back to the factory for a third pickup, making it a 370/12. It disappeared shortly thereafter, and McGuinn acquired another 360/12.

In 1988, Rickenbacker honored McGuinn's contributions to the company's success with a limited-edition signature version of the 370/12, offered in Mapleglo (natural, like McGuinn's original), Fireglo (red sunburst) or Jetglo (black). After the production run of 1,000 sold out, Rickenbacker continued to offer the 370/12 without McGuinn's signature and custom circuitry.

357

MODEL
Rickenbacker 370/12 RM

YEAR
1988

PRODUCTION
1988

RICKENBACKER

In February 1964, during The Beatles' first trip to America, Rickenbacker president F.C. Hall presented John Lennon with a new Jetglo 325 to replace Lennon's well-worn 1958 model. At the same time, Hall gave George Harrison one of the prototype Rick 12-strings and, later that same year, Lennon custom-ordered his own 12-string, based on his Rick 325, with three pickups and short scale length.

As the 325/12 model name would suggest, Lennon's guitar originally had a vibrato, but it didn't work well, and F.C. Hall removed it before sending it to Lennon. In 1985, five years after Lennon was killed by a fan, Rickenbacker began offering the 325/12 as a regular model (still without the vibrato and technically a 320/12). In 1989, the company officially teamed up with Lennon's estate to create the limited-edition 325JL and, a year later, the 325/12JL.

The limited-edition 12-string featured vintage-style "chrome bar" (aka "toaster top") pickups, five-knob control configuration, Lennon's signature and self-portrait drawing on the pickguard, and the same flat, non-vibrato tailpiece found on Lennon's original guitar.

MODEL
Rickenbacker 325/12JL

YEAR
1990

PRODUCTION
1990 to 1991

The German-made Roger guitars were *not* made by famed guitar designer Roger Rossmeisl; they were named *for* him. It was his father, Wenzel Rossmeisl, who started using the Roger brand as a guitar distributor in the late 1930s.

Rossmeisl began building jazz guitars in Berlin shortly after World War II. At the request of jazz guitarist Coco Shumann, and with the help of his then-teenaged son, Rossmeisl made what may have been the first electric guitar ever built in Germany. In the early 1950s, Roger Rossmeisl left for America, where he enjoyed a successful career designing guitars for Rickenbacker and Fender. Wenzel continued making mostly acoustic jazz guitars under the Roger brand.

This semi-hollow Model 54 was one of his few true electrics, but with a spruce top and a pickguard that appeared to be housing the electronics, it showed that Rossmeisl's heart was still with the acoustic guitar. The letter R in the tailpiece design of this 1960 Roger 54 no doubt inspired the "R" tailpieces that appeared on Rickenbackers in 1963.

359

MODEL
Roger 54

YEAR
1960

PRODUCTION
1960 to 1962

SUPRO

With an elegant "German carve" around the edge of the body and a Wedgewood Blue finish, the Supro Sahara had an expensive looking design that belied its place at the lower end of a budget-brand line.

The Supro brand started in the mid 1930s as an all-electric line made by the Valco company of Chicago, which had started in the late 1920s in California as the National company. In the post-World War II years, Valco abandoned the resonator guitars that had brought National to prominence and focused on electrics, with National as the main brand and Supro for budget models. Most of the company's amplifiers were also marketed under the Supro brand.

In 1960, Valco introduced new lines of Nationals and Supros with bodies that featured a front and back of molded fiberglass, secured together by a rubber gasket around the edge. Despite appearances, the Sahara's body was not solid, and its pickup was weak. The same could be said about its sales.

MODEL
Supro Sahara

YEAR
Circa 1964

PRODUCTION
1960 to 1966

From a brand known for angular solidbody electrics, garishly appointed with three or even four pickups and an array of pushbuttons and control knobs, the May Queen of 1968 was a relatively subdued and tasteful offering from the Teisco company.

Teisco was founded in Japan in 1946 and sent its first Teisco-brand guitars to the U.S. in 1960 through Chicago importer Jack Westheimer. After gaining a foothold, the company created new brand names for various distributors, including Kent, Apollo, and Teisco Del Rey.

Teisco fell on hard times and was acquired by Kawai (best known today for pianos) in 1967. A year later Kawai introduced a new wave of Teisco Del Ray models, including the May Queen. The body shape was based on the teardrop-shaped Vox Mk VI (which was a solidbody) but seemed to be distorted to accommodate a pickguard on the treble side. The May Queen was offered in red, mustard yellow, black or sunburst finishes, and it also appeared under the Apollo brand.

MODEL
Teisco Del Rey May Queen

YEAR
Circa 1968

PRODUCTION
1968 to 1969

VEGA

The "Duo" in the name of Vega's Duo-Tron models referred to its dual capability – it could be played as an acoustic or as an electric – thanks to its "floating" pickup.

The concept of a pickup suspended off the top of the guitar wasn't new in the late 1940s, but Vega did one-up DeArmond, Gibson, and other makers of add-on pickups by offering the Duo-Tron with two and even three floating pickups (the E-400 and E-500, respectively). Vega's tailpiece-mounted controls were also unique.

Based in Boston, Vega was a well-known name in the banjo world, starting in the classical banjo era of the 1890s and continuing through the Jazz Age of the 1920s and on into the folk era of the 1960s, but like most of the great banjo makers (Epiphone being a notable exception), Vega was never quite able to make a successful transition to guitars. Vega touted the Duo-Tron as "the finest guitar built in America or the world over today," but few guitarists ventured to find out if the claim was true.

MODEL
Vega Duo-Tron E-300

YEAR
1951

PRODUCTION
Late 1940s to early 1950s

"**S**tereo" was the buzzword in the recording industry in the 1950s, and the idea of splitting a sound into two separate channels caught the imagination of guitar makers, too, but this Vega 1200 Stereo model took it to a bizarre extreme.

Gibson's stereo guitars simply separated the bridge pickup from the neck pickup so that each could be played through its own amplifier. Gretsch's stereo system split the pickups so that treble strings were in one channel and bass strings in the other. Vega went the extra mile – or the extra ten miles – with the 1200, which featured 12 pickups (two for each and every string) and what appeared to be a woefully inadequate control system for so many pickups.

The 1200 Stereo proved to be a dubious high point in the history of Vega electric guitars, which quickly faded into the shadow of the company's banjos. The brand continued to be known for banjos, under the ownership of Martin in the 1970s and most recently as a part of the Deering banjo company.

363

MODEL
Vega 1200 Stereo

YEAR
Circa 1959

PRODUCTION
Late 1950s

VOX

Vox's Starstream XII was the hollowbody version of the teardrop-shaped Mk VI solidbody that Rolling Stones guitarist Brian Jones made famous. It was symbolic of the parent-company JMI's seemingly overnight change from one of the most promising companies of the mid 1960s – whose guitars, amps and combo organs were pervasive among the British Invasion Groups – to an importer of increasingly bizarre Italian instruments.

Introduced at the same time Vox had outfitted a guitar with organ electronics, the Starstream XII was overloaded with features, including a built-in tuner, distortion effects, treble and bass boost, percussion generators and even a hand-operated wah-wah – not to mention its 12 strings.

Vox's fall was even faster than its rise. In 1964, unable to produce enough instruments to meet the surging demand, owner Tom Jennings outsourced instruments to the Italian-based Eko company. At the same time, he sold a controlling interest to Royston, a British holding company. Guitar designs veered toward style rather than substance, and when Royston folded in 1969, that was the end of Vox guitars.

MODEL
Vox Starstream XII

YEAR
Circa 1967

PRODUCTION
1967 to 1968

WILKANOWSKI

The guitars of Willi Wilkanowski are among the most easily identifiable by any maker because their "rolled" edges make them look like violins.

Wilkanowski was born in Poland in 1886 and came to the U.S. around 1920, settling in Boston, where he made violins for the Oliver Ditson Co. Around 1938 he relocated to New York to work for the Gretsch company and, by 1939, he had opened his own shop in the New York borough of Brooklyn. Although he lived until around 1960, he only made guitars for a short period.

Most of Wilkanoswki's guitars had the squat, non-cutaway shape of this Airway model, with body points off the upper bouts. The rosewood pickguard was not his typical shape, but it was no doubt altered to accept the floating pickup. This example was unusual in that it sported modern "slash" soundholes (probably inspired by the "cat's eye" soundholes that appeared on Gretsch archtops in 1939) rather than Wilkanowski's typical violin-style f-holes.

365

MODEL
Wilkanowski Airway

YEAR
1940

PRODUCTION
Circa 1939 to early 1940s

YAMAHA

Yamaha is one of the oldest companies in the music business, founded in 1887, but its electric guitars of the late 1960s – exemplified by the SA-15 – looked like anything *but* the product of a long-established musical instrument company.

The SA-15 appeared to come from two different design teams, as if the first team got half of the way to creating a Rickenbacker and then the second team took over. The upper part of the body was actually a smoothed-down version of the infamous Yamaha solidbody SG-5A, better known as the Flying Samurai, which did in fact look like a reversed Rickenbacker; the lower body half was traditionally symmetrical. Also like the Rickenbacker, the Yamaha had a semi-hollow body with a soundhole, but again, the design inspiration appeared to be split between a Rickenbacker slash-hole on the upper half and a traditional (though reversed) f-hole on the lower half.

Despite its shaky start in the 1960s, Yamaha would go on to contribute popular and enduring designs to the electric guitar world in the last quarter of the 20th century.

MODEL
Yamaha SA-15

YEAR
1968

PRODUCTION
1966 to late 1960s

Although Yamaha stood apart from many Japanese companies in the "copy era" of the 1970s, establishing itself as a company with its own recognisable and successful designs, Gibson's ES-335 – the original semi-hollowbody model – was simply too tempting for Yamaha to resist copying in the late 1980s.

The SA-1100 had ever-so-slightly narrower horns than the ES-335, and the headstock had two dips in the top rather than Gibson's trademarked single-dip "dove-wing" shape, but it was unashamedly a copy of the legendary Gibson semi-hollow model. Actually, when it came to performance, the SA-1100 did the Gibson one better, by way of a coil-tap control (which the 335 had from 1977–81).

The SA-1100 was supplanted in the Yamaha line in the early 1990s by the SA-2200, which featured highly figured wood. Gibson did not fight back until 2000, when the company's import division released its own dot-neck ES-335 copy, called the Epiphone Dot. Still, the SA-2200 maintained enough attention that it carries on the 335-style guitars in today's Yamaha offering.

367

MODEL
Yamaha SA-1100

YEAR
1990

PRODUCTION
Late 1980s to 1993

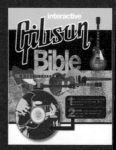